JUSTICE OVERRULED

JUSTICE OVERRULED

Unmasking the Criminal Justice System

Judge Burton S. Katz

WARNER BOOKS

A Time Warner Company

Warner Books, Inc., 1271 Avenue of the Americas, New York, NY 10020

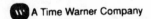 A Time Warner Company

Printed in the United States of America
First Printing: July 1997
10 9 8 7 6 5 4 3 2 1

Library of Congress Cataloging-in-Publication Data

Katz, Burton S.
    Justice overruled : unmasking the criminal justice system / Burton S. Katz.
        p.   cm.
    ISBN 0-446-52042-X
    1. Criminal justice, Administration of—United States.   I. Title.
    KF9223.K34   1997
    345.73'05—dc21   96-50043
                                                                              CIP

Book design by H. Roberts

In memory of my father, Henry Katz,
who if given the chance would have
made a brilliant trial lawyer

ACKNOWLEDGMENTS

This book could not have happened without the following people to whom I am deeply indebted:

My friend and agent Norman Brokaw, William Morris chairman of the board, who had the vision and enthusiasm to make it happen on the wings of a few spoken words; Norman's colleague and my friend and agent Mel Berger, who had the patience of Job to see the project through; Laurence Kirshbaum, president and CEO of Warner Books, who believed in the worth of this book; Warner Books senior editor Susan Sandler, whose humor and strong guiding hand made the project obtainable; copyeditor David Wade Smith's fine eye for detail, and all the people at Warner Books who made this project happen.

To Gavin de Becker, with whom I shared many creative and productive hours during long walks and fireside chats.

A very special thanks to Frank Francone, whose preliminary editing helped me transform a rambling, confusing manuscript into a coherent and tight draft. Frank's awesome intellect allowed me to test the mettle of my proposals.

My friends in the L.A. County District Attorney's Office, DA Gil Garcetti, William Hodgman, Scott Gordon, and newly appointed L.A. Superior Court Judge Norman Shapiro, who gave me access to my old cases and offered insight into our criminal justice system; Steven Kay, who provided valuable information on the current Parole Board procedures; to Steven Plumer, with whom I tried some cases, for assisting me in reconstructing their details. A special thanks to Sandi Gibbons, whom I first met when she was a reporter covering the Charles Manson murders, for her wealth of experience and insights into criminal justice as seen by the public and the media.

My friends in the L.A. County Public Defender's Office, re-tired L.A. County Public Defender Wilbur Littlefield, Paul James and Ken Green, regaled me with humorous and insightful sto-ries of justice gone amuck. Their constant support was an inspi-ration and a welcome opportunity to share some laughter and some colorful tales of systematic oddities.

To my lawyer-colleagues and friends who helped me recall many of the anecdotes contained in this book: thanks to Jerry Fogelman, a dedicated criminal defense lawyer who challenged my efforts to "bend the law" for the benefit of his client; to Don Wager, defense attorney par excellence, whose crafty and devil-ish wit made the practice of law challenging and rewarding—if not sometimes dangerous; to Marty Harwick, the first great de-fense lawyer I opposed in trial, who taught me invaluable trial strategies; to Chuck Rosenberg, fellow legal analyst and com-mentator, who read an early draft of the book and offered wis-dom on how to make it understandable; to Howard Weitzman, who helped me recall our mutual cases tried many years ago; to Michael Adelson, who helped me recall aspects of the John Sweeney murder case; to Jim Epstein, who helped me to recol-lect some of the intricacies of the McKinney-Sartain murder case; to my friends and outstanding criminal defense lawyers, Victor Sherman, Michael Nasatir, and Richard Hirsch, who al-ways challenge my alleged antidefendant biases; to my KABC radio talk show cohost and friend, Leo Terrell, whose civil rights expertise always challenges me to justify a position; and to my friend Lenny Levine, a brilliant lawyer who always has a humor-ous slant on our chosen profession.

A few special friends also gave me undying support: Ron Cohen who challenged me to "go for it," refusing to acknowl-edge my disgruntled complaints when things got tough; Dr. Melvin Kinder, whose acerbic and brilliant analysis of a work in progress helped me to articulate clear positions to the reader; my friend of many years, Vince Bugliosi, whose support and give-

and-take discussions allowed me to crystallize my own thinking; Hugh Sommers, our family lawyer, who stayed the course when some of us jumped off into uncharted seas; my friend and colleague Barry B. King, who appreciates my skewed view of the world, and for that I am grateful; Ken Harlan, who extended his hospitality, home, and friendship to a driven writer; Tom Catalano, who gave me tough love and challenged my hypotheses.

To my cop friends, a strong admiration for the many sacrifices you make to do society's dirty work; a very special thanks to my good friend Charlie Guenther, whose candid, humorous, and painful memories contributed to the soul of this book; to Paul Whiteley, Bill Gleason, the late Vinne Barrett, Michael Maloney, Casey Sturm, and Roy Hamilton, who put up with me as a demanding, nettlesome DA; to my old friend Phillip Vannatter and his dignified partner, Tom Lange, the "twin devils of deception."

To the press, especially Linda Deutsch and the late Theo Wilson, two of the greatest crime reporters, who always have reflected the highest values of their profession.

To Dr. Richard Saferstein, a renowned forensic criminalist, for his illumination of the murky world of DNA, hair, and fiber evidence.

To my fellow legal commentators, especially professors Stan Goldman and Laurie Levinson, with whom I argued vigorously on many fine legal points, such as the number of exceptions to the hearsay rule dancing on the head of a pin.

Finally, to my wife, Judith, and my daughters, Nicole and Alyssa, who saw me through this nonsense of writing a book, my lasting gratitude.

CONTENTS

JUSTICE OVERRULED

PROLOGUE

It's Not *L.A. Law*

JUSTICE BETRAYED

In the halls of justice, the only justice is in the halls.
—*Lenny Bruce*

This book is about a broken criminal justice system. A mythical system of dispassionate, evenhanded justice that never really was. A system that promised, but never delivered. A system that works for some and not for others. For much of our history, our criminal justice system has been a charade, a game to be played and won. Cops, lawyers, judges, and juries are the principal players. Today, more than ever, winning is everything.

Our criminal justice system can be improved dramatically. But to do so, radical changes must be made. Institutional attitudes must be revisited. I know. I spent twenty-three years in the criminal justice system as a prosecutor, as a criminal defense attorney, as a judge, and as a crime victim. I have seen the system from every possible angle and a lot of what I have seen is not very pretty.

My close involvement with the criminal justice system continues to this day as a close observer, critic, and commentator. Today, you may know me as television commentator Judge Burton Katz. Several times every month, I sit with one earnest television host after another, answering their questions about criminal justice. I tell them what I think about the trials of Eric and Lyle Menendez, of O.J. Simpson, of the cops accused in the Rodney King beating, and others. I talk of Randy Weaver and

Ruby Ridge. Of Koresh and Waco, and of the conduct of the FBI and the Justice Department. I tell them what I think about the criminal proceedings arising out of the Oklahoma City bombing and the arrest of the Unabomber. I let them know when I think police officers are lying in court, when defense counsel is hiding evidence or suborning perjury from witnesses, and when the prosecution is likewise engaging in unethical conduct. I tell them when the judge is losing control of his courtroom. I tell them who appears to be winning and who appears to be losing the game.

Or you may know me as a Los Angeles radio talk show host with KABC. Although I frequently get to answer questions from the television viewing audience, my real chance to talk with the public is on my radio talk show *Terrell and Katz*, where I engage in heated debates with my legal nemesis and friend, civil rights lawyer Leo Terrell.

Whether the callers with whom I speak are members of my TV or my radio audience, they have one thing in common: an entirely new level of interest about the criminal justice system today, as opposed to just five years ago. After the Simpson verdict, one might have thought the public's interest in the criminal justice system would wane. It has not. The questions are still intense. The callers are amazingly well informed about aspects of the criminal justice system. The variety of viewpoints is staggering. We talk about the handling of the JonBenet Ramsey case and other breaking cases.

Five years ago, these same callers would have had no idea what a preliminary hearing was, and how it differed from a trial. Nor would they have known that blood evidence was gathered in "swatches," transported in special plastic bags, dried in the lab, and preserved for later DNA analysis. They would have guessed that an *allele* was a new headache remedy rather than a version of a human gene. Today that level of knowledge is common. Today my callers have strong and sophisticated opinions about what were once arcane points of criminal law and evidence-handling techniques. But I have seen the system from the inside, and I know the crucial machinations they cannot know from the outside, looking in.

Why this intense public interest? The glib explanation would be the media feeding frenzy over big cases in recent years: Mac-

Martin Preschool, Rodney King, Damien "Football" Williams, William Kennedy Smith, Lorena Bobbitt, Menendez, and, of course, the *Tyrannosaurus rex* of media excess, the O.J. Simpson double murder trial. In each of these cases, the media stripped the proceedings and everyone involved of all dignity, reducing complex issues to the level of tabloid news and trial by sound bite. No news organization in this nation is innocent.

But the intense media coverage cannot be the full explanation. Media interest is fleeting. Normally, so is the interest of the viewing public. And yet, one and a half years after the O.J. Simpson verdict, the public is still intensely interested. I believe I know why. The public has seen the criminal justice system up close for the first time, closer than it has ever previously been allowed—too close for some of the players in the system. The American public has now taken a long look at the criminal justice system, and it doesn't much like what it has seen.

What unites almost all of my callers, regardless of their viewpoint, is a deep sense of unease. They sense that something has gone wrong. Worse, some things may never have been right. They feel lied to, cheated. American justice has been sold to us as a bright beacon of truth and justice, the greatest system in the world. But it does not look that great on TV. Has Uncle Sam played a cruel joke on us? Who gets justice? Who doesn't? And why? Is truth always irrelevant? Are defense attorneys, judges, police, and prosecutors interested in anything besides winning?

Public perceptions about justice are important. Even if inaccurate, they become self-fulfilling. My callers perceive that lawyers, judges, and the police care little about the truth. Procedures, rules, technicalities, strategies, clever practices, yes. Justice and truth, no. My callers are right. It is time for a little truth about the criminal justice system.

First, this book is about the titanic struggle between our cops and activist appeals courts for the past forty years. Truth has been the twofold victim of this battle. To begin with, crucial evidence is regularly withheld from juries. We don't let the jurors know the truth. Not only that, but court hearings about how the police gather evidence are often charades—the cops know it, the prosecutors know it, the defense attorneys know it, and the judges know it. Yet they all just look the other way.

Second, this book is about the adversary system—the engine

that drives criminal justice. It is about the roles of its principal
players: the lawyers, judges, and juries. The adversary system encourages adherence to arcane rules and procedures. It sanctifies
form over substance. It rewards trickery, deceit, and advocacy
skills at the expense of fundamental truths. To the adversary,
truth is but an inconvenience. Winning is everything. Guilt or
innocence is irrelevant. Judges have lost control of their courtrooms to the lawyers and must regain that control.

Third, this book is about how we have allowed our jury system to deteriorate. Modern juries are ill-equipped to deal with
the complexities of difficult litigation. They succumb too readily
to public pressure, hype, and rhetoric. They are often ignorant,
often biased. Those biases are exploited by unprincipled lawyers
whose only goal is to win. Increasingly, the few who serve on juries are unrepresentative of the community. Increasingly, they
use their time as jurors to return "payback" verdicts. Respect for
the jury system is at its lowest in modern history.

Fourth, this book is about legislatures and a public that look
for cheap ways to look tough on crime. We do have to get tough
on crime. It is exploding out of control. But we have to make the
system tough in reality—not on paper.

Finally, the increasing exploitation of "abuse excuse" and
other diminished-capacity defenses are like riptides pulling us
into the undertow of psychiatric fraud—far adrift from the calm
water of truth. Inflamed passions, prejudicial misinformation,
manufactured evidence, experts bought and sold, and outrageous "abuse excuses" must be dealt with firmly and quickly.

I want to end this prologue where I began. The callers in my
television and radio audience know something is very wrong.
The current players are so trapped in the system they often cannot see the trees in the smoke and fog. Without dramatic
changes, the criminal justice system will continue to lumber on
until it expires from its own immorality—and discourse about
truth and justice will then be a luxury for other civilizations.

Some tough reforms must be made in all quarters. Judges,
attorneys, juries, and cops must change their behavior and their
institutional biases. The law itself must be changed to allow truth
into our courtrooms. I value deeply my relationships with my
many friends who are cops, defense lawyers, prosecutors, and
judges. These are people with whom I have spent nearly all of my

adult life mired in the mud of criminal justice. They are special to me. But so are truth and justice. Some friends and colleagues will take offense at what I have to say. The truth does hurt. It is painful. No one likes to hear aired in public the dirty little secrets they have lived with for their whole careers. But you are about to hear them. And you are about to hear how I would fix the system.

O N E

Joining Forces

LESSONS FOR A YOUNG ADVOCATE

As a very young lawyer, from books that I read
I thought justice and law were the same;
But I soon put that juvenile thought from my head
And I studied the rules of the game.
—*Joe Swan*

I was a prosecutor for thirteen years. I had never intended to be one. Quite the opposite. I graduated from law school in the sixties. Revolution was in the air, and I shared many of the beliefs of the young people of that time. Having never seen a real criminal trial, I sincerely and naively believed our criminal justice system was filled with unjustly accused defendants, caught in the claws of a heartless establishment trying to imprison them. I wanted to defend innocent victims. So I applied for a job in the Los Angeles County Public Defender's office. They told me to wait for the next opening.

Anxious to start working, and worried that the public defender's office would never call back, I also applied for a job in the Los Angeles County District Attorney's office, which wanted me immediately. I put them off. But I had a young wife and a new baby, so I took the DA's job with qualms. My friends were not thrilled about my joining forces with, in the language of the day, "the oppressors of the people." Even my normally conservative Republican parents were surprised and cool to my joining the DA's office. But the DA's office gave me an impressive badge. It looked important. I felt important. So, except for a brief stint between 1964 and 1965 as a criminal defense attorney, this child of the sixties spent the next thirteen years putting people in jail.

As I started my new job, I was unsure how I was going to be able to prosecute all of those innocent people I had seen wrongly accused on *Perry Mason* and *The Defenders*. Much to my surprise, I found few victims of the system unjustly accused. In the vast majority of criminal cases, by the time a person has been arrested and the DA has filed charges, that person's guilt is obvious beyond any reasonable discussion. Period.

During my years in criminal justice, I had the privilege as a prosecutor to try a number of challenging cases, including double and triple murders and no-body cases. I was the DA who put Manson family members Bobby Beausoleil and Steve "Clem" Grogan in prison for the slayings of Gary Hinman and Donald "Shorty" Shea. I investigated and secured the grand-jury indictment in the Sal Mineo murder case, reviewed the findings of accidental death in actor William Holden's untimely demise, and tried the first "test" capital case for the Los Angeles District Attorney's office under California's new death penalty law. As a judge, I presided over many interesting and challenging cases.

I could wade waist-deep in the muck of the criminal justice system for only so long. I began to lose heart in 1983 while sitting as the judge in the John Sweeney murder case. John Sweeney strangled and killed actress Dominique Dunne. I will tell you a lot more about that case later. Suffice it to say that John Sweeney got away with murder. At that point I began to realize I had become part of the problem.

Three incidents from my early years as a prosecutor illustrate a system that at times worked and at other times was shamefully indifferent to the truth. In one of those cases I had the dubious honor of trying to put actor Rip Torn in jail for possession of marijuana. In another, a gang rape of a teenage epileptic recast me as a lawyer for the People. Finally, in *People v. MacDonald,* a circumstantial-evidence murder case, I watched helplessly as a more experienced and skilled adversary mangled my witnesses with trick questions. The result: a killer walked free.

Rip Torn Smoked Bull Durham—Not Marijuana

A few months after I joined the district attorney's office, I was assigned to "prelims." A prelim, short for preliminary hearing, takes place before trial. The purpose of a prelim is not to determine guilt—rather it is to let the judge decide whether there is enough suspicious evidence to hold the defendant over for trial. Otherwise the defendant is released.

Wet-behind-the-ears deputy DAs (like me at that time) were started on prelims because they were supposed to be easy. I would stand up, present a minimal case, and sit down. Usually I had an experienced cop beside me, whispering questions for me to ask. The most embarrassing moments were when, prompted by the cop, I would ask a question I did not understand. The judge would then rebuke me sternly for its irrelevance or incompetence. I would look sheepishly at the cop, who would shrug and feed me another question. Prelims were usually a walk-through because defendants usually did not even contest them; the evidence I presented was normally sufficient to hold a defendant for trial.

Ed McClarty was my supervisor. If anyone could have squeezed to the political right of General Patton, it was Ed McClarty. He told me my next prelim was a "special." That meant it was an important case and I had better do a good job. I grabbed the file and went back to my office, determined to make my mark. I shared my office with two other deputy DAs. The space left for three young attorneys among the mountains of files and books was barely large enough to accommodate three pigeons squatting side by side. We were in the old Hall of Justice, where Clarence Darrow and Melvin Belli and other greats had worked. I was about to become a part of history, or so I thought.

As I looked through the file on my "special," I realized to my horror that the defendant was one of my idols, the gifted actor Rip Torn. He was starring on Broadway in Tennessee Williams's smash-hit play *Sweet Bird of Youth*. Torn had been arrested for possessing a very small amount of marijuana found on the floor of a rental car he was driving. Ed McClarty was determined Torn would go to jail. What an example he would make! The damning evidence, in Ed's mind, was that Torn had been carrying Zig-

Zag cigarette papers in his pocket when he was apprehended. I was excited and I was appalled. Rip Torn. What would my friends think of me? What if they closed down the Broadway play?

This was 1964. The Beatles would soon be singing about "Norwegian Wood." Bob Dylan had already seared the radio waves with "Subterranean Homesick Blues" and with the anthemic "The Times They Are a-Changin'." Change really was in the air. In the middle of all that, my goal in my first big case was to try to put Rip Torn in jail for *felony* possession of marijuana.

It got worse. Torn had hired Russell Parsons as his attorney. To a fledgling DA, Parsons was a legend, best known for his prosecution of Rattlesnake James. Rattlesnake James had killed his fifth wife by thrusting her foot into a box filled with rattlesnakes. When she hadn't died quickly enough from the venom, he'd drowned her in the bathtub, then dragged her to their fishpond to make it look like an accidental drowning. Parsons had a flair for the dramatic; he had one of the live rattlesnakes (nicknamed "Lethal") "marked" as an exhibit at trial. Legend had it Lethal got loose in court during one of the lunch breaks. All young DAs, or at least this one, knew how Russell Parsons had sent Rattlesnake James to the gallows.

My first big prelim. A "special." And I had to draw Russell Parsons as opposing counsel. Events went from bad to worse. The prelim was before Judge James Tante, a tall, imposing man with a thin, perfectly cultured Don Ameche mustache. The good judge was a stickler for decorum, and had little patience for neophyte lawyers.

Despite my ambivalence and fear, I did my best. I called as a witness the officer who had stopped Torn for a traffic infraction. He testified he had seen some marijuana debris on the floor of Torn's car and that he had found Zig-Zag papers in Torn's breast pocket. He stated that Zig-Zags were commonly used in rolling marijuana cigarettes. Rip Torn sat through all this at the counsel table, indifferent, reading a paperback. I rested my case, expecting it to be submitted without contest, like most prelims.

Then the great Russell Parsons stood up and gravely called Torn as a witness. He was going to contest the hearing. My heart lurched. I was going to have to face Rip Torn and cross-examine him. In response to Parsons's smooth questioning, Torn testified he had no idea whose pot was in the rental car, but it wasn't his.

No, the car was not clean when he picked it up at the airport. The Zig-Zag rolling papers? He used them to roll his Bull Durham tobacco. Parsons thanked Torn, smiled at the judge, and courteously extended to me the invitation to cross examine Torn. Embarrassed, I conducted a typical rookie cross-examination that went something like this:

Q.: Isn't it a fact, Mr. Torn, that the Zig-Zag cigarette papers were possessed by you for the purpose of rolling marijuana cigarettes?

A.: No, sir.

Q.: You mean to tell us those Zig-Zag papers commonly used to roll marijuana joints were used by you solely to make hand-rolled Bull Durham cigarettes?

A.: Yes, you're correct.

Q.: Isn't it a fact Bull Durham is not commonly used in the form of hand-rolled cigarettes, Mr. Torn?

A.: No, sir, that is not correct.

I was stumped. I didn't know what else to ask. Finally an impatient Judge Tante stood up to his full, imposing six feet four inches. In flowing black robes, he looked to this scared young DA like the figure of Death out of Ingmar Bergman's *The Seventh Seal*. With a wave of his huge arm he dismissed the case against Torn. Clearly we had insufficient evidence ever to prove beyond a reasonable doubt that Torn knew there was pot on the floor of the car. I knew it. The defense knew it. The judge knew it.

There are lessons here about how our system can work. The attorneys treated each other, the witness, and the court with respect and courtesy. No one withheld evidence or lied to the court. Furthermore, no one in the courtroom, not even the legendary Russell Parsons (and certainly not I), had the slightest doubt that Judge Tante was in full control of his courtroom. While my special had been no more than a dubious case being pursued by an overzealous DA with a political agenda, the system caught and dismissed it early. In this case, the justice system seemed functional. Not perfect. Functional. Best of all, Torn went back to Broadway.

The Day I Became a Prosecutor: An Epiphany

I was excited at the prospect of learning the craft of a trial lawyer. Still, I had no commitment to being a career prosecutor and indeed just as easily could have been a defense attorney—until the day I was handed a special case. A case with a special victim, on a day I was baptized in hell—the day I became a DA.

The case involved a vicious gang rape. The teenaged victim was young and shy. She had flowing red hair and porcelain skin sprinkled with freckles. She was also an epileptic.

One day she was dragged into a garage on her way home from school. The gang kids knew her. They knew she was epileptic. They decided it would be fun to rape her while she was having a seizure. I do not exaggerate. Stuff like this really happens. One by one they terrorized her. One pinned down first her left hand, another her flailing right hand, another grabbed her right leg, still another her left leg. Another pulled her dress up and her panties down. Then, one by one, they mounted her. She went into seizures. The seizures were so forceful they stuffed her sanitary napkin in her mouth so she wouldn't bite her tongue off.

I knew after I had interviewed her what I needed to do, for her, for me, for my career. No more victimless crimes for me. I was going to be a real prosecutor of real predators. On that day I vowed to specialize in murders, rapes, and other violent crimes. On that day I was born a prosecutor.

Peter B. was the attorney for the rapists. A private lawyer, he looked like a bad caricature of a shyster lawyer out of a B movie from the 1930s. He was the kind of guy even Shirley Temple would have kicked in the shins. Swarthy and greasy, he wore a pinstriped, double-breasted black suit. The magistrate was a man in his sixties, and was completely passive in conducting his court; he never interfered with a lawyer's presentation of a case. As you will see, that was going to be a problem. A big problem.

We were now ready to proceed. I whispered to Mary to focus on me, to look only at me until she had to identify the defendants. She looked at me with hesitation. I began slowly with what I thought would be easy testimony so she could settle down. It was not to be.

DA: Mary, can you tell the court how old you are?

MR. B.: I object. This witness has no personal knowledge of her age.

I couldn't believe what I was hearing. Was this man really objecting to her testifying to her age? What was he trying to do? After some silly wrangling over what was a ridiculous objection, the judge permitted Mary to tell her age.

COURT: You may answer the question. How old are you?

MARY: I'm sixteen.

DA: What is your birthdate?

The defense attorney jumped up and again objected. He did this repeatedly throughout the prelim. Each time he popped up, the witness was distracted. The rhythm of her testimony was broken. At times she appeared agitated. I was beginning to get concerned she might have a seizure. I started watching her very closely for any signs of distress. Somehow we would get through the prelim. Mary testified to the rape ordeal. She had made it. We took a break.

I told her I was proud of her, that she was courageous. She seemed to breathe easier. I felt for the first time as a DA that I was doing something really important. If I could just let her know how special she was. But all I could feel was how we, in the system, were betraying her. I was afraid to touch her hand. She must have sensed that, because she touched mine. I turned away as the tears washed my shame. She smiled when we had a Coke. To see her smile burn through her fear and her tears was like seeing the sun burst through a dark cloud. It was to be too brief. We returned to court. The defense attorney began his cross.

MR. B.: Isn't it a fact that you were following the *young* boys?

MARY: No, sir, I was not.

MR. B.: You were pestering the *young* boys, isn't that correct?

MARY: No, I was not.

MR. B.: Now this "sun dress" you were wearing, how would you describe it?

MARY: I don't know what you mean, it was just a sun dress, you know?

MR. B.: No, I don't. Was it skimpy?

I could see Mary's face tightening up. I was afraid she might have a seizure. If he succeeded, then the prelim would be halted. Indeed, a dismissal would be required since the prelim could not be finished without interruption—as required by law. At best, even were there a waiver and stipulation that another date would be set to conclude the prelim, the reality was that she just might not be up to testifying on a future date. I objected, trying to give Mary time to calm down. But the judge let it continue.

MR. B.: All right. Let's take it one at a time. Were your breasts exposed? Could they be seen?

Before I could object, Mary answered.

MARY: No!

What made this lawyer do what he was doing? His humiliating questions were not designed to impress the judge. This was a prelim, and her direct testimony was all I needed to hold the rapists over for trial. There wasn't much he could do on cross to change that. I have always believed his questioning was designed to send her a message: *Hey, little girl, this and more is in store for you, if you testify against my boys.* The lawyer was right back with his next question.

MR. B.: Now, the hem of your dress, how high did it go up on your thighs?

DA: Your honor, I would ask the court to admonish counsel not to harass the witness. I am not referring simply to the content of the questions, but rather the tone and tenor of his voice—the aggressive and intimidating body language of counsel.

COURT: Well, Mr. B. will refrain from raising his voice. But he is entitled to explore the issue of any alleged consent, this being a forcible rape case. . . . This is cross-examination. Proceed, counsel.

MR. B.: I don't believe we ever got an answer to the length of her dress.

MARY: It was normal length, you know?

MR. B.: No, I don't. That's why I am asking. Was it two inches above your knee, three inches above your knee, maybe four?

Mary was showing signs of wear, and the defense had not even gotten to the actual rapes. How much more could she endure? She was near tears. With exasperation, she answered.

MARY: It wasn't above the knees, it was at the knees.

MR. B.: Thank you, that's all I was asking.

Without warning, he jumped to the rape.

MR. B.: You say you were taken to a garage. Did you scream?

MARY: No, I didn't.

MR. B.: Did you scream when you had sex with the first boy?

MARY: I couldn't.

MR. B.: Did you scream when you had sex with the second?

MARY: I couldn't.

The lawyer asked the same question as to each gang member, each time adding a little more disbelief to the tone of his voice. Finally these rapid-fire questions had what I believe may have been the intended effect. Mary started to slip into convulsions. Fortunately she suffered only a petit mal seizure.

I do not know whether the defense attorney actually intended to induce a seizure. He knew she was epileptic. He knew a seizure might result in the charges being dropped against his clients. Regardless, his overzealous behavior was reprehensible. But let me emphasize again that as long as the court and the law allow attorneys to act this way, some of them will. They see it as part of their job.

The judge eventually held the rapists over for trial. Mary moved out of state. I don't know what happened to her, except that she sent me a postcard shortly after the hearing, thanking me for kindness I had shown her. I felt humbled by her courage. My career was sealed in the fate of that postcard, which I kept until a few years ago, when a firestorm took everything.

An Advocate Smashes the Truth

According to F. Lee Bailey, "Those who think the information brought out at a criminal trial is the truth, the whole truth, and nothing but the truth are fools. Prosecuting or defending a case is nothing more than getting to those people who will talk for your side, who will say what you want said."

Bailey's compatriot on the O.J. Simpson case, Robert Shapiro, told Larry King on CNN, with the world listening, that *defense lawyers are not interested in the truth.* We all saw the so-called Dream Team at work. We know they were not exaggerating. The irony is that the system allows them to behave in that manner. In fact, in many ways the system encourages them to do so. It is not unethical for Bailey and Shapiro to be indifferent to the truth, for that is their job—it is the nature of our adversary system.

My very first murder case as a young DA illustrates Shapiro's statement perfectly. In *People v. MacDonald,* a twenty-nine-year-old woman's body had been found in a vacant field, riddled with thirteen M-1 carbine bullets. There were no eyewitnesses. Part of her brain was resting on a flowering bush. The coroner's photos of this formerly beautiful woman were burned into my brain. Her eyes bulged from the exploding M-1 bullet fragments. I stared at her, imagining she was trying to tell me who her killer was.

Her estranged husband was the suspect. He had previously

"And you like to watch cowboys shoot the bad men?" the attorney said, winking confidentially at the boy.

"Yes," said the boy, gratefully.

"And you saw the cowboy use the same rifle as the toy gun your daddy had?" the attorney asked, nodding his head with approval.

"Uh-huh—I mean yes," the boy replied.

"And that was the gun you told the nice DA you saw your daddy with, isn't that right?" the attorney said sweetly, as he looked at the jury, nodding as if they just had an epiphany!

Well, all was not lost because I had an adult backup witness, one who had seen the defendant with a *real* M-1 carbine in his trunk, two days before the killing. But all witnesses have a weakness. This one did not have enough confidence to withstand imaginative trickery by this skilled defense attorney.

"And you say you had a good look at the trunk?" the lawyer asked.

"Yes," said the eager witness.

"Well, how close were you to the trunk, in which you claim to have seen this rifle?" the attorney asked.

"Close enough to see it," answered the witness.

"Then obviously you were able to see the objects behind the rifle, correct?" the attorney asked.

"Don't remember anything else," the witness replied.

"Oh yeah, you remember the cathedral-shaped object in the back of the trunk, the one covered with a cloth?" the attorney pressed.

"Well, I'm really not sure I saw . . ." the witness said with hesitation, obviously confused.

"You say you saw the rifle, right?"

"Yeah, I saw that," the witness replied, to my relief.

"Then explain to the jury how you missed this huge cathedral dome in the back of the trunk," the attorney asked in mock astonishment, looking meaningfully at the jury.

"Well, maybe I did see it . . . yeah, I think I remember it," the witness replied with growing confidence.

"Right," the attorney said, "the birdcage in which you heard the birdie go 'tweet, tweet, tweet.' "

The People (namely me) were now in big trouble. There was no birdcage in the trunk. There was no bird going "tweet, tweet,

threatened to kill her if he couldn't have her. Sound fa
On the morning of the killing, the defendant's seven-y(
son, my star witness, had seen his father hide an M-1 carbin
under his overcoat. His father had then "escorted" the
mother out of the house. The boy never again saw his m(
alive.

At trial, a brilliant defense attorney destroyed the boy's c\
ibility by confusing him. By the time cross-examination was i
ished, the boy seemed unsure about whether his father had
real gun or was just playing cops and robbers with a toy gun. F
got the boy to agree that his father had bought the boy a "near
toy rifle, and that every time his father came by, they played cow
boys and Indians. Now take a look at how a great defense lawyer
turned a deadly M-1 carbine into a toy rifle.

"You remember the last time you saw your mother, you and
your daddy played cops and robbers, isn't that what happened,
John?"

"I don't remember," the boy said, looking confused.

"Sure you do, you know—when your dad snuck up behind
you, like he always does, and grabbed the toy carbine he had
bought you—the one you always left on the living room floor—
and pretended to be an outlaw?" the attorney asked, gently
prodding the boy.

"I don't. I don't know," the boy said, appearing confused.

"Well, when your daddy comes over to visit you, he always
plays with you, doesn't he?"

"Yeah," the boy replied cautiously.

"Now, do you remember leaving this toy carbine on the
living-room floor, the one your daddy bought you, and your
daddy telling you not to leave it there?"

"Uh-huh, I think so," the boy said softly.

"That's a good boy, John. You're doing just fine," the attorney said, smiling like Colonel Sanders enjoying a juicy fried
drumstick. "And the day you last saw your mother was the day
your daddy picked up your toy carbine and pretended to shoot
you—just like real cowboys and Indians, right?"

"I guess," the boy said, looking more confused.

"And you like to watch cowboys and westerns on TV?"

"Yes," said the boy, nervously wringing his hands.

tweet." The jury hung on the broken testimony of my key witnesses. The haunting image of the victim trying to communicate with me has never left my memory. Nor have I forgotten the lesson I learned about the justice system, about the adversarial roles of the defense and prosecution attorneys. I lost to a more experienced and powerful gladiator. Truth was the casualty. Mind you, my opponent was not acting unethically. According to the rules of the adversarial game, the attorneys are allowed to confuse small boys and to trick gullible witnesses. Artful cross-examination can be used to squeeze the truth out of hostile and biased witnesses. It can also defame and destroy a truthful witness. Jerry Spence refuses to put many of his clients on the witness stand for fear a skilled cross-examiner can make a truthful witness appear a liar. I have done that to witnesses myself.

Today we see much worse than what I have just described. F. Lee Bailey and Robert Shapiro said it all. The truth is irrelevant in criminal trials, and we adversaries often seem to be prepared to win at any cost. It happens every day.

The Bad News

Neither of the two incidents I have just related were extreme or exaggerated. Overzealous DAs do take cases for their publicity or political value rather than for their merit. Every attorney dreams of being able to destroy a witness on the stand with a strategy like the birdcage.

• Criminal attorneys—both defense and prosecution—routinely violate the law and rules of professional ethics. They hide evidence, they doctor documents, they deliberately play to the worst and basest instincts of the juries—with no apparent shame.

• Some expert witnesses will say anything the defense attorneys want them to. In fact, some experts specialize in inventing new and increasingly stranger psychiatric defenses. They know there will always be a market for an expert who can justify serious criminal behavior as being really not so bad, if we would just understand. The prosecution has its own stable of dubious experts. Disingenuous and lying experts are so much a part of the routine that no one really notices or cares.

• Starting in the 1960s, our appeals courts became obsessed with defining and enforcing rigid procedural rules based on newly invented constitutional rights that were never contemplated by the drafters of our Constitution. As a result, the principal focus of many trials today is not whether the defendant committed a crime, but whether the police strictly obeyed a set of byzantine, judicially crafted rules. Incredibly, most judges will admit they themselves have difficulty understanding these rules.

• The police know these convoluted constitutional rights are silly and unfair—and the police are right. The result is that otherwise honest cops now often lie about the details of searches and seizures to get around the complexities of the ever-changing and generally incomprehensible procedural rules. Many judges, prosecutors, defense attorneys, and police know this occurs. The practice is so common it has a name: *testi-lying*.

• Many jurors are undereducated and ill equipped to render judgment in complex cases. Even worse, juries often ignore the evidence they do understand. Increasingly, jurors seem to view their role as being a golden opportunity to pay someone back for one perceived wrong or another. To that end, prospective jurors often lie so they can become members of the jury, especially in high-profile cases, where instant celebrity is virtually guaranteed. Lying jurors are so common that no one takes even a second glance.

• Some of our judges have lost control of their courtrooms. They fail to hold lawyers, litigants, jurors, cops, and witnesses accountable for conduct that undermines the justice system. They fail to curtail repetitious and excessive behavior. They do not punish attorneys who violate discovery rules, lie, or suppress evidence. We court-watchers have seen this happening with virtual impunity over and over.

• Finally, and maybe worst of all, our society is becoming balkanized. The myth of a glorious melting pot died long ago. We are a matrix of competing cultures and ethnicities—all with special agendas, all fighting for a piece of the American dream. The phenomena of "group think," "them against us," and "payback time" are sadly upon us. The haunting image of cheering African-American law students at Howard University juxtaposed against the shock on the faces of white students following the Simpson verdict signified deep racial divisions in America. We seem to be unable to find an objective point of view where we all see justice the same way. We are in danger of adopting a system of justice by color.

No criminal justice system can be perfect. Period. The best system in the world will always convict some innocent people and acquit even greater numbers of guilty ones. As we evolve as a people, however, working together, we can refine our system to make it harder to ensnare the innocent and easier to find the truth. A system for all of us. Now we must take our first hard look at where it all begins. As Grover A. Whalen said, "There's a lot of law at the end of a nightstick."

T W O

The Secret Life
of Cops

MARKED MEN

From the moment of his birth, the customs into which
[an individual] is born shape his experience and behavior.
By the time he can talk, he is the little creature of his culture.
—*Ruth Fulton Benedict, 1934*

Cops work right where the criminal justice system rubs up against the people. The most likely encounter any citizen will have with the criminal justice system is with a cop. Most often it involves a routine traffic ticket; sometimes it is much more serious. So I begin by talking about cops.

In the last four decades, being a cop has gotten a lot harder. Ugly, violent crime has skyrocketed. Our population has grown at an explosive rate. Our crowded cities breed conflict and violence. Youth gangs in the 1950s and 1960s "rumbled." Basic weapons—fists, clubs, knives, brass knuckles, perhaps an occasional zip gun—were used. Occasionally people were injured, sometimes they even died. Now thirteen- and fourteen-year-olds in the cities and suburbs carry automatic pistols and AK-47s and we ask our cops to meet them with .38-caliber Police Specials—peashooters by comparison. We now have teenage serial killers, and cold-blooded killings by preteens.

In roll call, cops are constantly reminded of the dangers out there—from us, from you and me. Who is armed? Who is not? Who is dangerous? Who is not? I don't know one street cop who

does not have at least one harrowing story of how his or his partner's life was on the line in a day's work. Cops are marked men
and women. They wear badges and uniforms. We all know who
they are. No cop, however, knows who among *us* is the next
predator who will try to take his or her life, the life of a partner,
or the life of one of our fellow citizens. This is not theoretical for
cops. Even routine traffic stops are potentially lethal. Any driver
could have a gun, and might use it. That is part of what cops are
thinking when they stop you or me for driving too fast. It's nothing personal, it's just that if they let their guard down, they can
die. So there is *always* a line between cops and us.

Cops face more than mere danger, however. They also know
we entrust them with the license to carry and, if need be, to use
a gun. Every cop I know takes that responsibility very seriously.
They know that if they make a bad judgment call with the gun,
innocent blood will flow—and they will replay the shooting in
their nightmares for the rest of their lives. Bad judgment could
also cost them their career or, worse, jail. Real life is not always
clear-cut. Bad calls happen in fast-moving street situations—especially when cops are scared. Yes, cops get scared. This should
not be so hard to relate to, if we think about it. Suppose you are
a woman who works all day. It is late at night. You need to get
some breakfast cereal for your children, so you drive to a nearby
convenience store. You have read about carjackings and drive-
bys, so you have a .32-caliber pistol in the car for your protection.
As you park, an old car full of black teenagers pulls into the
parking spot behind you. Over the insistent rap music, you think
you hear lewd remarks and the word "bitch." Are they referring
to you? A car door slams and a teenager appears by your car
door suddenly, seemingly out of nowhere. Another is behind
him. The first one moves his hand toward the pocket of his over-
sized baggies. Is that a gun he pulled out? It could be. It's the
right size. Or is that a shadow? The image of being kidnapped,
raped, and killed cuts through all reason. Like a cop, you too are
scared. You pull your gun and fire. In a panic, you drive away,
leaving a mortally wounded teenager. His friends claim he was
just getting change for a parking meter. You still think his friends
hid the gun before the cops arrived.

You perceived your danger as real, and maybe it was—you
will never really know. You acted on the assumption that the kids

were dangerous because the media constantly headlines violent black youths. Maybe these *were* bad guys. They looked dangerous, wore baggy pants and baseball caps turned backwards, displayed the color red worn by the notorious Bloods, and had crude tattoos on their hands, and the one you shot had that sullen "bad 'tude" look on his face.

The shooting is now under police investigation. Black leaders call you a racist, and demand justice. The white mayor, seeing a cheap way to appeal to minority voters, has made *you* an issue in his campaign. You are not an issue; you are a person, but you feel you have become a scapegoat in a huge political passion play that you never even tried out for. It affects your personal life. Your black friends don't return your calls. Your white friends say, "Couldn't you have driven off, or locked the doors and blown the horn for help?" You ask yourself the same question over and over. You replay the shooting in your mind incessantly. If any of this resonates within you, that's a tiny bit of what it's like to be a street cop. They have to make this kind of decision in milliseconds, over and over, every day. Every stop, every detention, every arrest could get them killed, or it could be the one that brings on the nightmares in which are rerun incessantly the taking of an innocent life, the life of a person they were sworn to serve and protect, not to kill. It's a tough job.

Now let's go deeper. Cops see the very worst of human nature every day, in a way most of us do not understand. In effect, we hire them to be our buffer against human nature, to protect us from having to look too hard at the dark side of ourselves. The cops do their job, but they pay a price. Let me try to put this in perspective. Most street cops have seen more corpses than they care to remember. Many of those corpses are homicides. Suppose about twice a year in *your* job, you came to work and found someone murdered in your office—blood, a corpse, maggots, and the stench of death. And suppose it was your job to stay there and keep order until your boss got there an hour later. I have seen the corpses of murdered people, and have difficulty relating how disturbing it is. Try to imagine what I just described. How would you feel just before you unlocked the door to your office each morning? Would it affect your attitude toward your work, toward the people with whom you came in contact? If not, then let me tell you a little more.

I know the sheriffs who handled the Lawrence Bittiker case. Mr. Bittiker tortured and mutilated five teenaged victims with pliers, Vise-Grips, and an icepick. One of the victims, thirteen years old, was hammered to death. Two others were killed with icepicks thrust through their ears; Bittiker had seen the icepick-in-the-ear trick done in a gangster movie while in prison and thought it was a cool idea. He also tore the nipples from his victims' breasts with pliers. He photographed the murders and captured his victims' screams on tape—to sell.

The sheriffs saw it all—the bodies, the audio "snuff tapes," the photos. I would find cops, family men, sitting at their desk or in a bar, sometimes in a daze, just staring. Does that surprise you? It's not enough to say they are trained professionals. No one is trained to deal with this evil, ever. Suppose you personally encountered the bodies in the Bittiker case once every five years at work. Would that affect your attitude toward people?

Let's talk for a minute about being society's scapegoat. Did you feel uncomfortable at all when you imagined yourself the object of a cynical political campaign by the mayor? Well, police feel the same way. *We,* not the police, make the laws. Then *we* hire the police to go out and enforce *our* laws—the popular ones and the unpopular ones. We let them do *our* dirty work. Every day they are out in our violent, factionalized society, serving and protecting us. They are the ones who make our war on crime real. Transients, gang members, the mentally ill, wife beaters, drug dealers, serial killers—all of these become police problems. We have abrogated our responsibilities and now we want the problems to go away. Now. Don't bother us with details. We just want to get the job done.

What happens to the police when *our* kids are busted or when the confrontation with gangs that we have demanded so stridently becomes ugly and a fourteen-year-old Hispanic boy lies bleeding on the ground, his and his family's hopes snuffed out in one moment of violence? The cops say he had a gun. The boy's friends claim the gun was planted. Whom to believe? The media machine starts cranking, and we offer up the cops as a sacrifice to the gods of war. *Our* war gone awry, one in which "friendly fire" sometimes ends up killing our own people. We are angry and demand reform—for a while. But our memories and commitment are short, and we don't like crime. Society's unpopular members—illegal aliens, the mentally ill, the homeless, all gang members—are expendable in the war, so again we send the police out to "get tough on crime."

This time we want a war on real criminals, on *violent* crime. We want to arrest all the crack dealers. So the cops go after the violent criminals and crack dealers. But our war immediately butts up against some unpleasant facts for which the cops end up being blamed. Root causes aside, some minorities commit a disproportionately large number of crimes—especially violent ones. Crack is much more popular among black addicts than among whites, who tend to use the powder form of cocaine. If we, *as a society*, insist violent criminals be arrested, that crack dealers be jailed, much of that burden will fall on our minority communities. Period. The cops are just the messengers carrying *our* message. They do not like being unpopular in minority communities and called racists because they arrest violent criminals there, but find it more difficult to arrest white cocaine sellers and users in the suburbs and affluent areas of our cities. They see that as doing the job we hired them to do, *and they are right.*

This is not a pleasant topic. Police believe they are enforcing our values and our laws, not their own. So here's the line again between us and them. Nothing personal, but when things get rough, we and our politicians will leave them to twist slowly in the wind. When it was alleged that the CIA funded Nicaraguan contras with drug money derived from crack cocaine sales to black ghetto communities, the government, of course, denied complicity—leaving the police to deal with the angry and outraged citizenry.

They are the lightning rod of the justice system, the visible instrument of our values, and they will get the blame when we are not courageous enough to look in the mirror and admit that they were only enforcing our values and our decisions. If we don't like the cost, it is up to us to say so. Then we have to be willing to stand by what we say. The police don't think we will. They're probably right.

Then, too, the cops have seen years of hypocrisy by our appellate courts regarding the death penalty. Police risk their lives to apprehend serial killers and other vicious murderers. They live with the cases night and day. They hold the survivors' hands. The trial starts. The killer's guilt or innocence seems irrelevant;

what is important is whether the cops have complied with an impenetrable thicket of rules that change constantly. They get a conviction anyway. The killer is sent to death row. What follows is a Mad Hatter's dream. The victim is long dead but the killer languishes on death row, sometimes longer than his victim lived, filing appeal after appeal, writ after writ, until some high court finally finds a way to reverse the penalty (and sometimes even to let the criminal go completely). This happened over and over under the Rose Bird California Supreme Court, which reversed some sixty-five *consecutive* death-penalty verdicts. And that was in only one of fifty states. How could there be so much error? How could cops and DAs have made so many mistakes? The answer is they didn't. The court grossly magnified the importance and prejudicial effect of the perceived mistakes because it did not like the death penalty, and that was the only way to avoid it. Hypocrisy on high. As Justice Louis Brandeis said, "If we desire respect for the law, we must first make the law respectable." Only then will it be worthy of our respect, and that of the police.

Finally, when a cop like Mark Furhman (who ran the initial investigation in the Simpson/Goldman murders) is exposed, loud claques immediately claim he is typical—a slur that is beneath contempt. We witnessed the Mark Furhman drama unfold on TV like a Greek tragedy. We did not want to accept what we were hearing. How could we defend a racist cop who just "happened" to find a bloody glove? Was our only choice to disbelieve him and let a murderer go free? Were we to punish the prosecution for Furhman's bigotry? Which was the greater sin—perjury about racist attitudes, or double murder? And who is worse, the bad cop or the disingenuous pundits who falsely claim Furhman is typical? Furhman is not typical. Cops hate it when people bundle them up and throw them all in the same crate with Mark Furhman and Adolf Hitler. There's the line again, only this time *we* are drawing the line, not the police.

What amazes me is that anyone would want to be a cop today. Does it really surprise you that police have an insular society that few outsiders ever see, a society with its own peculiar rules and rituals? I have been privileged to see this society up close, and I would like to tell you about some of the wonderful people I got to know there, and a little about how their secret society works.

The great prosecutor J. Miller Leavy told me that if I wanted

to be a good DA, I had to put my nose in the muck and slime—
meaning I had to go where the cops have to go; to know them;
to be their friend; and to understand them. I took that advice to
heart, and today I number many cops among my closest friends
and the people I most admire. I got to know L.A.'s finest in Chi-
natown, where detectives from the LAPD gathered at General
Lee's. Just across from General Lee's, a few wobbly cobblestones
to the south, was Lipos, the sheriffs' watering hole. Sheriffs did
not enter General Lee's, and LAPD officers did not enter Lipos
unless they were up to no good or, on very rare occasions, when
they were invited. Why? Because even cops from other agencies
often distrust one another, wondering what the other group is
up to, what they may see and hear or may be looking for, and
whom they may suspect of some perceived wrongdoing. By nature cops are paranoid, living always near the edge—near the
backside of human decency.

The cops at General Lee's and Lipos were mostly robbery-
homicide officers. They lived with death on a daily basis. They
were accustomed to being rousted out of bed in the middle of
the night and dispatched to yet another gory crime scene. They
smoked inveterately to help kill the stench of death at the
morgue. They also chewed tobacco to cover up the lingering
taste of postmortem putrefaction. Many were overweight, puffy-
eyed, light-years from that lean and carnivorous look of their former selves, unable to share their burdens with outsiders, unable
to talk, except to each other in a private code. I became a part
of their world.

Meet Charlie Guenther

Charlie Guenther is one of my favorites, a sheriff's homicide
detective of German descent. Charlie's father marched his
stocky, blond, blue-eyed, beardless seventeen-year-old son to the
recruiting office, enlisting him in the U.S. Army, where Charlie
served as a soldier following VE Day, at the end of World War II.
No draft call. Enlistment was an honor and a duty. When Charlie returned from his term of service, he saw his father standing
outside their house in Cleveland, waiting. He began to greet his
father in German. In a heavy German accent, Charlie's father in-

terrupted, shaking his head, saying, "You're an American. Speak your country's language and be proud!"

Charlie's crewcut, his strong, regular features, and his sincere look made him seem solid and trustworthy. This look was not unhelpful to a detective. I first met Charlie and his partner, Paul Whitely, when I was assigned to prosecute Manson family member Bobby Beausoleil for the murder of Gary Hinman. One of my earliest memories of Charlie is seeing him kneeling in front of one of the Manson girls, "Mr. Sincere," looking up at her with those baby blue eyes and trying to persuade her to cleanse her soul by confession.

Charlie saw the dark side of police work early. Tears still curl around the edges of his eyes when he relates a story he can tell only when buffered by a couple of beers. New to homicide, Charlie went to a crime scene. Just inside the front door, a little girl in a pretty white starched Communion dress lay in a lake of blood, which connected her to the bodies of her four brothers and sister. The mother had shot her children, a friend, and then herself with a rifle. Six murders and a suicide. Welcome to homicide.

Like most cops, Charlie used humor to dull the pain. He could even find humor in the homicides themselves. Charlie used to relate with great amusement how he had once responded to a report of a man hanging by the neck from a tree in a park. On the way, Charlie saw several patrol units parked outside an apartment. Charlie stopped to investigate and went inside. To his right and left, two women rocked back and forth in matching rocking chairs. Straight ahead, a man was seated with his arms spread across the top of the couch. On the floor, facedown, with two bullet holes in his back, was a male corpse lying in a pool of blood. Guenther asked who owned the house. The lady to his right said, "I's pay the rent, and where is your search warrant?" Guenther learned the speaker's name was Liza. So he asked, pointing to the woman in the other rocking chair, "Well, Liza, who is that woman over there?"

Liza: "That's my sister Louise, and Louise can come in anytime she want, 'cuz I's pay the rent, and where's your search warrant?"

Guenther: "Well, who's that on the couch?"

Liza: "Well, that's Rolfe, and he can come in anytime he wants, 'cuz I's pay the rent, and where's your search warrant?"

Guenther: "Who's that fellow lying on the floor?"

Liza got very quiet. Then, leaning forward, she stared at the body for a long time. She cogitated. She then looked over at the man on the couch. "Rolfe, who's dat motherfucker laying on the floor?" Rolfe sat there for a moment, deep in thought, then replied, "Shit, woman, you's pay the rent!" That's a good day in homicide.

Meet Vinnie Barrett and Michael Maloney

Just to be evenhanded, I want you to meet a couple of my LAPD friends. I was the DA assigned to the murder of a husband and wife in their own home. They were killed with a .22 High Standard automatic outfitted with a silencer, hands cuffed behind their backs. It looked like an organized-crime hit. One of their employees, a waitress, was found dead in her car. We knew that Jerry Sartain had killed the waitress, but there were problems with our case against him. Sartain was a crafty and streetwise felon who had served eighteen years in federal and state penitentiaries for armed robbery and other serious felonies. He was smart, and wrote writs for other inmates for money and favors, securing their early release from prison. Oddly, he never succeeded in winning one of his own! We offered Sartain three concurrent life sentences (as opposed to the death penalty) in exchange for his testimony against the killer of the husband and wife, George Patrick McKinney.

Vinnie Barrett and his young partner, Michael Maloney, worked the case with me. Vinnie was one of the youngest and last of the old-time "Hat" squad of the robbery division, the kind of cop Nick Nolte depicted in the film *Mulholland Falls*. Barrett had more of a sense of humor and definitely had more fun than Nolte's character. The "Hats" were the crack LAPD robbery detectives after World War II. They dressed impeccably and wore felt hats, à la Dick Tracy. Barrett loved to play the horses and go to Vegas. The deep lines in his face came less from his work than from watching the horses at Hollywood Park and Santa Anita and playing golf.

Barrett's partner, Sergeant Maloney, was an easygoing, fast-rising cop. Barrett had finally penetrated Maloney's compliant good nature and by-the-book mentality. What was the point of keeping it, since, time after time, the grizzled Barrett broke departmental regulations, using his guile, charm, and wit to solve crimes his way.

Barrett, Maloney, and I needed Jerry Sartain's cooperation to convict McKinney, the hit man. Hence the deal about life in prison. But Sartain's testimony would not be enough. He was an accomplice, and we had to have corroboration. No deals unless Sartain could produce verifiable evidence! So Sartain agreed to take us to the place in the desert where he claimed to have buried the gun, the silencer, and the handcuffs used on the husband and wife.

A caravan of three cars embarked upon a strange odyssey. In a sheriff's van, Jerry Sartain, wearing steel bracelets, rode with several armed sheriff's deputies. A sheriff's car led the group, while Barrett, Maloney, Don Wager—Sartain's attorney—and I trailed the group. The four of us went in Barrett's unmarked car to find the damning evidence. It seemed strange to pass occupants of other cars who hadn't a clue that sitting in just another sheriff's van was a natural-born killer, a very, very bad man. A person who, if given the chance, would have killed the four of us quickly and with as much emotion as it took to stub out four spent cigarettes.

Barrett promised Sartain that if he took us to the evidence, Barrett would treat him to the best steak dinner he ever had. This was against every imaginable regulation. Barrett just winked at me and rolled his eyes. I sat back, skeptical that Sartain would lead us to anything, believing he only wanted to get out of jail for a few hours, looking, perhaps, for a chance to escape. Maybe Sartain was setting us up. Maybe we'd meet some killers waiting for us in a remote desert location. Or maybe I had seen too many B movies. I looked at Don Wager for some sign that Sartain was acting in good faith. Don, dressed in a dark striped suit, made me think of Batman's nemesis, the Penguin. His frozen, enigmatic smile told me nothing.

Sartain led us to one location. We got out of the car. He suddenly bolted down a sloped embankment. My thoughts raced. I could only think of him running to a spot where he had secreted the hit weapon, in a readily accessible place. A place where quick access could give him a loaded gun for a few precious moments. A place where killers hiding behind sagebrush would be waiting. Of course, I also felt like Woody Allen in one of his films, wondering what a nice Jewish boy was doing in this bizarre situation. After all, our killer was still loosely handcuffed, or was he? I couldn't tell from where I was. Couldn't see the cuffs! Then he slowed down, appearing to study the terrain. Maloney and Barrett joined Sartain, followed by Wager and me and the sheriffs. Sartain, Barrett, and Maloney relieved themselves. They casually smoked a cigarette and stretched their legs. Wager did likewise, engaging in easy banter with his client. Sartain looked at Barrett and Maloney, then the sheriffs, as if sizing them up. Would he run? Would they shoot? He looked at me as if I were a tasty dessert. I walked to a bush, but was unable to urinate in front of the killer. I suggested we move on, mumbling to myself that this was a complete waste of time.

We got back into the car and drove another twenty minutes across the same numbing scenery, when suddenly Sartain motioned for us to stop. It was even more desolate than before. More desert. We got out and he nodded toward a sandy location. What was he up to? What was he going to try? I imagined Sartain with a gun, and me fleeing his shots, darting in a zigzag pattern in a vain effort to avoid being killed.

Barrett acted as if nothing were wrong. He opened the trunk of his car. He had forgotten to bring a shovel, but not his golf clubs. With his sand wedge he lumbered to the location Sartain indicated. Like a dog circling some buried treasure, Sartain pawed the dirt with his foot. His eyes darted back and forth across the sagebrush. Barrett stepped in with his trusty sand wedge, and Sartain stepped aside. Within minutes he uncovered something. I heard the distinct sound of clanking metal. Then Barrett produced a rusty beer can! I smiled, giving him my best I-told-you-so shrug, as my eyes quickly darted toward the large tumbleweed balls that appeared to be encircling us, moving.

Barrett moved a few feet over, exploring with his sand-wedge. The defendant's eyes never left the head of the probing golf club. He looked intense. So did Wager. Another metallic clank. Carefully, Barrett began to probe some rusted objects. At first I did not recognize the rusty silencer-equipped automatic and three sets of handcuffs, similar to the ones binding two of the murder victims, buried just a few inches below the surface. But there they were. This was the hit weapon preferred by many "wise guy" assassins. Success. I turned to thank Wager, who appeared self-absorbed. A strange expression of surprise, even shock was written over his face. Even Sartain's attorney was unwilling to believe until this moment. Now all that was left was to get this killer back to jail.

We drove back to L.A. Instead of taking Sartain back to jail, Barrett headed for his favorite watering hole and steak house, Taylor's, on Ninth Street, frequented by high-ranking cops, city politicians, reporters, John McKay, and the USC football team. I realized with growing horror that Barrett was going to deliver on his promise of a steak dinner, at which we were captive guests! Not only that, but Barrett was going to pull this off right under the noses of the LAPD brass, with the complicity of the sheriffs. Barrett was personal friends with the owner, Tex Taylor. I don't know how Barrett convinced Tex and the sheriffs, but Barrett sneaked Sartain up a seldom-used side entrance under Tex's intense, reproving gaze. We were to eat in a private dining room upstairs, a place where Heisman Trophy winners rubbed shoulders with the city's elite.

Sartain, in cuffs, was placed at one end of a rectangular table between two bulky deputy sheriffs, as if he were a slab of sandwich meat. Wager sat next to one of the sheriffs, and Maloney, across from Wager, sat next to the other deputy. Barrett, at the opposite end, faced Sartain. I sat next to Barrett, buffered by two more sheriffs sitting between Maloney and me. Then the moment came. Our salads were served. Sartain sat rigid, staring at his salad. Seeing this, Barrett bellowed, "C'mon, he can't eat with the cuffs, take 'em off!" Reluctantly a deputy removed the cuffs. Jerry gave a steely glance down the table and began to eat with great intensity, without a word. Barrett looked at Maloney, who raised his eyebrows. Then at Don Wager. He looked at me, taking special delight in my obvious discomfort. Barrett squinted at Sartain. Then suddenly he said to the sheriff, whose gun was perched on his hip within inches of Sartain's grasp as if it were a sacrificial offering, "Since he's uncuffed, don't you boys think you should take your guns off?" The sheriffs, embarrassed at their potentially fatal oversight, quickly removed their guns and placed them on the table well out of Sartain's reach.

Sartain continued to attack his salad. The craggy veteran, uncharacteristically somber, suddenly broke the embarrassed silence, asking Sartain, "How come you didn't go for the gun, Jerry?" Without missing a motion of his fork, Sartain replied, "Because you're holding on me under the table!" And there I sat, thinking this was like a Dirty Harry movie—only this time there were real guns, and a real killer. I stared at Sartain's hands, remembering how he had told me of firing eight bullets into the back of the waitress's head with about the same emotion as stepping on a cockroach. Sartain looked intensely at Barrett, searching. Something was bothering him. Barrett responded, "You're still wondering what would have happened if you went for the gun, is that it, Jerry?" Sartain blew smoke rings toward Barrett's nose, one after the other, like heat-seeking missiles. He smiled with his mouth, not his eyes. Slowly, Barrett produced the snub-nosed .38 he had been holding under the table, laying it next to his plate. Given the fact that Wager's and my knees were ostensibly in the direct path of a Barrett bullet to Sartain's gut, I began to exhibit a Nixonian bead of perspiration.

All I could think was, *How did I get myself into this?* These *goyische* cops were crazy! I couldn't wait to go home and hug my wife. And regale her with a few stories!

One final fact, when revealed to me, made me wonder if this was not an episode out of a famous comic strip. The Penguin sidled up to me as we were leaving Taylor's and showed me a huge sheet of paper, folded five ways, on which he had written in enormous block letters, I'M ONLY THE DEFENSE ATTORNEY, DON'T SHOOT! He smiled like that other penguin—the one who gave Batman so much *tsuris*—and then waggled away.

Was That Really Funny?

I learn more about a group of people from their humor than from anything else. Police society has strange, macho, and sometimes bizarre humor rites. I believe that cops seize on anything to dull the inhumanity they experience every day. So they find humor where perhaps humor seems inappropriate to outsiders.

The rivalry between the LAPD and the sheriff's department was a source of raw cop humor. Guenther was assigned to the Firestone station. The Firestone station had its own doghouse with its own separate address. The cops housed their shaggy mascot in this special doghouse. The mutt was surely one of the ugliest dogs alive, its genetic heritage and alleged male gender a constant source of debate. Remember, Guenther was a sheriff. One day the rival LAPD kidnapped the mutt and had a veterinarian cut off all his hair. Not only that, but the vet used vegetable dye to color the pooch pink all over. As a final touch, the vet left two strands of hair between the mutt's ears, to which a pink bow was tied. The pink bow was carefully chosen to match the mutt's now-pink skin. Oddly enough, the sheriffs found this funny, especially when the Firestone station started receiving calls asking about gay dogs. LAPD brass did not find the incident so funny, at least not officially. They gave the four dognappers four days off without pay—a sentence substantially greater than the one detective Mark Furhman received for committing perjury in the O.J. criminal trial! They also demanded that the sheriffs testify against the chastened LAPD officers. The sheriffs refused—cops do not testify against other cops, even if the other cop is from the rival LAPD and recently kidnapped and dyed *your* dog. There the matter ended. As you can see, even police departments have a tough time dealing with the cops' code of silence, not to mention their fraternal mischief.

THREE

The Ten-Thousand-Pound Gorilla

THE EXCLUSIONARY RULE

Tell me not of technical rules of evidence! They have
excluded the light of day from the jury box long enough.
Not only open wide doors and windows, but unroof the
temples of justice, that all the rays of truth may beam
brilliantly upon those who are set for the administration
of the law.
—*Hon. Joseph H. Lumpkin, 1858*

The exclusionary rule is the ten-thousand-pound gorilla
of our criminal justice system. Cops, prosecutors, and
trial judges spend much of their time tiptoeing
around the beast, hoping it is sleeping soundly. Like the mythical beast, it is wiser not to stir up the exclusionary rule, lest we
suffer the consequences of a runaway train. Defense counsel,
when faced with damning evidence against their client, do their
utmost to keep it awake and mad. An extraordinary portion of
the resources of our criminal justice system is devoted to servic-
ing the beast's ever-changing whims. The exclusionary rule is
bad law. It is demeaning, an insult, a slap in the face to our cops.
Worse, it makes the truth irrelevant to the criminal justice system. The exclusionary rule has failed in its only goal, to prevent
cops from violating the Constitution. The cost of feeding this
creature is almost unbelievably high. The rule should be elimi-

nated and replaced with measures that will preserve our constitutional rights and let the truth back into our courtrooms.

The exclusionary rule is simple to state and difficult to apply. Any evidence seized by cops in violation of a "fundamental" constitutional right may not be used as evidence against a criminal defendant. There are some extensions, exceptions, and permutations, but for now this definition will suffice.

The Bill of Rights, the first ten amendments to our Constitution, was ratified in 1791. These amendments protected all citizens against illegal acts committed by the *federal* government. For 123 years there was no exclusionary rule. There is a good reason for that.

In 1914 the United States Supreme Court decided that evidence secured by the *federal* government in violation of the Fourth Amendment protection against illegal searches and seizures could not be admitted into evidence. This became known as the exclusionary rule. Until 1961 the rule under the U.S. Constitution applied only to the federal government. In 1961, in *Mapp v. Ohio,* the United States Supreme Court, after 170 years, decided the rule should apply to all of the states. *Mapp* was the culmination of an activist judicial trend that began in the supreme courts of some states in the 1950s. Since *Mapp,* I have no doubt but that entire rain forests, formerly filled with precious trees of great antiquity, have been sacrificed so that judges, lawyers, and scholars could write endless pages of cases and commentaries about the exclusionary rule and its infinite permutations.

From the start, the exclusionary rule had but one purpose: to deter misconduct by the cops. The theory behind the rule was that cops will beat or intimidate prisoners until they confess, and that cops will seize evidence illegally unless they are punished for doing so. The exclusionary rule is the punishment and deterrent crafted by the United States Supreme Court. Implicit in the rule is the judgment by our appellate courts that it is as important to deter misconduct by the cops as it is to deter criminal behavior by putting the criminals in jail. In a sense, the exclusionary rule reflected a shift in the perspective of our appellate courts to a liberal, activist perspective in which "newly discovered" criminal procedural rights were divined— "rights" that were said by some to be more important than the quest for the truth. Sometime in the 1950s and 1960s our appellate courts started to believe that cops, not criminals, were part of the problems to be addressed by the criminal justice system. Even trial judges, who are in the trenches and who should know better, frequently exhibit strong anti-cop biases. I can talk about this in the abstract all I want, but reality is much more powerful. A recent example illustrates both the biases of one particular judge and a bit about how the exclusionary rule works.

In 1995, U.S. District Court Judge Harold Baer Jr. suppressed eighty pounds of cocaine and heroin seized from a drug courier's car because he ruled the search was illegal. The effect of the ruling was that the criminal defendants would go free. Here is how the courier was arrested. Early in the morning, in a drug-infested neighborhood, cops observed four men putting heavy bags into the trunk of a car with out-of-state plates. When the men saw the cops, they ran away. The police thought that behavior was suspicious, and investigated. Judge Baer did not think the behavior was suspicious at all because "many people in the upper Manhattan neighborhood . . . view the cops as corrupt, abusive, and violent." So? Does that mean that running away was not at least a little suspicious?

Judge Baer did not even have the courage of his personally biased convictions against the cops. Under enormous political pressure, from no less than President Clinton, Speaker of the House Newt Gingrich, and Senate Majority Leader Robert Dole, demanding a reversal of the ruling or his removal from office, the judge held a second hearing and reversed himself, claiming there was new evidence, namely another cop's testimony (the same testimony as given by the first cop). Even though he was wrong and biased against cops in his first decision, the cops would have respected him more had he stuck to his guns, and not yielded to extraneous political pressures.

The most common uses of the exclusionary rule are to exclude *physical evidence* seized by the police, or to prevent the jury from hearing *confessions* or *admissions* of a criminal defendant. When a judge applies the exclusionary rule, the usual result is a dismissal of the charges or an acquittal of a guilty person because of the weakness of the remaining evidence, if any. Let's look at some actual examples of the exclusionary rule as it applies to both physical evidence and confessions.

Whether physical evidence should be excluded often comes up in the context of whether the police have conducted an improper search or seizure under the Fourth Amendment. Judge Baer's decision above would have excluded the presentation of the seized drugs as evidence in the trial against the courier. The exclusionary rule has also been used to prevent juries from seeing such physical evidence as the murder weapon in murder cases, and incriminating financial records in white-collar-crime cases.

Defendants also claim frequently that their confessions or admissions were coerced because the cops did not read them their Miranda rights (the Fifth Amendment) or when, after being formally charged, they are asked a casual question by the cops that they now regret answering (the Sixth Amendment). In these cases, their confessions and admissions are often withheld from the jury under the exclusionary rule.

You might wonder how important this really is. After all, how many criminals are stupid enough to admit they committed the crime, and to a cop, no less? Actually, it happens a lot. For example: "I killed her because she tried to hide money from me," or "I hit her 'cause the bitch stole my rig." Or they make factual admissions: "Yeah, I took her home from the bar, but I dropped her off at her apartment—never saw her after that." Well, if the police have no other evidence that the defendant was with the woman who got killed that night, that is a pretty important admission.

When there are no eyewitnesses to a crime and little physical evidence, a confession is often the *only* way to bring a guilty person to justice. For example, in 1971 I handled a case in which a conviction would probably have been impossible without a confession. I prosecuted Manson family member Steve Grogan for the murder of cowboy stuntman Donald "Shorty" Shea. We had a problem in that case: we knew Shorty Shea had disappeared, but there was no corpse to show the jury. Fortunately, Grogan had confessed his participation in the murder to Manson family member Paul Watkins, describing how he, Manson, Tex Watson, and Bruce Davis had killed Shorty at Spahn Ranch. Listen in on a portion of his confession:

Charlie told me to cut his [Shorty Shea's] head off. So I had this machete and I chopped his head off and it went, bloop, bloop, bloop rolled over out of the way . . . it was real groovy. . . .

Needless to say, if the defense had been able to exclude this confession, my case against Grogan would have been very weak—I had no body to show the jury. I was lucky in that Watkins (who heard the confession) was not a cop, so the defense could not argue that the exclusionary rule applied. (The Fourth and Fifth Amendments, and consequently the exclusionary rule, do not apply to acts of private citizens, but only to government agents.) The jury got to hear this confession and returned a murder verdict. The point here is confessions are often *very* important to the people's case.

A side note: seven years later, Grogan contacted me. He admitted killing Shea. He also drew a map depicting where Shorty's body was buried at Spahn Ranch, insisting that Shorty was never beheaded or cut into pieces. That Grogan had not really chopped Shea into pieces, as he had boasted in his confession, seemed to make the killing more palatable to him. We found Shorty's body from the map. Sure enough, it was in one piece.

The exclusionary rule is actually much more far-reaching than I have described. The "fruit of the poisonous tree" doctrine requires the exclusion of all evidence obtained from exploitation of evidence that was illegally seized.

Suppose the cops fail to read the Miranda warnings to a suspected rape-murderer. Then suppose the suspect tells the cops he killed the victim and he hid the knife used in the killing in his garage. The police secure a search warrant for the garage, based on the confession, and they recover a knife. Sure enough, the defendant's prints and the victim's blood are on the knife. The confession, the knife, the fingerprint analysis, and the blood evidence will all be suppressed as "the fruit of the poisonous tree." Even though the search warrant for the knife was valid, the confession on which the warrant was based was given without the reading of Miranda rights. Therefore the jury cannot hear anything about the confession, the knife, the fingerprints, or the blood evidence, because every bit of that evidence is the result of an illegal confession. (Some exceptions reduce the harshness of this doctrine, but it remains one of the most potent weapons in the arsenal of defense counsel who is faced with damning evidence against a client.)

You now have a pretty good grounding on the basics of the exclusionary rule. Let's step inside a courtroom during a typical evidence-suppression hearing. You can listen as a cop and defense counsel duel over the intricacies of the exclusionary rule and the search-and-seizure decisions under the Fourth Amendment. I should add that the cop here is very smart and has been well trained in her search-and-seizure law. What follows is a sort of mating dance—a fascinating and bizarre ritual exacted by the Ten-Thousand-Pound Gorilla from those who would practice criminal law. It also may involve more than just a little dishonesty by the cop.

To understand the duel you are about to witness, you need a little background on one tiny corner of the intricate law of search and seizure. When cops stop citizens but do not arrest them, that is called a *detainment*. Many cops have been seriously injured or killed in what they thought were routine detainments. Even though a cop has no knowledge that a particular detainee is armed, the overriding public interest in not having cops killed means cops may frisk a detainee for weapons—a sensible rule, not always observed by some of our more liberal courts. Usually the cop's privilege to frisk a detainee means he or she can only feel the outer clothing of the detainee to detect the possible presence of a weapon.

In this case the fun began when the cop claimed she found marijuana during a frisk of a detainee. A routine stop thus became an arrest for possession of marijuana. Remember, the cop may only search for weapons. If she feels a *hard* object, which might reasonably be a weapon, she can retrieve the object. But if she feels a *soft* object, which cannot rationally be said to constitute a threat, she cannot ordinarily retrieve it. In reality, when the cop feels something soft, what usually follows is a kind of cop-detainee dance in which, if the cop has much experience, she will be able to "induce" the detainee to produce the "suspicious" bulge "voluntarily."

If the bulge is marijuana, the case will likely end up in a suppression hearing before the judge. The issue: Should the judge apply the exclusionary rule and prevent the jury from learning that a baggie of marijuana was seized? The predictable duel begins:

DEFENSE ATTORNEY: You felt no hard objects. Correct, officer?

COP: That's correct, counselor.

Cops like to say "counselor." It must be taught at every police academy. I suspect it is a very pejorative term in cop-speak, but, as a counselor myself, I never quite had the courage to ask.

ATTORNEY: At that point, you were not concerned for your safety, is that a fair statement?

COP: I can't say that.

ATTORNEY: But you can say you were satisfied there were no hard objects on the defendant, right?

COP: It appeared there were none, counselor.

ATTORNEY: You certainly didn't think this soft rounded object was a grenade or a bomb, did you, officer?

COP: Well, I really didn't know, I couldn't say. There are plastic explosives . . .

The cop just doesn't want to give any quarter. The defense attorney is the enemy.

ATTORNEY: Oh, come now, officer.

COP: Officers have been assaulted with explosives and acid . . .

ATTORNEY (rolling his eyes): Right, and alien Martians . . . withdrawn, your honor . . .

The defense attorney knows he has overstepped his bounds, but sometimes it is hard to resist.

ATTORNEY: The truth is, you thought it was a bag of marijuana, isn't that right?

COP (coyly): It did cross my mind, counselor.

ATTORNEY: Indeed. So you reached in and retrieved it, isn't that right?

COP: Not exactly. You see, your client started to *pull away* from me. I asked him what was in his pocket, and . . .

What we have here is a ritual being enacted in which *each* word has a particular legal consequence, such as the phrase "pull away." Just that additional fact, if true, could be the difference between a legal search and an illegal one in *some* courts. The ritual continues:

ATTORNEY: Officer, did you have a warrant for the arrest of my client, or a warrant to search his person?

COP: I did not, no I didn't.

ATTORNEY: And my client was not free to go, was he?

This is very important because many Fourth Amendment exclusions are triggered by this fact.

COP: He was not under arrest at that time, counselor.

This cop is sharp. She knows involuntary detention is a critical fact to be weighed by the court in looking at the totality of the circumstances for the reasonableness of the search.

ATTORNEY: Officer, we all know he was not under formal arrest then. But try to answer my question. Was he free to leave? Could he just walk away? That's what I am asking you. If that is too difficult, I will break it down for you.

COP (with disdain): Your question assumes I had completed my investigation, counselor. I had not.

ATTORNEY: This so-called investigation was a narcotics investigation, correct?

COP: That's correct.

ATTORNEY: So in your own mind, your suspicions of narcotics activity were confirmed when you felt the soft pouch, isn't that a fact?

This is a dangerous area for the cop, because if she concedes she thought the pouch was contraband, it can be argued she made up her mind to arrest the defendant *before* she lawfully confirmed that fact. If that is so, even his "voluntary" retrieval of the pot from his pocket might be held to be a submission to unlawful authority. We can see the two combatants walking on a tightrope, each carefully looking for an opening to pass the other.

COP: The soft pouch was suggestive of narcotics, counselor. I hadn't yet verified that pouch was in fact contraband.

ATTORNEY: But he was not free to leave. Correct?

COP: Yes.

ATTORNEY: It is a fact that you reached into his pocket. Do you deny this, officer?

Again, we are at dangerous crossroads. Here the *exact* sequence of events will determine whether this search is constitutionally permissible. Listen to how well this cop has done her Fourth Amendment homework.

COP: Only after the defendant reached inside his pocket. I was fearful he might try to destroy evidence or perhaps do something to me.

The cop didn't take the bait. Because of the defendant's own suspicious actions, she has now made a case that she responded in a reasonable fashion. She even threw in a possible threat to herself, which would entitle her to intercede for her own safety.

ATTORNEY: Let me see if I understand this. You stopped the defendant, who was walking on a public street in broad daylight, you had no arrest or search warrant, he had not, to your knowledge, committed any crime, he was not free to leave, and you did not find any weapons on him. Does that fairly sum up the facts, officer?

COP: You left out something very important, counselor. This was a high-frequency narcotics area. The defendant looked in my direction and then turned around and walked the other way.

ATTORNEY: Oh, is that a crime, officer? Are you saying that citizens of the United States can't walk away from the police if they so desire? Since when is—

COP: That's three questions, counselor. No, it is not a crime. Yes, under most circumstances, a citizen is free to walk away from the police, but under *the totality of the circumstances,* including a *quick motion* he made with his left hand, I felt it warranted a brief investigation.

This is one sharp cop. She has just clobbered the defense attorney between the eyes. She used the magic phrase *totality of circumstances,* and added a new twist of constitutional significance. The quick movement suggests suspicious activity, which might be held by the court to give the cop a rational basis for the detention. Defense counsel is in trouble. If the judge believes the cop—and we will discuss that issue later—then the bag of marijuana will probably be admitted into evidence.

Let's look at what has just happened in this duel. A ritual was played out—a serious ritual, because life and liberty are at stake, as well as our precious constitutional principles. Who prevails may depend as much on *what* the search has turned up as on the niceties and principles of the Fourth Amendment. This is the real world. No academia here. If all the cop got was a bag of marijuana, many judges would probably suppress the evidence. They would simply say they did not believe the cop—the cop's testimony was too pat—or that once it was confirmed there were no deadly weapons, the cop had no right to reach into the defendant's pocket without probable cause to believe he had contraband. But suppose that search revealed two expensive diamond rings wrapped inside soft, spongy foam, and those rings were taken from dead victims of a burglary-murder down the street. Then the judge is much more likely to "believe" the testimony of the cop, even though her testimony was awfully pat. The judge might also interpret what is reasonable under the Fourth Amendment differently when a more serious crime is at stake.

Note that three remarkable things are going on here:

First, in my opinion, the cop's testimony above *is* too pat. I'll bet every arrest she makes for narcotics on a detainment just happens to go almost exactly the same way, with minor variations, depending on the actual circumstances. She found a formula that works for narcotics arrests on a detainment and she sticks with the formula, *even if it isn't exactly true.* That is what insiders in the criminal justice system call "testi-lying." It happens all the time. Note this well. You will hear a lot more about testi-lying.

Second, when the stakes are high—in a murder case, for example—the judge frequently is willing to overlook the cop's lie. Focus on this, because it is important. *The judge admits the evidence even though he or she suspects the cop is lying.* It happens all the time. You will hear a lot more about this practice also.

Third, during the hearings, nobody even comments about how odd it is that everyone is spending a lot of time and money arguing about whether the most relevant evidence in the case should be shown to the jury. Isn't criminal justice a quest for the truth? About whether the defendant is or is not guilty? How could a jury make that decision if they do not get to see the most important evidence?

Obviously these observations raise profound issues about justice and the integrity of our system.

I believe it is time to reevaluate the exclusionary rule in light of its original purpose and in light of the very high cost it has imposed on our judicial system. Here are the points to keep in mind about the exclusionary rule:

1. The exclusionary rule is a recent judicial add-on to the Constitution. Therefore we would not have to amend the Constitution to change it.

2. The exclusionary rule makes the truth irrelevant in criminal proceedings. The whole proceeding focuses not on whether the defendant had eighty pounds of cocaine and heroin in his car, but on whether the cops got the search right, or read the Miranda warnings soon enough. Needless to say, cops believe strongly that the focus should be on the cocaine and heroin. They notice when the truth "seems" unimportant. This sets the stage for testi-lying and all of its negative consequences.

3. The exclusionary rule is either/or. Either the heroin comes into evidence or it doesn't. If the heroin is excluded, the defendant usually goes free. Thus, the stakes are high. The draconian result of suppressing the evidence makes the testi-lying even easier. A virtual certainty. The high stakes also make it more likely that the trial judge and the prosecutor will ignore what they know or suspect is false testimony.

It is important to understand clearly that the exclusionary rule is different from our constitutional rights. The exclusionary rule exists only as a sort of mechanical tool devised to protect our underlying rights by deterring police from violating them. While the rule itself is of recent origin and has caused no end of problems, the underlying constitutional rights are precious and must be preserved. The next chapter talks about some of those rights that can trigger the exclusionary rule—the Fourth through Sixth Amendments, which prohibit unreasonable searches and seizures, coerced confessions, and which guarantee you the right to counsel before you make a statement to the police.

F O U R

That Sucker Didn't Read Me My Rights, Man!

THE CONSTITUTIONAL TEA PARTY

We are under a constitution, but the constitution is
what the Judges say it is.
—*Chief Justice Charles Evans Hughes*

Our Constitution has rules against the police searching your home without a warrant. It has rules against searching you or your effects without probable cause. It has rules that guarantee you can have a lawyer if you are ever arrested. It does not allow the cops to beat a confession out of you. These are very important rights. Unfortunately, the manner in which the appellate courts have chosen to enforce these rights has created more problems than it has solved. We have already seen how the exclusionary rule has hurt the justice system. But there are other problems. Our constitutional protections should be defined clearly—something the appellate courts have failed to do. Our protections should not emphasize form over substance. The famous Miranda decision and its progeny do exactly that. I believe strongly that our constitutional rights will be better protected by eliminating the Miranda decision and the exclusionary rule and substituting other and better protections.

The Bill of Rights defines our personal rights as against those of the police. When can a cop search our homes or cars? The flip side is that it defines what we can allow the cops to do to other people for the purpose of protecting us. The Bill of

rs allowed British soldiers to break into any home at any
, using so-called general warrants? A general warrant was
blanche to search anyone, anywhere, anytime. Nor did the
sh governors have qualms about forcing Americans to "con-
with what can only be euphemistically described as "per-
ve" techniques.

magine living in prerevolutionary America. You and your
ds are having beer at a local tavern before going home after
irteen-hour workday. You complain out loud, goodna-
lly, to no one in particular that the government takes too
1 of your money, jesting that the group should form a beer
kers' guild to fight the beer tax. Unfortunately, the wrong
n hears you complaining.

ive hours later you are in bed, comfortably snuggled up
your wife, your dog at the foot of the bed. Your three-year-
on sleeps in the next room. Suddenly you are awakened by
xplosive sound of your front door being smashed inward.
son is frightened and cries out for his parents. You start to
p, but the butt of a musket slams your head into the wall.
1 you come to, your wife is trussed up, her shredded night-
es exposing her naked breast, your dog is lying in a pool of
1, and your child is screaming in terror. The soldiers ran-
your house, drawer by drawer, item by item, looking—just
ng. This is why the Constitution has rules against searches
ut warrants.

he Bill of Rights also prohibits the police from coercing
essions out of you. There's a good reason for the rule
st forced confessions. It hasn't been that long since torture
outine in so-called civilized countries. Poison administered
turously small quantities sufficient to prolong an agonizing
1, spikes driven slowly beneath your fingernails, bodies
hed on turning drums, limbs dipped in acid, and heads
hed in vises are but a few of the devices used to get you to
1e "truth." Forced confessions are not an artifact of olden
Hitler, Stalin, Mao Tse-tung, Ho Chi Minh, Fidel Castro,
'ol Pot used them, and current dictators worldwide still do.
ember the staged trials in China and Russia, in which re-
int political prisoners confessed to truly unbelievable
s against the state? Our Fifth Amendment privilege against

Rights is a sort of "rules of the road" for the cop
very important that the courts define those rig'
Cops have to apply the rules on the street in the
real people. Cops need to know what the rul
nately, over the last four decades, the rules hav
than a greased pig slithering from the clutches
were left holding a bag full of wind. The rules m
to year and from court to court. So the cops
form of evolving species, adapted to these mut
ting their testimony to each new scenario.

The courts have tried again and again to
clearly. In the last thirty years a hurricane of cri
has blown through the appellate courts. Th
mightily to articulate clear standards for cop
streets. But I think it is fair to say they have fai'
a judge, I had law clerks, a law library, and, mc
to make decisions on search-and-seizure mot
often had to struggle to comply with contra
Even then, I frequently had no idea whether
the higher court rulings correctly. And I was
turing at judicial symposia and law schools! I
ing to make sense at the Mad Hatter's tea part
asks if Alice has guessed the riddle he pc
replies:

> "No, I give it up. What's the answer?"
> "I haven't got the slightest idea," said th
> "Nor I," said the March Hare.
> Alice sighed wearily. "I think you migh
> better with the time," she said, "than waste
> with no answers."
> "If you knew Time as well as I do," said
> wouldn't talk about wasting it."

That's the law of search and seizure. In
situation, however, cops have no law clerks
no time, much less time to waste.

Our Bill of Rights was added to the C
fide reasons. Our founding fathers knew a
ernment firsthand. Did you know that the

self-incrimination was born of such abuses, and stands today as a guardian against the bad old days. We can't forget that.

Of course, it is a long way from torture by acid to the highly formalized Miranda warnings required by the Supreme Court. Torture by acid was one of the reasons for the Fifth Amendment. The Miranda warnings are what the Supreme Court says the Fifth Amendment means today. So here is a brief, guided tour to the Fourth through Sixth Amendments to the United States Constitution. It is also a tour through the insanely complex and changing interpretations of those amendments by our courts.

Search and Seizure

The Fourth Amendment protects us against *unreasonable* searches and seizures of our houses, persons, effects, and papers. No search or seizure may be conducted, except by written search warrant issued on *probable cause*. That means that a *neutral magistrate* must review and approve the factual basis justifying the search and seizure *before* it can be conducted lawfully. In short, it isn't enough that the cops *think* they have just cause; the judge must also independently conclude there is probable cause for the issuance of the warrant.

So why do cops stop and search automobiles all the time without a warrant? The Supreme Court has struck a balance between our reasonable expectations of privacy in the car and its contents, and society's compelling interest to investigate (invade our privacy) and protect against crime. In so doing, the Court has created hierarchies of protection under the Fourth Amendment, in which our homes are afforded the highest level of protection, while trash and open fields get the least. So our homes, except in extraordinary circumstances, may never be searched without a warrant. Because of the movable nature of cars and the obvious risk that evidence will be destroyed or lost, police are sometimes permitted to search the entire contents of the automobile without a warrant. In other words, cars lie somewhere in the middle of the hierarchy of Fourth Amendment protection against warrantless searches and seizures.

All of this theory is fine, but Fourth Amendment search-and-seizure law is unbelievably complex. Every situation has its own

special set of rules, each of which has volumes of articles, legal
treatises, and case law devoted to it. For example, there are detailed and particularized rules about arrests; detentions; auto
stops; stop-and-frisk; search of third-party premises; search of
third-party personal effects; closed-container searches; searches
of trashcans; searches of trash that has been dumped into a
garbage truck but not yet mixed in with the rest of the trash;
searches of trash that has been dumped in a garbage truck and
that has been mixed in with the rest of the trash; flyovers; open
fields; contraband in plain view; searches conducted pursuant to
a warrant; probable cause for issuance of a warrant; consent to a
search; hot pursuit; exigency; wiretapping; eavesdropping; bor-
der searches; institutional searches; and on and on. I would like
to talk about some real-life examples of searches and seizures to
give you a feel for how it works in the real world and the real
courts. We will take a trip through the looking glass into the
world of searches of personal residences, closed containers, and
trash.

Searches of Personal Residences

   Most of us remember the extensive testimony in the O.J.
Simpson double murder trial from detectives Vannatter and
Fuhrman. Soon after they discovered the dead bodies of Nicole
Brown and Ron Goldman, they visited Simpson's Brentwood estate, jumping the fence and searching the grounds and subsequently the house. There they found the bloody glove that
contained Simpson's, Nicole's, and Ron Goldman's blood. They
found Simpson's blood in the foyer, Simpson's blood on the drive-
way. They found the bloody socks covered with Nicole's blood.
Explosive evidence.
   Remember how careful Vannatter, Lange, and Fuhrman
were to emphasize that they jumped the fence because they believed more victims might be in the estate? All of the testimony
centered on what Vannatter, Lange, and Fuhrman were thinking
when they jumped the fence: Were they looking for victims, or
were they thinking that Simpson was a suspect? As is typical in
exclusionary-rule hearings, Simpson's guilt was irrelevant. What

was important was what the cops were thinking and what they did.

The reason the hearing focused on the cops' state of mind is that Vannatter, Lange, and Fuhrman entered without a search warrant. They had to justify the entry on grounds of exigency. Police may not enter a person's home in the absence of an emergency. The home and its environs constitute the most sanctified of places. Any governmental intrusion requires extreme justification. A belief that there may be more dead bodies or injured persons is an exigency that permits police entry without a warrant. So are we surprised that Vannatter, Lange, and Fuhrman explained that they thought there might be additional victims, dead or alive? No time to get a search warrant, they emphasized. When asked if Simpson was a suspect, they protested innocently that of course Simpson was not a suspect. As a DA, I had had cases with Vannatter. I knew him to be a good cop, and I liked him immensely. Lange also has a reputation as a straight shooter, a good cop.

In my experience as a DA, the spouse of the victim, in a circumstantial evidence case, is almost always the number-one suspect at the beginning of a case. It is also the experience of cops—Vannatter and Lange had nearly sixty years of experience between them—especially when, as in the Simpson case, a history of domestic violence existed. (That Simpson was, in fact, a suspect would be reinforced later by testimony from two gangsters *and* an FBI agent—Vannatter having allegedly told them Simpson was a suspect. In fairness to Vannatter and Lange, they distinguish between a suspect and a "probable cause" suspect. The former cannot be arrested, while the latter can.) Were Vannatter, Lange, and Fuhrman testi-lying about the search and seizure? Perhaps. Were they shading, embellishing? Perhaps. Look what was at stake. Had the court found that the initial search was constitutionally improper, all of the blood evidence at the house, the glove, and the later search revealing the bloody socks would have been suppressed (the socks because they would have been the fruit of the poisonous tree).

The defense would argue that Vannatter should have waited for a warrant. That's tough for a cop to swallow. Remember, when the cops arrived at the Brentwood estate, Vannatter did not know Simpson had left town. As far as Vannatter knew, Simpson was in the estate at that moment, destroying evidence. The defense wants Vannatter to wait a couple of hours to obtain a warrant? Not likely. It is therefore not surprising that Vannatter directed Fuhrman, a younger man, to jump the fence. Nor is it surprising that Vannatter claimed he was concerned for other possible victims, which I am sure was true. Nor is it surprising that Vannatter's explanation allowed the court to find that there was an exigency, thus allowing the bloody glove, bloody socks, and evidence of blood on the foyer of Simpson's home to come into evidence.

A lot of experts felt the court had winked at Vannatter's explanation, not really believing it. This was reinforced when Judge Lance Ito made a later finding that Vannatter had shown reckless disregard for the truth in a subsequent search-warrant affidavit. Given the many years of experience Judge Ito has with police procedures, as a DA and as a judge, I too find it hard to believe the court was not aware that Simpson, as the spouse, was almost automatically a principal suspect at the time Fuhrman leaped the fence. This is particularly true because Fuhrman and Detective Ron Phillips knew about Simpson's history of domestic violence against Nicole.

Closed-Container Searches

The law regarding when police can search closed containers—paper bags, lunchpails, and so forth—is wondrously complex and at times about as logically consistent as the ramblings of Daffy Duck. Take one famous California case. A man was acting bizarrely in public—he seemed to be under the influence of PCP. He was carrying a closed lunchpail at the time of his arrest. The cops told the defendant to put the lunchpail down, and took him to jail. The defendant and his pail were separated—the cops now controlling his lunchpail. Naturally, the cops looked in the lunchpail. They found narcotics. A California appellate court said that because the cops had exclusive control over the lunchpail, there was no emergency. Therefore, the court reasoned, the cops had to get a search warrant to open the pail, even though a normal booking search would have inevitably revealed the drugs in the pail. Imagine what would happen if, in every arrest where the defendant had a lunchpail or a pouch or some closed object, the police had to take time off patrolling the streets to go to the DA and get a search warrant.

In the lunchpail case, the California appellate court *thought* it was applying a U.S. Supreme Court ruling. But the U.S. Supreme Court later ridiculed the California court for misunderstanding its ruling:

> Under this fallacious theory no search or seizure incident to a lawful arrest would ever be valid; by seizing an article even on the arrestee's person, an officer may be said to have reduced that article to his exclusive control.

How can we expect cops to understand what is expected of them, when the courts can't even figure it out? The confusion does not end there. Courts in other divisions of California and in sister states were at odds with each other on the same issue. One division would allow a warrantless search of a tote bag found in the trunk of a car following an arrest for suspicion of robbery. Another division would disallow a search of a woman's purse following her arrest, or the search of a briefcase in the possession and control of a lawful arrestee.

Here's another example of the confusion about closed-container searches. Suppose a cop effects a proper arrest of a person in his car. The officer can legally search the car and the *unknown* contents of any closed containers in the car for evidence of the crime, as an incident of the arrest. The contents of the container may be completely unknown and the search is okay. But some courts have held that as soon as the cop has *probable cause to believe a particular container might actually contain specific evidence or contraband,* she cannot search the container until she gets a warrant. In other words, the officer cannot search if she has good cause to believe she is in fact going to find something illegal. But it is okay to search if she does *not* have any particular knowledge of the container's contents and is just fishing for something illegal. Honest, I'm not making that up. That was the law. You figure it out. I can't.

And then there were cases about footlockers, luggage cases, cardboard cartons, and more paper bags, each of which was afforded differing privacy expectations, depending on which ju-

risdiction you were in, depending on which philosophically liberal or conservative judge you were in front of, and depending
on what kind of evidence the cops found. Is it any wonder the
cops look at the courts with a contemptuous distrust? If judges
and lawyers could not read the shifting sands of the Fourth
Amendment, as is obvious from their different readings, how
could the cops be expected to have a firm grasp of what was expected of them?

Trash Searches

When I was a relatively new judge, my old friend Howard
Weitzman appeared before me on a motion to suppress bookmaking evidence found at the residence of his old childhood
chum. Howard wanted to win this motion very badly, and he told
me confidently that he had a good motion.

I read the search warrant and the supporting affidavit.
Howard was moving to "traverse the warrant." Traversal means
going through or behind the face of a warrant, valid on its face,
to the underlying affidavit. Howard was contending that the officers had acquired information in the affidavit by means of an
illegal trash search. Therefore, he argued, the probable cause
supporting the warrant was invalid, hence the subsequent search
pursuant to the "invalid" warrant produced nothing but another
fruit off the poisonous tree. That takes us into the wonderful
world of searching and seizing trash.

Howard proved early on that some of the information establishing probable cause in the warrant was obtained by searching
through trashcans on the defendant's property. At that time in
California, trash that remained on the defendant's property
could not be searched—the defendant had, according to the
California courts, a reasonable expectation of privacy in his discarded trash. Now, the various state courts have been completely
unable to agree on whether a defendant retains any reasonable
expectation of privacy when the trash is placed alternately onto
a sidewalk, or a curb or a public street, awaiting pickup. Side-
walks, curbs, and public streets have different constitutional protections in some jurisdictions. California courts have been very
protective of our privacy rights in our trash, holding that defen-

dants have not abandoned their trash, or their privacy interest in it, until the trash collector has collected it and placed it into the garbage truck along with other trash. So what did the cops do? Like old dogs learning new tricks, they tipped the trash collector with money taken out of their vice fund, instructing the trash collector to put the trash in the truck, but not to mix it up with the other trash. Defense attorneys soon got wind of this ploy and asked the California courts to protect this "crucial" privacy interest. God bless the California courts, who responded by deciding that trash was not abandoned by the defendant until it was all mixed up in the garbage truck with other trash. *Commingled* was the operative word used by the courts. Your discarded trash unceremoniously dumped into a bed of rotting refuse retained its Fourth Amendment privacy interests until someone shook up the trash and mixed your trash up with the rest of the garbage in the truck. Of course, if you happened to live in a federal jurisdiction or a state that followed federal law, you had no such expectation of privacy. The happy accident of where one resides now apparently had constitutional significance. Makes perfect sense to me. How about you? These rulings resulted in hilarious scenes of vice officers flailing around in the odoriferous beds of commingled trash, looking for evidence as the trash truck gingerly turned the corner a few short yards away from the suspect's house—being careful not to shake up things too badly. See what I mean? It seems like a game, except that people's freedom and lives are at stake.

Anyway, given the above California law, and based on the case Howard Weitzman had expertly built, I found the officer had violated California law by searching through the defendant's trash. Therefore *some* of the probable cause supporting the warrant was tainted. My next task was to determine whether the warrant could survive this defect. Howard asked me to invalidate the warrant on the ground that the officer swearing to its veracity had demonstrated a reckless disregard for the truth in failing to mention how he acquired his information that was in the warrant—namely by searching surreptitiously through the defendant's trashcans. The affidavit supporting the warrant contained an intentional *omission*, not an intentional *misstatement*. Well, here we go again. Believe it or not, an intentional lie under California law, but not under federal law, required the suppression of all the ev-

idence, regardless of the sufficiency of the remaining untainted
evidence—which, standing alone, could justify the issuance of
the warrant! If the defect in the warrant was an intentional omission, then I, as the judge, could weigh the balance of untainted
evidence to determine whether the warrant could survive the attack. Ultimately I found against Weitzman's client, who thereafter
pled to the bookmaking charges. Years later, Howard told me
that my decision denying his motion was the best thing that had
ever happened to his client, who gave up bookmaking and became a successful businessman.

Cops and Confessions

Prohibitions against unlawful searches and seizures are only
a portion of the rights given to criminal defendants in the Bill of
Rights. Your right to an attorney and not to have a confession
beaten out of you are equally important and closely interrelated.

Criminal defendants often attack the admissibility of confessions because they claim questioning continued after the defendant asked for an attorney. Frankly, it is hard to find a defendant
who does not distinctly "remember" that he asked for a lawyer
just before he confessed to the crime. And that brings us to the
Miranda rule.

No other aspect of criminal justice has captured the imagination of the people as the Miranda rule. Every crime show and
every movie we see seems to accord to Miranda some minor role,
if not a starring one. People no longer think much about it; they
take it for granted. We're all entitled to our Miranda rights. As a
judge I used to hear juveniles reprimand their attorney for not
asserting their Miranda rights in a suppression hearing. "Hey,
that sucker didn't tell me my rights, man." "Didn't you volunteer
to talk to the cop?" the attorney asks. "Yeah, but he didn't give
me my rights, I'm tellin' ya," the boy spits out angrily. We're talking about rights that the juvenile has seen on TV and received
firsthand during his dozens of previous encounters with the
cops, rights that are encoded in his little brain.

It was not always so. For some 175 years after the adoption of
our federal Constitution and Bill of Rights, there was no Miranda rule. Before Miranda, the Fifth Amendment privilege

against self-incrimination prevented the prosecution from using confessions extracted by physical abuse or unacceptable mental coercion. Unacceptable mental coercion meant such conduct as fourteen-hour interrogations of a retarded boy without letting him sleep. No magical words had to be read, until the Miranda decision. With a stroke of its mighty pen, the Warren Court turned its back on a long line of precedent standing for the proposition that imploring a suspect to confess without an attorney being present did not violate constitutional standards.

Miranda was one of the defining moments of Chief Justice Earl Warren's active move to expand criminal rights. The public was polarized. At the heart of the Warren Court's concern was its fixed belief that anyone in custody was in an inherently coercive atmosphere. Any confession in such an atmosphere conjured up for the Court images of confessions extracted by beatings, twenty-four-hour interrogations, and so forth—historical images of a lone, helpless individual pitted against the might of the state. The Warren Court distrusted the police. One could argue that the Warren Court members by and large believed that any custodial confession was probably obtained improperly by a cop. So the court set up rules that would make confessions in custody less frequent and more voluntary. They would level the playing field.

Note that the concept of custody comes up over and over. The Warren Court believed custodial interrogations were inherently a star chamber, and that a helpless defendant had no free will in the absence of specified warnings. Only then could the pressurized atmosphere of custodial police interrogation be mitigated so a suspect could act of his or her own free will. Note further that this rule is entirely formulaic. All that matters is that the right magical words are said.

Miranda Defined

The Miranda rule comes into play only when three circumstances coalesce: first, the defendant must be a prime suspect in a crime; second, there must be a process of interrogation designed to elicit incriminating statements; third, the interrogation must be custodial. That last item means the suspect is not free to leave. So if a cop briefly detains a suspect on the street, without a formal detention or arrest, asking but a few questions, such interrogation would not be custodial. When a suspect is under arrest, however, or being transported in a police car, he is in custody and Miranda applies.

When all three of the above elements are present, Miranda requires that a suspect be advised (1) of the right to *remain silent,* (2) that anything said will be *used against him or her* in a court of law, (3) that the suspect has a right to the *presence of counsel,* and (4) that if the suspect is *unable to afford* counsel, one *will be appointed prior to questioning,* if the suspect desires. In practice this becomes a ritual mating dance; if it is delicately handled, a cop may be able to finesse a waiver of these rights, even where the suspect appears to be initially reluctant. That is why experienced officers rarely jump right into a discussion of the suspected crime. Instead, they usually soften up the suspect by chatting about common things—football, armed forces, movies, the news, anything but the case—until the suspect is sufficiently warmed up and some rapport is established. Then the Miranda mantra is stated. Finally, before a statement is admissible, it must be clear the suspect understands and gives up each right and wishes to make a voluntary statement.

These rules in the abstract seem simple enough; it is in their live application that things become sticky. I can't tell you how many cases I handled as a DA, or heard as a judge, in which defense claimed that there had been a substantial interrogation of the defendant and consequential admissions taken *before* the Miranda admonition. Usually the defense would insist the defendant had asked to see an attorney, even before any Miranda rights were given. If this were true, any subsequent waiver of any rights would be invalid.

A favorite police procedure was (and is) to chitchat with the defendant about the case and get all the information they could from him. Of course, that conversation was not tape-recorded. If there were any points at which the defendant said, "Maybe I shouldn't talk to you guys about the case without my attorney," or "Hey, I don't want to talk about it anymore," or "This is bullshit, I want to talk to my attorney," this would be omitted from any formal report. After they had worked through the defendant's reluctance to talk, they would turn on the tape recorder.

Usually you would hear something like this, in the friendliest, most conversational manner:

"How's the coffee, still hot? Charlie here'll get you some more. All's you got to do is ask, okay? We'll be sending out for some food in a while, and we'll get your order. Man, they have some gooooood food over at Lucy's. Outstanding enchiladas, man, outstanding. Now, we were talking about your Miranda rights. I want to read them to you again, Johnny, and make sure you understand them, okay?"

You might hear the scraping of a moving chair and a grunt. The cop then meticulously, and with perfect elocution, reads Johnny his Miranda rights. His voice is so solicitous you would think he was sweet-talking his favorite grandmother. Then he continues,

"Now, Johnny, you've indicated you want to talk with us, is that what you want to do?"

A "Yeah" from the defendant reveals an utterly defeated voice. No more bravado left there.

"And you're willing to tell us what happened, of your own accord, without an attorney?"

The "Yeah" from the defendant is even more pathetic.

After the cop secures the waivers, we will usually hear him tell the defendant to "go back to the beginning, because I just want to make sure I get it right in my own mind." Then we hear the confession flowing in a smooth narrative, with some prompting from the cop. "Ah, John, I think you left out that point about, you know, the one where you said the codefendant gave you the shotgun shells. I believe he went out and got them, not you, is that correct?" (The cop accomplishes two things: first, he gets the defendant to admit he had shotgun shells; and, second, he befriends the defendant by implying the other guy provided the shells to him, as if that would make one whit of difference in his culpability in this shotgun robbery-slaying.)

More problems arise if the tape recorder has been turned off for a period of time, then turned back on. Even if nothing untoward has occurred, it raises suspicions that something was happening when the tape was off that the cops didn't want anyone to know about. It doesn't mean it did happen, but a skillful defense attorney might argue that the defendant never confessed, the tape had been doctored, evidence planted, and improper promises made. In today's post-Simpson climate, that is a very real concern for the DA and the cops. We need only to recall in Simpson the tape-recorded interview of the nurse, Thano Peratis. On tape, he told DA Hank Goldberg that he had probably been mistaken earlier when he said he had taken a full 8 cc of blood from Simpson. (If he had taken the full 8 cc, the cops could not account for 1.5 cc of Simpson's blood.) The defense was able to debunk this "new" evidence, in part because of a thirteen-minute gap in the taped interview. Why would the videotape have been turned off for thirteen minutes unless the witness was being told what to say? Why else would this interview be conducted with no defense attorneys present? What did they have to hide? What was really said when the recorder was off?

In the early years of Miranda, some troubling problems had to be worked through, problems that exacerbated the gulf between law enforcement and the courts. Anomalous results would sometimes arise as the high court tried to craft rules to meet each permutation of the Miranda legacy on a case-by-case basis. Even more confusing were the interpretations given to the Supreme Court's ruling by the different courts. Remember Charlie Guenther? Well, Charlie learned the hard way just how strange this rule can be. Homicide detective Guenther was investigating the killing of a sixty-five-year-old widow whose head had been crushed with a brick. Her body was found in her El Monte, California, home, stuffed behind a couch. Someone had tried to set the place afire. There were no leads. Her car was gone, and in the bathroom was a man's shaving kit with the monogram KB. Guenther checked with the phone company and found a long-distance call to Plainsville, Ohio. He ran the phone number and inquired of the person to whom the number was registered if they knew anyone with the initials K.B.? He was told that a distant cousin, Kenneth Brandhand, had called from El Monte, California out of the blue. Guenther ran his record, and it came back with other arrests. An all-points bulletin was put out. Soon he received a call from the Salt Lake City cops, who had Brandhand in custody for "drunk and disorderly."

Guenther went to Utah and read Brandhand his Miranda rights according to a written Utah waiver form. Brandhand waived his rights and told Guenther he had met the victim in the parking lot of a market and helped her put her shopping bags in the car. He had had no place to stay that night, so she'd invited him to stay at her house. He admitted he had taken her car to Arizona. Brandhand told Guenther where the car was, which was confirmed by the Arizona cops, who recovered the car and retained it for prints. Guenther took the suspect to Arizona, where he identified the car.

Murder charges were filed against Brandhand. Brandhand's attorney made the predictable motion to suppress his client's damaging admissions. Brandhand's counsel argued that the defendant had originally demanded an attorney (while he was still drunk) after being Mirandized by the Salt Lake city cops on the drunk-and-disorderly charges. The trial court suppressed Brandhand's admissions in the murder case, reasoning that once Miranda had been invoked in *any* case, the cops could not talk to the defendant without an attorney present—even though this was a separate, unconnected interview about a separate and unconnected case in which the defendant fully waived his Miranda rights. The trial court also expressed disbelief that a defendant (even though he was drunk at the time) would invoke his rights on a misdemeanor but would waive them on a murder case. Another judge, in another court, on those very same facts, would have held just the opposite. This judge simply didn't know Guenther's charm and persuasiveness. As a consequence, the DA went to trial with no way to establish that Brandhand was with the murdered woman. Brandhand was acquitted by a jury kept ignorant of the truth. When the defendant walked out of the courtroom a free man, Guenther invited him to come down to the sheriff's office to pick up his shaving kit, to which the defendant replied nonchalantly, "I've got another one." He brushed passed the tearful detective, who could think only of a helpless woman who died alone with a crushed skull.

The conservative Rehnquist Court has limited some of the wildest excesses of Miranda and its progeny. For example, when a *second* interrogation is about a *different* case, a previous invocation of rights will not invalidate a voluntary waiver given in the new case. In addition, we now understand that Miranda does not apply to questioning conducted by an informant or cellmate working for the police because the defendant does not know he is being interrogated. Thus the coercive atmosphere of a police interrogation is absent. A request to see a probation officer is not the same as a request for an attorney (yes, some creative defense attorneys actually made that argument, and our appellate courts actually had to waste their time making that ruling). Of course, if the defendant executes a free and voluntary waiver of her Miranda rights, her statements are admissible.

Notwithstanding the cutbacks at the margins of the Miranda rule, it remains a very important tool in the arsenal of a defense attorney who does not want the jury to hear his client confess to a crime. As a result, the Miranda rule has generated its own form of testi-lying. A confession is admissible if the defendant is advised of her rights and, understanding them, voluntarily waives them. If you were to read a random sampling of reports of arrests made by cops, or sit through a criminal calendar or twenty or so preliminary hearings in downtown Los Angeles, you would be amazed that every single arrest occurs in almost exactly the same way, and that the suspect confesses in almost exactly the same words. For example, an arrest report for an ax murderer might read as follows:

> Officer ——— then read the suspect his full Miranda rights. Officer ——— asked the suspect if he understood the rights and the suspect stated that he did. Officer ——— then asked the suspect if he freely and voluntarily waived those rights and the suspect stated that he did freely and voluntarily waive his rights as read to him. Officer ——— asked the suspect <u>who had chopped the decedent into small pieces and the suspect stated that he had done so</u>. . . .

To change this into a typical police report for drunk driving, all you have to do is change the last sentence to: "Officer ——— asked the suspect if he was driving while drinking and the suspect stated that he was."

I find it amazing how many criminal defendants, from drunk drivers to ax murderers, waive their constitutional rights, confessing in almost exactly the same words. Yes, I know that police departments provide officers with a Miranda advisement card that they carry in their wallets, and print the Miranda advisement and waiver form on their arrest reports. Perhaps that is why everything sounds the same. Or is this just more testi-lying? Maybe. DAs and judges often just check off on their laundry list each of the elements required by Miranda, as the cop, by rote memory, repeats the magic incantation.

FIVE

The Bitter Harvest

TESTI-LYING AND THE CODE OF SILENCE

The citizen is the law. In this country we haven't got around
to understanding that. We think of the law as an enemy.
We're a nation of cop-haters.
—*Raymond Chandler*

B y now you know I believe that some cops are not always
truthful on the stand, and that it happens more than occasionally. You have undoubtedly heard about a code of
silence that infects our police departments: Cops don't rat on
cops. So how bad is the code of silence? How bad is the testi-lying?
How many cops do it? Can we believe our cops about anything?

The Code of Silence

Cops are like any other group of people; some of them will
always be bad. Our problem, as the people in a democratic society, is to deal effectively with cops who are prejudiced, violent,
abusive, and corrupt without ruining the reputations of the
good cops and without paralyzing our ability to deal with criminal violence. How many really bad cops are there among the
men and women in blue? We all listened with horror to Mark
Fuhrman's virulent ideas about criminal justice in the Laura
Hart McKinney tapes.

FUHRMAN: Well, I really love being a policeman when I can be a policeman. It's like my partner now. He's so hung up with the rules and stuff. . . . I get pissed sometimes and go, You just don't fucking even understand. Fuck the rules, we'll make them up later. . . . He's a college graduate, a Catholic college. He was going to be a fucking priest. He's got more morals than he's got hairs on his head. He doesn't know what to do about it.

McKINNEY: What do you mean, he's got more morals?

FUHRMAN: He doesn't know how to be a policeman. "I can't like lie." . . . Oh, you make me fucking sick to my guts. You know, you do what you have to do to put these fucking assholes in jail. If you don't, you fucking get out of the fucking game. He just wants to be one of the boys.

McKINNEY: So, how does he deal with it?

FUHRMAN: He doesn't lie. Well, I know for a fact in this Internal Affairs investigation he had a ten-day suspension. He'll roll.

McKINNEY: I'm sorry. I don't understand.

FUHRMAN: He'll drop the dime on me, squeal, tell the truth. He won't take any time. . . .

McKINNEY: You serious?

FUHRMAN: Not a policeman at heart. He's considered one of the good guys.

McKINNEY: He won't take any suspension at all?

FUHRMAN: He'll say . . . he didn't realize. He goes: "I got a wife and kid to think of." I says, "Fuck you. Don't tell me because you've got a wife and kid. . . . You're either my partner all the way or get the fuck out of this car. We die for each other. We live for each other. That's how it is in the car. You lie for me, up to six months' suspension. Don't ever get fired for me. Don't get indicted for me. But you'll take six months for me 'cause I'll take it for you. If you don't, get the fuck out of here. . . . It shouldn't have to be said."

Now, I know a lot of cops personally, and I've worked closely with many times that number. I will tell you right now, and I will tell you emphatically, *Mark Fuhrman is not a typical cop.* The cops I know were sickened by what they heard on the Fuhrman tapes. They felt that a public servant had betrayed his trust. A cop who took the Fifth Amendment. Cops don't do that; the bad guys do. I know some cops who were so ashamed at Fuhrman's testimony and at his taking the Fifth that they started refusing to tell people they were cops. Charlie Guenther tells no strangers of his colorful past. Nor does he invite questions about it.

The vast majority of cops, like Phil Vannatter and Tom Lange, are decent and caring people. People with families and loved ones. People who worry about whether their sons and daughters will have a good education and safe environment in which to grow up.

To be fair, Fuhrman is not an anomaly. He is real, and he represents a certain aberrant police mentality. On rare occasion, corrupt cops have planted evidence—as when New York cops planted fingerprint evidence or when a Saturday-night special is planted next to the body of a slain suspect. But that is rare, very rare.

Alan Dershowitz and others have leapt upon Fuhrman's testimony, claiming that it shows him to be typical of all cops. They say all police are indoctrinated to look the other way when something amiss takes place. In fact, good officers will not do so; corrupt ones always will. They claim cops are taught one thing at the police academy and another in the streets; at times they have accused the police of teaching rookie cops to lie at the police academy, an allegation that I believe is unsupported and slanderous. We've heard it said often that when a cop abuses a suspect, his partner looks the other way. That cop knows his life may depend on his partner someday. He also knows you don't rat on another cop. He knows it is dangerous to be treated as a pariah, as an outcast, in a profession in which collegiality and support are critical to one's survival. Dershowitz is right about the enormous pressure to support a fellow cop, even a bad one. Weak cops will look the other way—joined at the hip in a code of silence.

Yes, a code of silence *does* exist in one form or another, to some degree, in most if not all police departments. Frankly, however, there is a lot less to the code of silence than meets the eye. If we back off for a moment from the dramatic term *code of silence,* we can look at what is really going on. We should be shocked if there were not a code of silence among cops. Consider their isolation. They are a group that is marked, that stands separate and apart from the rest of us. Of course cops see each other as brothers and sisters. Of course they see the world as a them-against-us proposition. The hostility of the high courts toward police over four long decades has just made that isolation worse. Millions of new immigrants unfamiliar with our ways have added to this estrangement. The existence of a code of silence among cops should not surprise us because it is not much different from how *we* conduct our daily lives. We keep secrets in the workplace, in our families, with our friends. This is a code of silence we may not even be aware of most of the time.

Remember the film classic *Stalag 17*? William Holden and his fellow Americans are prisoners in a German POW camp. Holden plays a cynical and glib loner who is content to amuse himself through his many scams and schemes—which make his life more bearable, but infuriate his fellow prisoners. Holden will have nothing to do with a planned escape attempt that goes awry, killing two prisoners. He is mistakenly and unfairly suspected of being an informer, and everyone makes life miserable for him. The Academy Award–winning film examines the deep values ingrained in our society about betrayal of one's fellows. None of us wishes to think of himself as a Judas.

Have we not heard of doctors who refused to testify against their errant colleagues who have butchered unsuspecting patients? Of a pathologist who ignored the presence of surgical instruments left in a deceased patient's body cavity? Of military officers covering up friendly fire or fragging incidents? Or of cigarette companies and politicians . . . well, need we say more? So why are we surprised when Mark Fuhrman tells us cops cover for each other, just as the rest of us do?

When Good Cops Lie

The misbehavior of atypical cops like Fuhrman does not concern me nearly as much as the low-level dishonesty that many cops practice every day. What pains me is to see cops I know, good cops, telling what they regard as white lies under oath—testi-lying, by which I mean testifying dishonestly about how they got the evidence against a defendant. Lies about whether a cop has read Miranda rights to a defendant, and whether the defendant waived them, and lies about why the cops had to search a suspect's house without a warrant. Lies about all of the procedural rights the appellate courts have invented over the past forty years. Am I exaggerating the problem of lies by our cops? The Honorable Alex Kozinski is a highly regarded member of the Ninth Circuit Court of Appeal. He says,

> It is an open secret shared by prosecutors, defense lawyers and judges that perjury is widespread among law enforcement officers. . . . [The exclusionary rule is a] great incentive for . . . police to lie to avoid letting someone they think or they know is guilty, go free.

I want you to understand one crucial fact: *Cops may lie about how they got the evidence. But they rarely lie about the evidence itself. They rarely lie about the defendant's guilt.* Cops who regularly testi-lie about searches and seizures would be appalled to discover another cop lying about something they regard as critical to due process, such as planting evidence, or falsely claiming the defendant confessed, or stating that the cop saw the defendant shoot someone when he saw no such thing. Does that sound funny to you? It's okay to lie about "judge-made" procedures, but not about guilt? You may not like it, but that's the way it works.

Let's look at an example of how the testi-lying game gets played in the real world, and how it compromises our courts. Suppose the cops have a bookmaking search warrant for a house. They know the bookies keep their records (pay and owe sheets) on dissolving paper located next to a bucket of water, a toilet, or a portable flame. But the law requires cops to knock and then give notice of their presence, identity, and purpose for being there, and to demand entry. If they don't, any evidence they recover, even under a search warrant, will be suppressed. Of course, in the real world, the cops know if they do give "knock and notice," the bookie will throw his disposable evidence in the tub of water. By now you will probably not be surprised that the court testimony on the exclusionary-rule suppression motion almost always sounds something like this:

"Officer," says the young DA (that's me), "after securing the search warrant for the location known as 123 Lotus Street, what did you do next?"

"We proceeded to that location." (Cops always "proceed," they never just go.)

"Upon your arrival at that location, what happened?"

"I positioned myself just to the left of the front door. My partner went to the rear of the house, keeping the rear entrance under surveillance."

"I see. What happened next?" (Young DAs always say "I see" when they see nothing.)

"Uh, well, I knocked loudly on the front door, yelling 'police officers, open up, we have a search warrant.' I heard muffled sounds inside. Then the sound of retreating steps."

"Muffled sounds" and "retreating steps" are legal words of art under the exigent circumstances exception to the "knock and notice" requirement. Somehow, the cops usually hear them.

"What, if anything, did you do, officer?" I ask, with rising concern in my voice.

"Fearing for the safety of my partner, and fearing the evidence might be destroyed, we effected forcible entry," the officer says, looking at the judge with his most sincere expression.

(The words cops use to describe events like the destruction of evidence, bashing in a door, choking a suspect, or even hitting a suspect always amazed me when I was a young DA. They "feared" for the loss of evidence. They "effected" forcible entry. They "employed a bar arm control" on the defendant. "Officer Terrell sustained injury to his knuckles on contact with suspect's teeth." You may think I'm joking about this last one. I'm not; I've seen it on more than one police report.)

The judge has heard the same officer give the same testimony before, word for word. Frankly, he does not believe things happened exactly the way the cop just described. In a routine bookmaking case, you are likely to see this ruling from the judge:

You know I have great sympathy for the police, they have
a difficult job. But I am not convinced they complied with
the knock-and-notice requirements. After all—these requirements make it safer for everyone. A startled occupant
is more likely to resort to sudden force or, worse yet, shoot
an unidentified police officer. So it is for the protection of
all that we must support this rule. Accordingly, the evidence
is suppressed. Case dismissed.

What happens when the cops make a forcible entry, just as
before, but what they find is a huge quantity of heroin and a
large cache of automatic weapons? Enough heroin to ruin the
lives of thousands of people? The cop's testimony is still hard to
believe. You will probably not be surprised to learn that the
judge is, nevertheless, going to be open to a little more testimony before she rules. So the judge asks for more, hoping the
cop and the DA will give her some way not to exclude the evidence. Obediently the DA elicits from the cop that he heard the
sound of a flushing toilet; in his experience, that means dealers
are disposing of heroin. The cop says he has lost evidence this
way before. He looks up for an approving nod from the judge,
who is listening intently. Mind you, this judge knows this officer
"hears" flushing toilets pretty much every time he "effects a
forcible entry." But this time the judge wants to admit the evidence. She is still not sure a ruling admitting the evidence will
stand up on appeal. So now the judge takes over the questioning. She asks the officer whether he had any information from
informants about the heroin dealer's habits when confronted by
the cops. The cop, of course, knows exactly what the judge is
looking for. With the most earnest expression he can muster, he
tells the judge that he heard on one occasion that the defendant
had destroyed evidence when suddenly confronted by the police—after knock-and-notice had been given.

What is happening here? The testimony by the cop is just as
contrived as it was when the defendant was a bookie. But now it's
a heroin dealer with a huge amount of heroin and a cache of automatic weapons. This time the judge rules,

Having heard muffled sounds, retreating footsteps, and
flushing water, they reasonably feared evidence would be

destroyed if they did not effect immediate entry. This, in addition to the officer having knowledge, prior to the forcible entry, of defendant's successful efforts to destroy evidence in the past. Exigent circumstances existing, defendant's motion to suppress is denied.

Testi-lying goes on every day in our halls of justice. No matter how tough the high courts get with their precious exclusionary rule, trial judges and cops face the real-life dilemma of either being a little sloppy with the truth or letting really bad guys go free. Given the stakes involved, testi-lying is a seemingly rational and sane reaction to an insane and ever-changing set of rules. After all, the high courts have made the truth irrelevant at trial with the exclusionary rule. Why should the cops stick strictly to the truth? When judges ignore the testi-lying, that too is a rational and sane reaction to an ever changing set of rules.

Just because lies are rational and sane responses does not mean they are right, nor does it mean the justice system should encourage that kind of behavior. Look at the damage such lies do to our justice system. For one thing, the justice system ought to be about the truth. Not only that, but, unlike the cops, juries do not distinguish between little white lies about seizing evidence and big lies about planting evidence. How do you explain to a jury that a cop who easily lies about the details of a search and seizure would never plant or falsify evidence? Marcia Clark couldn't do it. Most profoundly, testi-lying is a symptom of a crazy judicial system, a system out of control.

Of course, all cops do not testi-lie and all judges do not overlook such practices. This brings us to the other horn of the exclusionary-rule dilemma: When cops and judges are rigorously honest, killers walk free.

There is an alternative to all the testi-lying and the code of silence. We can have a criminal justice system that protects us from criminals and preserves our constitutional liberties—one in which lies are no longer necessary. We can have a system in which our good cops can really be good.

SIX

Toxic Tides

AN AGENDA FOR CHANGE

Now and then an extraordinary case may turn up, but
constitutional law like other mortal contrivances has to
take some chances, and in the great majority of instances
no doubt justice will be done.
—*Oliver Wendell Holmes, 1911*

The tides that had ripped through our criminal justice
system for the past four decades are toxic. It is not acceptable when dishonesty works its way into the system
as part of the everyday routine. Period. It is not acceptable when
judges wink at the dishonesty. Period. Yet it has become systemic.
The question is, How do we get out of this mess?

Harvard law professor Alan Dershowitz believes he knows
what the problem is and how to solve it. He believes the problem
is runaway cops abridging our rights. He does not see the problem as runaway crime. He would have us be steadfast in enforcing the exclusionary rule until the cops finally come around to
his way of thinking and at last get it right. Dershowitz's total
focus is on protecting our constitutional rights at the expense of
the truth. To Dershowitz, justice is not the same as the truth. He
would therefore make the enforcement of the exclusionary rule
even tougher and acquit more criminals, regardless of whether
the criminals are guilty. Just put him in charge of the police commissions and he will whip those cops into line!

That is the kind of thinking that got us where we are today. If
you want to make things a lot worse, follow Dershowitz's advice.

He will only drive the cops further into isolation, and increase the amount of testi-lying and the pressure on trial judges to ignore it. Nor would the Dershowitz approach protect our precious constitutional rights one whit. Every change the high courts have made to prevent cops from violating constitutional rights have been met with change by the cops. Cops adapt like a mutating organism perceiving a new threat. They would grow gills if it would help! Remember the garbage search and seizure stories? Every time the high courts have expanded the constitutional protection of garbage, the cops have figured out a clever way around it. You see, cops really believe their job is to arrest bad guys. If they have to climb into the back of a garbage truck and pick through fetid guacamole to find evidence that will put bad guys in jail, they will.

The problem is not the cops, but a system in which lies seem to be the only reasonable way for a cop to do his or her job. Dershowitz's assertion that "law enforcement officials—from the attorney general of the United States down to the cop on the beat—[must realize that] police perjury undermines their cases and must therefore stop it" is straight from academia. It is naive, wishful thinking. It ain't going to happen unless the system changes. Why? Because cops, like most of the rest of us, want to see guilty people pay for their crimes.

Let's do a little role-playing. We are now going to put you in the position of a cop, a DA, and a judge in exclusionary-rule hearings. At the end of the role-playing, I think you will agree the exclusionary rule has failed, and that we need a new approach to seizing evidence, getting confessions, and protecting our constitutional rights.

Let's pretend you are a young cop who has an older and more experienced partner. Every day, you and your partner get into a police vehicle and work the streets of L.A. You work the Ramparts Division—it's a rough and treacherous town. Your life depends on your partner, and vice versa. In fact, your partner is a hero; he saved your life about eight months ago. Now you are sitting in court. It's an evidence-suppression hearing in a murder case. The perp killed his girlfriend and her two kids with a crowbar. The defendant doesn't want the jury to know about the crowbar. Your partner takes the stand and swears to tell the truth. He says the perp consented to a search, and when the two of you searched the car, you found the crowbar. Part of this is true; the two of you did find the murder weapon, and it had the perp's prints on it. Lab tests on the crowbar also found his girlfriend's and her kids' blood and a matted, bloody mass, barely recognizable as blond hairs from a ten-year-old girl. All of that is true. You got your killer. But part of what your partner said isn't true. The perp *did not* consent to the search. Your stomach lurches. You look around the court. You look hard at the DA, at the judge. What are they thinking? You suspect they know your partner is not telling the complete truth, and they don't seem to think much of it. You respect your partner. Is this okay with you?

Now you take the stand and swear to tell the truth. The attorney for the defendant asks you whether the defendant really consented. Here's the sixty-four-thousand-dollar question: What do you do—back up your partner and send the killer to jail? Or do you call your partner a liar and let the killer walk? Most cops back their partners. Before you answer, read on.

This time you are a veteran cop patrolling a freeway. You spot a car traveling the highway in the quiet early-morning hours. From fourteen years of experience you have a hunch something is amiss, but you can't articulate any reason. You follow the car. The driver seems to be trying to keep as much distance between you and him as he can. But he does not speed, and all of his lane changes are completely legal. You decide to stop him anyway and investigate. In fourteen years you have learned to trust your instincts.

The driver appears nervous. You say, "You don't mind if I have a look in your trunk, do you." It is clear the driver does mind, but he says nothing. You open the trunk. A swarm of flies buzzes out of the trunk. What you see makes you gag. A severed head has been tossed onto a pile of greasy rags. You draw your gun, force the driver out of the car and onto the ground, and cuff him. Your partner looks under the driver's seat. She finds a bloody ax.

Your initial stop of the ax murderer's car was not a proper stop. A hunch is not enough. You are interviewing with the DA before the evidence-suppression hearing. The DA keeps asking you questions that would make the stop legal if only you said yes. Was the car driving too slowly? Was it straddling lanes? Was it weaving at all? Was it changing lanes too often? Did the driver dip his shoulder to the floor when he saw you? Maybe even almost lose control of the car when he dipped his shoulder because his head disappeared for a moment? That might suggest he was concealing something—maybe the ax? If you do not say yes to one of these questions, the ax murderer is going to go free. You know what the DA wants. He wants a yes to one or more of his questions. The severed head and the ax are the product of an illegal stop. What are you going to do? Again, before you answer, read on.

Now suppose you are the DA in that severed-head case. You are meeting with the cop before the evidence-suppression hearing. You keep asking a bunch of questions. The cop keeps saying no, the driver wasn't weaving, he wasn't straddling lanes, and so forth. You are getting to the end of your list, and the cop finally tells you that he recalls that the driver did dip his shoulder to the floor. But the cop doesn't seem convincing. You don't believe him. Do you put him on the stand to testify? If you do not, the ax murderer walks free. Before you answer what you would do as the cop or as the DA, please read on.

A beautiful model turns up missing. A suspect has told a friend that he may have "accidentally" killed the model. His friend tells the cops. The suspect's story is implausible—it is almost impossible she could have died in the manner in which he describes. The model's parents are beside themselves, wanting to know what happened to their daughter. Is she really dead? Where is her body? You take the suspect into custody. You are in charge of the interrogation. You take one look at this guy and you *know* he is the killer. The suspect asks for an attorney twelve times. You are angry and ignore his requests. You keep telling the suspect to come clean, to take you to the body so the parents can give their daughter a proper burial. After much resistance, the suspect takes you to the body. She was murdered.

You violated the defendant's Miranda rights—no question about that. The defendant now moves to suppress his incriminating statements and the body as a product of the unlawful interrogation. What do you do as the cop? As the judge? What would you like to see done as a citizen? Before you answer any of my questions, read on.

Consider what Sir Robert Bolt had to say in his brilliant play about Sir Thomas More, *A Man for All Seasons,* about the consequences of bending the law. More, his daughter Alice, and her husband, William Roper, are engaging in a heated argument.

MORE: The law, Roper, the law. I know what's legal, not what's right. And I'll stick to what's legal.

ROPER: Then you set man's laws above God's!

MORE: No . . . The currents and eddies of right and wrong, which you find such plain sailing, I can't navigate. I'm no voyager. But in the thickets of the law, oh there I'm a forester. I doubt if there's a man alive who could follow me there, thank God. . . .

ALICE: And while you talk, he [the criminal] is gone!

MORE: And go he should, if he was the Devil himself, until he broke the law!

ROPER: So now you'd give the Devil benefit of the law!

MORE: Yes. What would you do? Cut a great road through the law to get after the Devil?

ROPER: I'd cut down every law in England to do that!

MORE: Oh? And when the last law was down, and the Devil turned round on you, where would you hide, Roper, the laws all being flat? This country's planted thick with laws from coast to coast—man's laws, not God's—and if you cut them down—and you're just the man to do it—d'you really think you could stand upright in the winds that would blow then? Yes, I'd give the Devil the benefit of the law, for my own safety's sake.

Now consider my questions again. What would you do? They present a moral conundrum that will always exist in a civilized society. We must maintain order, and we must hire cops to do that. But we cannot let the cops become all-powerful. I am sure the Roman Empire had this problem two millennia ago. And I am sure it will continue to exist two millennia hence.

Cops should not lie. DAs should not use evidence they suspect is not true. Judges should not allow perjured testimony. On the other hand, people should not murder, and drug dealers should not destroy families and entire cities with their heroin and cocaine and go unpunished. In this world of moral relativism, we weigh the relative wrongs. I don't know what decisions you have made about the questions I asked. Most cops, DAs, and trial judges choose the lesser of the two evils. If the bad guy is really bad, they choose to put him in jail. In so doing, however, they have unclean hands. They feel dirty.

Every one of these scenarios I have presented is a direct result of the existence of the exclusionary rule.

Look at the real consequences. Cops develop disdain for the system. If lying about procedure is okay, that creates a culture in which other, more serious lies about whether the defendant is guilty may also be okay. It also creates a climate in which a Mark Fuhrman might, in some twisted way, think his behavior is justified. On the other hand, jurors are disinclined to believe an otherwise truthful officer on the fundamental issues of guilt because of lies told on tangential issues. Fuhrman is a racist. Fuhrman lies about his racist attitudes. Fuhrman is to be disbelieved. Vannatter, an honest cop, says Simpson was not a suspect when the world saw him as one. As a consequence, the jury disbelieves an otherwise competent and honest cop on more important issues relating to the spurious claim of a planted glove or a sample of Simpson's DNA.

Look at the cost to society. Killers are free to kill. Rapists are free to rape. Again. Not only that, but huge amounts of our judicial resources are devoted to putting the cops on trial. What were those cops thinking when they jumped the fence? Did they keep questioning the defendant after he asked for an attorney? Our system is already grossly overburdened, even without the added cumbersome weight of exclusionary-rule hearings. Finally, when the defense gets to put the cops on trial, bad guys often go free. We all saw it happen on TV, and it is not pretty.

The system is broken. Here is how to fix it:

1. The exclusionary rule is a judicially crafted rule of historically recent origin. It should be overruled in its entirety, including the "fruit of the poisonous tree" doctrine.

2. The Miranda rule is also a judicially crafted rule of recent origin. It should be overruled in its entirety. No voodoo incantations, no mantras, no magic words should determine justice, nor should they shackle and smother our core values of fairness.

3. To determine whether physical evidence that is the result of an illegal search and seizure may be seen and heard by the jury, the court should ascertain whether it was acquired in such a way as to be *shocking to the conscience of a civilized society*. By "shocking to the conscience" I do not mean the tender mercies of the psychiatric apologists for criminal behavior, or the self-esteem crowd. I mean such activities as forcibly pumping the stomach of a defendant for evidence of drug use, or beating the defendant until he tells where the murder weapon was hidden. If the evidence was acquired in a manner that is not shocking to the conscience, the evidence may be viewed by the jury, as long as it is otherwise legally admissible and not inherently unreliable.

4. To determine whether a confession or an admission may be heard by a jury, we can return to the pre-Miranda standard that served us well for 175 years. What I propose is that if the DA plans to use a confession or an admission, there will be an evidentiary hearing before the judge. The DA and the defense may introduce all evidence that bears on whether the confession or admission is voluntary. If the judge determines the confession or admission was extracted by physical or extreme mental abuse in a manner shocking to the conscience, it may not be heard by the jury. Otherwise the DA must show, by a preponderance of the evidence, that a jury might reasonably conclude that the confession or admission was voluntary. If the judge finds that the DA has carried that burden, the jury may hear the confession. The defense may still introduce evidence and argue to the jury that the confession was not trustworthy or credible. The jury always retains the power to disbelieve the confession and to reject it.

5. Failure to advise a suspect of his right to an attorney, or to provide a requested attorney, is a fact, among many, that can be considered in determining whether a suspect's confession or admission is free and voluntary. These facts will not, per se, invalidate an otherwise free and voluntary statement.

Commentators like Alan Dershowitz will complain that if we do this, the cops will violate the Constitution. My first response is it happens anyway. The exclusionary rule and the Miranda rule just let us pretend the cops do not conduct illegal searches or interrogations. My second response is that if the consequences of an illegal search or an illegal confession were less draconian, or were personally directed at the offending cop or police department, as explained below, maybe we could get the cops to be more careful and respectful of the people's constitutional rights.

The exclusionary rule and the Fourth Amendment should not be confused. We must always vigilantly enforce the Bill of Rights. Always. We also must work hard to prevent police violations of our rights. The difference in my program and the current law is that truth and justice will not be casualties of my program. The system itself will not be party to the suppression of truth. DAs and judges will not have to choose between believing a lying cop and suppressing vital evidence. They will not have dirty hands.

Here's what we can do to help prevent the cops from violating our constitutional rights:

1. New and expanded civil rights laws would empower government prosecutors to prosecute cops who willfully or with reckless disregard violate our constitutional rights. Cops would be subject to substantial fines and sanctions, including the loss of their jobs. Special provisions would impose higher penalties on repeat offenders.

2. Cops who commit crimes in the violation of our Fourth Amendment rights would be prosecuted criminally.

3. Law enforcement agencies that know or should have known of a cop's illegal behavior, or that failed to take reasonable measures to eliminate it, would be subject to civil rights violations and loss of government grants and funding.

These sanctions are real. Today, juries return multimillion-dollar verdicts against police officers and the governmental agencies that employ them. The County of Los Angeles and the L.A. County Sheriff's Office suffered a judgment of nearly $16 million for beating some Samoan partygoers and violating their rights. Another jury returned a verdict of in excess of $3.5 million against the City of Los Angeles and the LAPD cops who shot a felon.

Look at how these sanctions work. A cop can be fined or lose his job. He can lose everything he owns. That is a far greater deterrent to illegal behavior than suppressing evidence, the absence of which compromises our quest for truth and justice. Of course, some cops may lie at the civil rights trials. If so, they risk perjury charges for lying. The critical fact is that lying in the civil rights trial compromises only the liar's integrity. It does not compromise the integrity of the entire system by forcing the complicity of DAs, judges, and other cops.

Our civilian review boards must be functional and proactive. We must be informed of, and track, the number of police shootings and abuses. We must demand an independent oversight director whose sole function is to monitor all police abuse cases independent of the police, and who is answerable directly to the mayor or city council. Our mayor, our council. We must create an efficient mechanism for removing bad cops immediately, without costly and endless procedural entanglements from police unions.

There is one final thing we must do, you and I.

We own the police departments. The cops are our servants. We make the policies. We tell our leaders what we want for our communities. We must set the tone and the values we want them to reflect. If our desire is to remain a bastion of white refuge, insulated from others who are different from us, we need only give the signals to our leaders and to our cops. Stop African Americans or Hispanics who drive through white communities in old cars—heck, stop 'em if they are in new cars, because they might be stolen. Hassle the undesirables or the strangers who land on our precious terra firma, the people who don't meet our community standards or personal criteria. The cops cannot survive without our support, implicit or otherwise. What they do in our name is a reflection of our morals, our humanity, and our values. We must stop blaming the cops—and assume responsibility ourselves.

Juries on the Rampage

ABSOLUTE POWER
CORRUPTS ABSOLUTELY

Send a message . . . to stop this cover-up! If you don't stop
it who will? [I]t has to be stopped by you. [I]f you don't do
what's right, this kind of conduct will continue on forever.
—*Johnnie Cochran, 1995*

We love juries and we hate them. It has been so since
the emergence of the modern jury in 1670. Our ambivalence about juries is a tension built right into the
system. The whole problem is one of power. Jurors in criminal
cases have power, and they have a lot of it.

We like it when our juries use their power to protect us
against tyrannical government. The phrase *tyrannical government*
is not just some political science catchphrase. The power to lock
me up and throw me in jail is an awesome power, easy to abuse.
Of all the constitutional protections that stand between me and
overzealous prosecutors or judges who don't like the way I look,
the right to trial by jury is the most important.

Juries really do bring a fresh sense of the values of the community into a musty, jaded courtroom. Judges and DAs have
seen it all after a few years. Over and over. They lose their sense
of outrage. Ho-hum, another murder case. Another guy the
State of California or the State of Texas is trying to send to the
gas chamber. Another day's work.

But there is a downside to juries. For them to protect us
against tyrannical government, overzealous prosecutors, and

bad judges, we have to give jurors power. A lot of power. We like it when the jurors bring *our* values into the courtroom. When the jury agrees with *us*. Throughout American history, and especially in the last five explosive years, we have seen stupid and bigoted juries render one bad decision after another. When that happens, we are not so certain we like *those* jurors to have all that power. *Their* community values don't seem so good.

As you can see, we both love and hate juries for precisely the same reason. Jurors have lots of power: the power to prevent the government from abusing its power to imprison citizens; the power to do horrible injustice, to free murderers or to convict innocent people because they do not like their looks or the color of their skin.

Jurors decide the facts. Not judges. Not appellate courts. If jurors decide a criminal defendant has a good alibi, that's it, it doesn't matter how unbelievable or stupid the alibi may be. If jurors decide DNA typing, accurate to one in 1.6 billion, is not enough to prove the defendant was at the crime scene, that's it. There is *no* appeal when a jury wrongfully or incredibly acquits a criminal defendant.

Jurors can ignore the law completely. Even if everyone agrees on the facts, and the law is clear that the defendant is guilty on those facts, the jury may still acquit the defendant. This is known as *jury nullification.*

A jury in a criminal case may do pretty much as it pleases when it comes to acquitting a defendant or convicting a defendant of lesser charges. That tremendous power makes the modern Anglo-American jury system unique.

The jury system needs to be changed. Not the core of the system; the jury system has served us fairly well for many hundreds of years. Recently, however, jurors have increasingly run amuck, with the willing aid of shameless attorneys and the media. Judges have failed to control their courtrooms. Juries, attorneys, and judges need to be reined in without taking away the essential power of the jury.

Bushell's Case: Where It All Began

You may think complete independence of juries is a recent development. It is not. The modern jury emerged in 1670 in the famous Bushell's case. In 1670, recalcitrant jurors did not land lucrative book deals. Instead, jurors were under extreme pressure to convict in criminal cases. When I say pressure, I mean that angry judges, appointed by and beholden to the monarch, could *imprison, fine, or banish* a juror who refused to convict a criminal defendant. That is, until Bushell's case.

This is fascinating even today. The crown had arrested William Penn for preaching the tenets of the Quaker religion. Because England had an official church, preaching other religions was against the law. So William Penn *was* guilty of violating the law of England. At trial, Penn defiantly admitted preaching the word of God to an assemblage of people—a clear violation of the law. All that remained was for the jury to convict him. Or so the crown thought. Penn defiantly proclaimed to the jury that since people have the right to worship God, *any* assembly for such a purpose is legal. And any law to the contrary is wrong. The judge, however, had other ideas. He instructed the jury as follows:

> You have heard what the Indictment is. It is for preaching to the people, and drawing a tumultuous company after them, and Mr. Penn was speaking. . . . [If Penn is not punished], you see they will go on [preaching]. . . . [N]ow we are upon the matter of fact *which you are to keep to, and observe, as what hath been fully sworn at your [the jurors'] peril."* (Emphasis added.)

At the jurors' peril! Quite a bit different from the situation today.

The jury attempted to return a partial verdict against Penn, but refused to convict him of unlawful assembly or disturbing the peace. The jurors also acquitted a codefendant, William Mead. Both verdicts were clear violations of the court's instructions. The judge was angry. He ordered the jury to be locked up without "eat, drink, fire, and tobacco," and to resume deliberations. He ordered the jurors to follow the court's instructions and return a proper (i.e., guilty) verdict. (This is the true mean-ing of being sequestered!)

The jury again refused to change its verdict, and the furious court threatened to starve them. Their backs to the wall, the jury returned a unanimous verdict of not guilty. This was jury nullifi-cation, pure and simple. The jurors gave the fist to the law, re-fusing to acknowledge its moral or legal authority. But Bushell's case was far from over. In fact, it was just starting.

The furious judge fined the jurors. One of the jurors, Ed-ward Bushell, was an uncommonly stubborn man. He refused to pay his fine, the judge threw Bushell in jail. Bushell appealed his imprisonment to the Court of Common Pleas. Chief Justice Vaughan then made history by ruling that *jurors may not be fined nor imprisoned for their verdicts.* Stop and think about this for a minute. It seems so simple, it is easy to miss how important it is. Jurors can do pretty much whatever they want, and we cannot punish them.

The Right to Trial by Jury: A Defense of Colonial America Against King George

America enthusiastically adopted the English system of pow-erful juries. Before the American Revolution, the colonies saw jurors as a way to protect themselves against the tyranny of the English monarch. For example, in 1735 a jury refused to convict John Peter Zenger, a printer, of the crime of seditious libel against the New York colony's royal governor. Zenger had pub-lished a completely truthful article in his newspaper, the *Weekly Journal,* in which he revealed that the corrupt colonial governor had dismissed the chief justice of the New York Supreme Court for ruling against the governor in a court case. Although the ar-ticle was truthful, the law still regarded it as criminal libel at that time.

The only real issue for the jury was whether Zenger had, in fact, published the article. Truth was no defense. Zenger's lawyer, Andrew Hamilton, argued that the jurors had the "right beyond all dispute to determine both the law and the fact, and where they do not doubt of the law, they ought to do so. [Jurors should] see with their own eyes, . . . hear with their own ears, and . . . make use of their consciences and understanding in judging of the lives, liberties or estate of their fellow subjects."

The jury acquitted Zenger, refusing to follow a law it felt was unjust.

Most of the colonies had enacted laws requiring trial by jury by the time of the American Revolution. The royal government in the colonies appointed judges who were lackeys for the crown and often denied defendants the right to jury trials—especially in politically significant cases. Our British overlords knew that American juries were not likely to convict Americans in political cases. This was such an incendiary issue that, in our Declaration of Independence, Thomas Jefferson wrote:

> The history of the present King of Great Britain is a history of repeated injuries and usurpations, all having in direct object the establishment of an absolute Tyranny over these States. To prove this, let the Facts be submitted to a candid world.
>
> He has made Judges dependent on his Will alone, for the tenure of their offices and payment of their salaries.
>
> He has . . . subject[ed] us to a jurisdiction foreign to our constitution . . . giving his Assent to their Acts of pretended Legislation. . . . For depriving us in many cases, of the benefits of Trial By Jury.

That says it all. The government appoints lackeys for judges, and we need the common sense of the citizens to protect us from the government. As a result, in 1774 the First Continental Congress declared that all colonists were empowered with the right to the "great and inestimable privilege of being tried by their peers of the vicinage."

The Blessings of an Independent Jury System

I have seen every possible side of our independent jury system. Sometimes it is a great blessing, sometimes a curse. Not surprising, since jurors are but human. Of course, in the historic cases, an independent jury sounds wonderful—everyone ought to be protected from the tyranny of old King George, right? But even in modern times I have seen many examples of a jury genuinely serving as a protection against abusive government.

Consider the famous MacMartin Preschool case. I watched with horror as a politically ambitious district attorney brought utterly unsubstantiated claims of bizarre sexual molestation against Raymond Buckey and his mother and grandmother. The charges were made by schoolchildren, apparently egged on by their parents and therapists. I watched with incredulity as the therapists were caught on videotape, asking the children over and over if they had been touched "down there." The therapists would just not take no for an answer. Eventually the children said yes. Based on that evidence, and on claims by the preschoolers of secret tunnels and bus rides to churches where sexual rites were performed and animals were sacrificed (not one shred of which was ever confirmed by any physical evidence), the State of California undertook to put poor, hapless Raymond Buckey and his mother in jail. Raymond spent five years in jail and his mother over two years, awaiting the conclusion of the trial. Thank God for an independent jury. They acquitted the defendants rapidly after a preliminary hearing and a trial that lasted several years. (A few unresolved remaining counts were dismissed by the DA, but for the Buckeys, justice came awfully late—long after their lives were smashed and wasted.)

On a lighter note, jurors often refuse to convict defendants of crimes they consider silly. For example, betting is legal at the track. But a few blocks away, if "Lefty" takes a few bets, the DA is after him. Frankly, judges and DAs would prefer not to be bothered with these cases. But DAs don't want to be perceived as soft on crime. Nor does a judge. So, periodically, Lefty gets arrested for illegal bookmaking. Of course, young deputy DAs get to try these cases, which no respectable veteran would take. Juries usually refuse to convict a mom-and-pop bookmaking operator who conducted his enterprise a few miles away from the legalized betting of a race track. After a few witnesses with nicknames like "Squirreley," and "Joey the Juice," jurors usually give twelve hearty thumbs down to a conviction, exercising their power of jury nullification. But not without a smile and wink to the hapless young DA, and perhaps placing a small bet with the bemused defendant.

Sometimes juries try to exercise their power to get rid of silly cases, and just miss the mark. For example, in the Heidi Fleiss pandering and drug case, the jurors wanted to convict Fleiss on a charge on which she would do no jail time. So they compromised their verdict and acquitted her of the drug charges, convicting her only on the pandering charges. As it turned out, they got it completely backwards. Pandering carried a mandatory minimum three-year prison term, the drug charges did not. When Sheila Mitrowski, the jury foreperson in the Fleiss case, found out Fleiss was going to jail for three years, she was appalled: "Three years in prison for what she did? Give me a break. That is outrageous." The Fleiss case was recently reversed for juror misconduct. This illustrates an interesting limitation on the power of juries. Jurors have absolute power to *acquit* a criminal defendant, whether they are right or wrong. If they wrongfully *convict*, however, the appellate courts can send it back for a new trial. So Fleiss may now be retried on the pandering charges. But she *cannot* be retried on the cocaine charges.

The Curse of an Independent Jury System

So the independent jury system seems pretty good. Well, not always. Imagine how difficult it was in 1940 to convict a white man of raping a black woman or lynching a black man in the deep South. Or in 1950. Or in 1960. Or to convict KKK members for murdering civil rights protesters. That too is jury nullification, and it is not so pretty. Bigotry and hatred never are.

Take the 1991 murder of Yankel Rosenbaum in Crown Heights, in which an African-American and Hispanic jury acquitted Rosenbaum's black killer, Lemrick Nelson. The murder took place during an emotionally charged race riot. Frankly, the race riot continued in the jury room. Here is how the United States Court of Appeals described the uncontested facts:

An automobile driven by a Hasidic Jew struck two black children playing in the Crown Heights neighborhood of Brooklyn during the evening of August 19, 1991. One child was killed, and the other was seriously injured. Rumors spread throughout the community, during the course of the evening, that ambulance personnel responding to the scene of the accident first treated the Jewish driver rather than the two seriously injured children pinned beneath the automobile. A large crowd gathered at the accident scene. . . . [A crowd of black men, including the murderer, Nelson, headed for a nearby Jewish neighborhood.] Yankel Rosenbaum had the misfortune to be espied by Nelson and some ten other black individuals. One of them shouted, "There's a Jew, get the Jew," and they chased Rosenbaum across the street and attacked him. Rosenbaum, having been stabbed in the midsection of his body by Nelson, was left bleeding in the street.

The police apprehended Nelson approximately one block away from the stabbing scene. They found in Nelson's pocket a bloody knife with the word "Killer" on the handle. When Rosenbaum confronted Nelson during a "show-up" identification, he positively identified Nelson as the person who had stabbed him. Rosenbaum died in the early morning hours of the following day at the hospital to which he had been taken following the incident. Shortly thereafter, Nelson orally admitted to the police that he had stabbed Rosenbaum.

For causing the death of Yankel Rosenbaum, Nelson was charged as an adult with second degree murder under New York law on August 26, 1991. *After a six-week trial in Kings County Supreme Court, Nelson was acquitted in October 1992 of all charges arising out of the events of August 19, 1991.*

Ouch. It's payback time. (Nelson was subsequently retried under federal civil rights laws and convicted by a federal jury in 1996.)

Or consider the acquittal of the murderer of Rabbi Meir Kahane, founder of the Jewish Defense League. Kahane was assassinated in 1990 while giving a speech at the Marriot Hotel in Manhattan. William Kunstler defended El Sayyid Nosair, an Egyptian-born Arab. Sayyid shot a man in the leg as he fled from the hotel. A short distance away from the hotel he commandeered a taxi at gunpoint, then fled from the cab when it stopped for a red light, running into a postal security officer with whom he exchanged gunfire. Both were wounded and the murder weapon was found laying next to the wounded Sayyid.

The jury consisted of five African-American, one Hispanic, and six white citizens. They acquitted Sayyid of the Meir Kahane murder count, yet convicted him of the lesser charges, including possession of the murder weapon.

During jury selection, Kunstler targeted whites for preemptories. He also tried to ask if jurors were Jewish. After the verdict, Kunstler did not pull any punches—he admitted that he wanted "a third world jury of non-whites, or anyone who's been pushed down by white society." Dershowitz, commenting on this trial, said, "Kunstler knows better than anybody in America how to manipulate the ethnic prejudice and biases of a jury." Of course, that was before the Dream Team.

Kunstler directed a defense in which he suggested that the cops, in a rush to judgment, had just arrested the first Arab they could find near the crime scene. That this particular Arab was carrying the murder weapon did not, apparently, figure in the cops' "rush to judgment." Then Kunstler blamed the Jewish Defense League for the murder, accusing the JDL of assassinating Kahane and framing Sayyid Nosair. Lawyers and juries—a volatile mixture. Ouch. It's payback time.

The acquittal of the police who beat Rodney King was an affront to our sensibilities. The Simi Valley jury returned a verdict that seemed to defy the damning evidence captured on video. The world was indignant as Los Angeles burned in the thunder of public outrage.

Consider the acquittal of O.J. Simpson in the slaying of Nicole Brown Simpson and Ronald Goldman. In the double murder trial, the racist appeal could not have been more obvious. On the very first day of cross-examination, Johnnie Cochran made sure that a predominantly African-American jury knew that a police detective on the case lived in Simi Valley (the community that had refused to convict the police of beating Rodney King). Cochran emphasized over and over how the detective had driven from his home in Simi Valley to investigate the double murder. He lingered on and emphasized the words "Simi Valley," in case any jurors missed the point. In closing argument, Cochran was even more direct. He exhorted the jury to punish the "racist" police department, to "send a message beyond Department 103 . . . to stop this cover-up! If you don't stop it, who will? It has to be stopped by you. . . . If you don't do what's right, this kind of conduct will continue on forever." The jury deliberated less than four hours, following nine months of testimony, 133 witnesses, over 45,000 pages of transcript, and over 1,100 exhibits! And it sure sent a message. Ouch. It's payback time.

The cases I have been talking about are the ones you have probably heard of—the notorious cases. But the rot goes much deeper in the system. In courthouses in predominantly African-American neighborhoods of New York, Los Angeles, and other major cities, it is increasingly difficult to convict a black man for assault on, or murder of, a white man. I am sure the reverse is true today in other parts of America. Although no one wants to talk about it, that is another of the ugly little facts about our justice system today.

In each of the above cases, a jury refused to convict an obviously guilty person. It's thrilling to read about how Edward Bushell made history by refusing to convict William Penn for preaching the word of God, or John Zenger for printing the truth about a corrupt colonial governor. Modern jury nullification is not so thrilling. Johnnie Cochran's argument to the jury seems wrong to many of us. Look how much things have changed in the world of jury nullification. Neither William Penn nor John Zenger was a murderer. Nor was Zenger's attorney playing the ugliest card in the deck, the race card. Nor was Zenger or Penn dealing from the bottom of the deck, as codefense attorney Bob Shapiro accused Cochran of doing. Modern defendants are getting away with murder and mayhem, and our powerful, independent juries are responsible. What is going on? Why the change?

One explanation may lie in the fact that the jury is supposed to bring the conscience of the community into the court system. A community conscience, as historically envisioned, probably no longer exists. That notion related to a homogeneous society where a single community more or less shared common values and mores. In England and colonial America, blacks, women, and minorities could not serve as jurors. Verdicts therefore reflected the conscience of white male landowners of a certain class standing. Today our multiethnic society makes it hard to define, let alone capture, the essence of the community conscience. It is far more difficult today to reach a community consensus of right and wrong, of shared values. Egregious verdicts or hung juries happen when jurors vote in accordance with their ethnic or religious affiliations or on the basis of the politics of special interests, without regard to the merits of the evidence. Political essayist George Will refers to this phenomenon as "group think."

Is the jury system dead? Should it be replaced? I still regard a powerful, independent jury as one of our most important protections against government tyranny. Juries can and do bring the conscience of the community into the judicial system. But what we are seeing are not isolated cases. The trend is clearly toward ever-increasing use of the jury system to "get even" with society for "past wrongs." To punish the system. Worse, to punish an entire society. The myth of the melting pot has long since died. There is a real danger that this nation of increasingly segregated and hostile cultures, each carrying baggage of perceived hurts, paranoia, and ill will, could become as polarized as the Serbs and the Croats.

Jurors are getting their say today, just as juries did in 1670. Too often, however, their "say" has all the judiciousness of a temper tantrum. Too often the modern conscience of the community allows murderers to walk free because of the color of their skin, or because of the color of the skin of the person they murdered. Or because all cops are pigs and liars. Or because of past wrongs, real or imagined.

I regard this trend of acquitting dangerous criminals as the most serious assault on the integrity of the jury system since 1670, when the judge fined poor William Bushell for refusing to imprison William Penn. If this trend continues, and if juries continue to "group think" their way to injustice, the independent jury will not survive as an institution. It will not take many more Simpson or Rodney King verdicts to build a political consensus that the jury system needs major changes—and perhaps needs to be discarded altogether. This would be a tragedy. But the system can be repaired.

EIGHT

The Jury Selection Scam

WHO CAN PICK THE STUPIDEST
AND MOST BIGOTED JURY?

When you see a lawyer trying to pick a smart jury, you know he's got a strong case. Percy Foreman and I once had an argument as to which of us had picked the most stupid jury. I think I won with one that returned a verdict which amounted to "Not guilty with a recommendation of clemency because of reasonable doubt."
—F. Lee Bailey

The most interesting part of F. Lee Bailey's remark that serves as the epigraph to this chapter is what he does not say. He should have added, "When you see a lawyer trying to pick a stupid jury, you know he's got a weak case." Clearly, Bailey is a master of representing clients with weak cases—the jury he describes was not, shall we say, composed of wizards. The composition of the jury is extremely important to the prosecutors and to defense counsel. As important as the evidence? No, probably more important than the evidence.

Another dirty little secret of our judicial system is that we do a terrible job of choosing fair juries. Much of the jury selection process—especially in federal court—is designed solely to make judges' lives easier, to move the trial along efficiently and quickly. Much of the rest of the process of jury selection is spent by the lawyers trying their utmost to get the most prejudiced, narrow-minded jury they can find.

Our jury selection process encourages cynical defense attorneys to pick the dumbest jurors they can find. F. Lee Bailey is not kidding when he brags about selecting the stupidest jurors. He is proud because that is an important skill for a defense lawyer to possess. Most defense lawyers will tell you in their more candid moments that in tough cases they automatically eliminate educated or smart jurors from the panel. Any juror who is too educated might become the leader who explains to the rest of the jury that the defense is grasping at straws.

Worse, the system also encourages both prosecutors and defense counsel to pick bigots when they are trying a racially charged case. Of course, they want different kinds of bigots, but each side wants as many of its kind of bigot as possible.

The jury is a microcosm of the outside world. But all the hate, distrust, and ignorance is compressed, in the jury room, into an unnatural setting—a setting where ordinary people are asked to make life-and-death decisions about people they despise and fear as their enemies in ordinary life. Thus, bias and bigotry are heightened and more lethal in the jury room than in society at large. If we can't fix this problem, I fear the jury system will not be with us much longer.

How Attorneys Pick Biased Jurors

Both the prosecutor and the defense try to select jurors who will be biased in their favor. Each side looks for particular biases, prejudices, and capabilities in a juror. It is axiomatic that jurors see things through the lenses of their own experience. That is what informs their views. That is the basis for how they will weigh and consider evidence. It probably will not surprise you that in the Simpson trials, Johnnie Cochran and Marcia Clark, and Dan Petrocelli, John Kelly, and Robert Baker were looking for different sets of biases, prejudices, and capabilities.

The place where a trial is held greatly affects the character of the jury pool and hence the kind of jurors who will sit as the trier of fact. One of the most crucial decisions in the Simpson case was where to try it. The reason? If the criminal trial was tried downtown, the biases of the jury pool would be completely different than if it was tried in Santa Monica. Court policy usually favors the trial being heard in the jurisdiction in which the crime occurred. This is for the convenience of witnesses as well as to reflect the community conscience of *the people who live in the place where the crime occurred*. In the Simpson double murder case, that meant the Santa Monica district serviced by the Santa Monica courthouse. DA Gil Garcetti gave several reasons for the case being tried in downtown L.A. instead. He failed to mention what I believe is the real reason. Before Johnnie Cochran publicly joined the Dream Team, prominent black leaders met with Garcetti. They argued vehemently that the appearance of fairness demanded the case be tried downtown, where African Americans would feel Simpson could get a fair trial. They told Garcetti there could be another Rodney King–style race riot if Simpson was convicted by a predominantly white Santa Monica jury.

Garcetti is a fair-minded man. He believed the prosecution had more than enough evidence to establish guilt. He believed no reasonable juror, regardless of skin color, could fairly conclude otherwise. Public perceptions of fairness are important. So Garcetti bent over backwards to preclude any possible claims of racism—all for the noble purpose of averting rising racial tensions and another possible riot. In acceding to the black leaders' demands, Garcetti miscalculated the explosive potential of the race card in a case involving a black national icon, thereby sealing the fate of the prosecution. The prosecution could not win downtown if the defense team played the race card; they could only hope to get a hung jury. Well, the rest is history. Incredibly, Johnnie Cochran was one of the prominent black leaders who met with Garcetti, imploring the DA to keep the case downtown—*before* anyone knew he would lead the Dream Team. History sadly reflects that instead of ameliorating racial tensions, the swift verdict rendered by a predominantly black jury exacerbated them, setting relations between blacks and whites back decades.

To summarize briefly, the Santa Monica jury pool more closely matched the biases the prosecution wanted and needed on the jury. Downtown they matched the defense. Let's look at each side's ideal juror.

The People needed jurors who could understand and appreciate scientific evidence and expert testimony. They needed jurors who could embrace the science of DNA and not be intimidated by it, because DNA evidence is not intuitive.

They also needed jurors who were intelligent, educated, and

sophisticated enough to understand that in a big investigation there will always be mistakes in handling the evidence, that is, to understand that a mistake does not equate with a "corruption" of evidence or sinister motives. The People wanted jurors who would be able to look at the mistakes one by one and to assess analytically whether a particular mistake affected the validity of the evidence. The People also wanted jurors who had upper-class, yuppie values. These jurors would likely be sympathetic to Nicole Simpson as a battered wife, but basically nonjudgmental about her lifestyle. They would not approve of domestic violence as a necessary by-product of a dysfunctional relationship. Remember, there was one incident in which Simpson sneaked up on Nicole's home to spy on her. He watched through the window as she had sex with another man. That is what Simpson was yelling about on the infamous 911 tape: "You were f———g a man in the living room while the kids were upstairs." How did Simpson know? He was hiding outside, watching through the window. The prosecution needed a jury that would judge Simpson as the wrongdoer in that situation for sneaking around, spying.

The People also needed jurors who would be inclined to accept the testimony of police officers and law enforcement lab technicians. Jurors who did not regard the cops as enemies.

Simpson's defense team, on the other hand, was looking for a very different juror. The defense team wanted to find a "show me" jury that fulfilled the following criteria:

• Jurors who had bad experiences with the police, and who would therefore be skeptical, if not downright distrustful, of police evidence.
• Black jurors, who could relate to Simpson *both* as a black man and as a national icon. Jurors who might be so resentful at the system they would use the case to send a message. Payback time! A recent report from the Washington-based Center for Equal Opportunity, titled *Race and the Criminal Justice System: How Race Affects Jury Trials,* examined 55,000 felony cases throughout the major counties in the United States, and found that whites were more likely to be convicted of major crimes than their black counterparts. For example, in rape cases, 51 percent of blacks won acquittals versus 25 percent of whites; in assault cases, 49 percent acquittals for blacks versus 43 percent for whites; in

drug trafficking cases, 24 percent of blacks were acquitted compared with 14 percent of whites; and in weapons charges, 32 percent of blacks were acquitted compared to 22 percent of whites. We can speculate about the reasons; certainly one is that blacks are getting off easier through the leniency of black juries, who believe that too many of their own are disproportionately being sucked into the system and sent to prisons.

   • Jurors who would be more inclined as a matter of disposition to believe in outlandish conspiracy theories.
   • Less educated jurors. The elaborate conspiracy at the heart of the defense case would have been virtually impossible to carry off in the real world. Likewise, less educated jurors would be less inclined or likely to understand the intricacies of DNA science. A juror who had a hard time understanding the DNA testimony could take the easy path and pretend to himself or herself that the DNA evidence was unimportant by buying into the conspiracy argument. In short, less educated jurors have an extra reason to believe in conspiracies, in that they don't have to resolve discrete discrepancies and ambiguities or, indeed, understand the scientific evidence at all.
   • Jurors who, from experience, might accept domestic violence as part of the hard realities of life.
   • Jurors who would be unsympathetic to Nicole Brown Simpson and disapprove of her morals and lifestyle.

What I have said is not pretty, nor is it politically correct. But I assure you that is how the Dream Team decided what jurors they wanted to pick. Aside from the fact that black jurors were more able to identify with Simpson as an African American, they posed a very serious problem for the prosecution on two other counts.

First, as mentioned, an inner-city black jury is more inclined than a predominantly white Westside jury to believe in outlandish conspiracies. Researchers in urban folklore have found widespread support in the inner city, if not significant segments of the black community, for the rumor that the AIDS virus was invented by white people to kill black men. Aside from Oliver Stone devotees, most Westside L.A. residents (like those from Santa Monica) would rank white conspiracies to kill African Americans with AIDS as being less likely than Elvis Presley's appearance with Ted Koppel on tonight's edition of *Nightline*. Isn't it interesting that the Dream Team tried the case as a conspiracy by whites and Asians (the cops, the forensic people, and the technicians) to get a black man? This theory was tailored to the biases of a substantial portion of the downtown jury pool.

Furthermore, focus-group studies before the trial revealed that the prosecution had a particular problem with black women jurors. Polls before the trial showed that 23 percent of black men but only 7 percent of black women thought Simpson was guilty. Several factors account for this discrepancy. One is that black women in focus groups, when told about Simpson's history of domestic abuse, shrugged it off because "every relationship has these kinds of problems." A critical part of the prosecution's case was Simpson's alleged long history of wife beating. A Santa Monica jury would have recoiled at that history. It turned out it was no big deal to the actual jury. Second, black women were resentful of Nicole Simpson, a rich white woman. Nicole was perceived as having taken Simpson away from his first wife, Marguerite, a black woman. Finally, black women did not like Marcia Clark, the lead prosecutor. She was regarded as a pushy white bitch trying to bring down a prominent black man.

In the downtown L.A. jury pool, the jury inevitably would be dominated by black women if the defense exercised its peremptory challenges to exclude other groups—and that is exactly what happened. Excusing males, whites, and Asians because of their gender or ethnicity is as illegal as excusing blacks because of their skin color. It is constitutionally prohibited. But they did it, and they got away with it. Unwittingly, Marcia Clark played into their strategy with her erroneous belief that women, black or white, would condemn Simpson because of his history of abuse.

Much has been written about the jury selection in the Simpson criminal trial. Everything that has been said applies to the Simpson civil trial in spades. Think about it. Anyone who denies having formed some opinion about O.J.'s guilt or innocence or of the evidence is a flat-out liar. Associated Press veteran correspondent Michael Fleeman, attending the O.J. civil trial, echoed the frustration all of us had with the prospective jurors: "He's guilty. He's innocent. He's probably guilty, probably innocent, maybe perhaps probably guilty but I'm not sure because I really didn't follow the case except when I did. But I do know this, Your Honor, I can be fair. I think."

When a prospective black male juror who believed O.J. was "probably innocent" claimed that he only vaguely followed the case, writing in the jury questionnaire nothing about what he had heard regarding Mark Fuhrman, he was being disingenuous if not willfully mendacious. When pressed on voir dire, he admitted he had heard something about Fuhrman testifying, but offered nothing further. When pressed again, he offered something about hearing "racial bias." When pressed further, he admitted hearing something about the "planting" of some evidence! But the juror quickly added that he wouldn't make judgments on hearsay. Yeah, and his brother is Pinocchio. Then there was the white male juror who strongly felt there was domestic abuse. When pressed by the defense, he admitted he had formed some opinions based on the slow-speed Bronco chase, the passport, the gun money, and the disguise. When prompted for more, he admitted that the 911 tapes and the DNA evidence were compelling. However, the juror said, he could be fair and he could set aside his opinions. Yeah, and I'm Donald Duck.

What has crystallized is the ugly fact that in the absence of reforms, more trials throughout our troubled nation will be resolved not on the merits of the evidence, but on racial and group demographics. The strength, richness, and diversity of America rests in its multiethnic population. Yet focus-group studies, polls, jury consultant analysis, and shadow juries used by lawyers cynically exploit this diversity to ensure the selection of skewed juries. So are jurors so hopelessly biased that justice is defined by their special agenda and "group think" mentality? Or is there something we can do to mitigate this very real problem?

Peremptory Challenges and Challenges for Cause

A prospective juror may be eliminated from the jury panel for either of two reasons: First, the juror may be challenged for cause. If either the prosecution or the defense can show that the juror has prejudged the case or is biased against one side or the other, that juror should be and usually is excused for cause. Second, either side may exercise what are referred to as *peremptory challenges*. A peremptory challenge may be exercised *without stating any reason*. The Supreme Court will not, however, allow a peremptory to be used to dismiss a juror because of race, gender, or ethnicity. So lawyers must be clever. They must give another reason, if challenged about their motivations. Any other stated reason for the peremptory is usually good enough for the record, unless a pattern of discrimination can be shown. In any event, if prosecutors, for example, suspect but cannot prove that a potential juror is against the death penalty, they will likely exercise one of their peremptories in a capital case.

The number of for-cause challenges is unlimited. The number of peremptories is limited. In federal criminal cases, the prosecution has six peremptories and the defense has ten. State court judges generally allow up to ten peremptories for each side. In capital cases, both sides get twenty peremptories. Needless to say, both sides treasure their peremptories because they are tools to sculpt a jury to the proper set of biases.

Voir Dire and the Art of Jury Challenges

Voir dire is an Anglo-French phrase, meaning "to speak the truth." The ostensible purpose of voir dire is to select a *bias-neutral jury*. In fact, effective voir dire combined with peremptories is one of the best tools available to pack a jury, that is, to use its biases.

The judge must seize hold of the voir dire process so that the lawyers do not hijack its proper purpose. Because of the way the adversary system pits adversaries one against the other, a volatile framework is thus forged. When life hangs in the balance, tensions often reach critical mass. Voir dire can be explosive.

Voir dire questioning allows the lawyers to probe, giving them information that assists them in the exercise of peremptories. By itself, voir dire is not a bad thing. Remember, we said the purpose of voir dire is to ferret out jurors who harbor actual bias. Getting rid of those jurors can only improve the justice system. But lawyers can get rid of biased jurors by exercising a challenge for cause. And those challenges are unlimited. When voir dire is combined with extensive peremptories, the lawyers now have a powerful means to make sure they have a biased jury—precisely what we, the public, do not want. The more information a lawyer can get concerning a juror, the more the lawyer will be able to judge whether the juror is likely to have the right set of biases. Most attorneys use voir dire for that purpose. There are several approaches on the bench to controlling voir dire. Each has its own champions.

Federal judges are case-management-oriented; they have heavy case loads and do not look kindly upon anything that prolongs a case. So, in federal court, the judge alone usually asks questions of the jurors. The attorneys are required to submit suggested questions in writing, which the judge may or may not choose to incorporate in his or her voir dire. The problem in the federal courts is that the judges generally ask few questions and the questions are usually very unhelpful in ferreting out actual bias. Some federal judges limit voir dire to exactly four questions, posed by the judge: "What is your name?" "What is your occupation?" "Are you married?" "Can you be impartial in this case?" And that's it. So, in a typical federal case, the attorneys do not have enough information to exercise challenges for cause effectively.

Peremptories are a different matter. While voir dire helps the lawyers exercise their peremptories, it is not necessary. Lawyers know a lot about a potential juror's biases simply by knowing his or her age, sex, marital status, occupation, residency and ethnic background. The way lawyers find this out is through surveys and jury consultants. They can tell you, statistically, that a second-generation Chinese-American woman between forty and fifty is more likely than a randomly chosen juror to have a particular set of opinions and attitudes. If you do not like her statistically calculated opinions and attitudes, you excuse her on a peremptory. If you think her opinions and attitudes will help your client, you will do everything in your power to keep her on the jury. Because jury consultants can slice the population's biases up about any way you want, peremptories have become a simple matter of stereotyping in federal court.

On the other hand, the amount of lawyer-conducted voir dire in the state courts varies. In California, for example, prior to 1990, before the passage of a criminal justice reform initiative, attorneys had enormous latitude in conducting voir dire. Today California judges are disinclined to allow open-ended questioning because it dramatically lengthens the voir dire process. If courtroom efficiency is at the top of the list of priorities, then such questioning is discouraged or forbidden.

I want to show you how powerful a tool voir dire can be in selecting a bias-neutral jury.

In the trial of Manson family member Steve Grogan for the murder of cowboy stuntman Donald "Shorty" Shea, I had to find a jury that could properly consider the death penalty in a case where we had no body. The court had conducted a typical perfunctory voir dire, using leading questions that suggested what answer the court wanted. For example, "Would you automatically *refuse* to vote for the death penalty, regardless of the evidence?" Each juror answered that he or she would not.

At that point I believe the jurors thought they were telling the truth. Many potential jurors have no general philosophical objection to the death penalty. But when they are confronted with the reality of making that kind of decision themselves, they often find they cannot act in accordance with the law. After its perfunctory questioning, the court then turned over the questioning to the lawyers. I was worried that the court's questions about the jurors' attitudes toward the death penalty were far too shallow. It turned out I was right. The voir dire of Mrs. Jones (name changed) produced some surprises.

KATZ: Does it offend your sense of justice and fair play to know that in this state a person can be convicted of murder in the first degree based wholly upon circumstantial evidence, there being no production of a body or eyewitness to the killing?

JUROR: No.

It was time to push Mrs. Jones (as well as the other jurors) until she personally felt the weight of the problem with which she would be confronted. It is not only her answers that are important, but her body language as well. Does she look at me? Do her eyes dart nervously away from my gaze? Is she confident? Is she shaken? What is she doing with her hands? Does her expression belie her answers?

KATZ: [So if] the circumstantial evidence created an abiding conviction to a moral certainty of the truth of the charge, you would not hesitate to vote guilty even though we didn't produce a body. Is that correct?

JUROR: I wouldn't—I wouldn't hesitate.

I watched her very carefully. She shifted her weight several times before answering that question; I am now concerned the People may have a problem with this juror. So I keep asking questions.

KATZ: Mrs. Jones, let's take this one step further. Let's suppose you know now that upon the return of a first-degree murder verdict you would have to go on to the very difficult task of determining whether another human being shall live or die. [Y]ou are in the jury room and you're deliberating. Do you think that because you have knowledge that if you voted for murder in the first degree, that fact and that fact alone would cause you to compromise your verdict to a lesser degree such as second-degree murder or even acquittal merely to avoid the difficult task of going on to the penalty phase?

JUROR: No.

KATZ: So what you are saying is that regardless of the consequences of your voting for murder in the first degree, if that was the proper verdict in accordance with the facts as you find them to be and in accordance with his honor's instructions, you would vote that verdict, is that correct?

JUROR: I *think* so.

Now I am pretty sure I have a problem. This juror has been unequivocal in her previous answers. She has told the judge she would not automatically refuse to vote for the death penalty in an appropriate case. But now she equivocates about returning a first-degree murder verdict. My problem is to convince the court that she is biased so I can challenge her for cause. As you will see, that wasn't easy.

KATZ: [D]o you generally oppose capital punishment?

JUROR: Yes.

Here, open-ended questioning should be allowed such as "Tell us your thoughts about the death penalty," "What have you told others about your feelings?" It is time to make this juror understand that we are serious about seeking the death penalty in this case. Therefore we must make it clear that her personal involvement is essential and will be demanded. Is she up to it?

KATZ: Now, what I am asking you is this. Can you conceive of yourself in some circumstances in which you would vote the death penalty as a juror?

JUROR: That I would vote?

KATZ: Yes, you, yourself.

JUROR: *I wouldn't!*

There it is. This juror is biased. Now it is necessary to elicit her answer in a way that allows for a challenge for cause, despite what she had told the judge in answer to his perfunctory question about the death penalty.

KATZ: Are you telling us that, regardless of the facts that would unfold during the course of this trial, you would under no circumstances yourself vote the death penalty?

JUROR: That's right.

Eureka! A challenge for cause should exist right now. But I wanted to make the record stronger. If the judge excuses her for cause and an appellate court disagrees with the challenge, the case will be reversed, regardless of the strength of the evidence.

KATZ: Just so I understand it, and the court understands, you are telling us that regardless of the evidence in this case before you, you would *automatically* vote against the death penalty yourself?

JUROR: Right.

If ever there was a good challenge for cause, this was it. Much to my surprise, Judge Call refused to grant it because of her one answer to his perfunctory and leading question about the death penalty at the very start. I asked the judge if he would help clear things up by re-asking his original question. The court had the reporter read back the original question and answer where the juror said that she would *not* automatically vote against imposing the death penalty.

COURT: You heard your answer there, did you, Mrs. Jones?

JUROR: Yes.

COURT: Well now, you have found some confusion. . . . I will ask you this question again. Would you automatically vote against the death penalty without regard to any evidence that might be produced at the trial of this case?

JUROR: I answered no.

COURT: All right. Well, I will take the answer no. I will refuse the challenge.

This was unbelievable! Here a careful record had been made that the juror would refuse to participate in a death verdict, regardless of the evidence. Yet this judge refused to look at the total record. We were in trouble.

KATZ: Excuse me, Your Honor. May I continue my questioning, then?

COURT: Challenge is refused.

KATZ: No, I appreciate that, Your Honor. Based upon this juror's last response.

COURT: All right.

KATZ: Mrs. Jones, now I am totally confused. I just asked you a moment ago whether or not you, yourself, would automatically refuse, regardless of the evidence, to vote the death penalty, and you told me that you would.

JUROR: I misunderstood you. I am sorry.

KATZ: Well, you misunderstood the judge or you misunderstood me?

JUROR: I misunderstood the judge. I automatically oppose the death penalty.

KATZ: Your Honor—

COURT: Well, I refuse. . . . I don't know, she tells me no, she would not.

KATZ: If Your Honor pleases, I did break down my question, I think, in very fundamental terms and I would ask Your Honor once again to rephrase the question and make sure Mrs. Jones understands it. I appreciate the court's indulgence.

COURT: Mrs. Jones, if you are voting for the death penalty or life imprisonment . . . would you automatically vote against the death penalty without considering all of the testimony in the case?

JUROR: Would I vote against the death penalty?

COURT: Now is the answer yes or no?

JUROR: Yes.

Finally the judge dismissed the juror for cause. The point of this voir dire excerpt is to show how a judge's perfunctory questioning cannot possibly elicit enough real information with which to determine if a challenge for cause exists. That is why one of my major recommendations for reform of the jury system is to reinstitute active attorney participation in the voir dire process in both federal and state court. When used fairly, in the manner intended by the law, it is virtually the only way to expose gross biases. If the judges will not do it on their own initiative, then we will have to ask the legislature to require the judges to make the change.

Limit the Peremptory Challenge

You may be thinking I've given you conflicting messages about peremptory challenges. In truth I have. As an advocate trying cases, I loved peremptories when I was selecting juries. As an advocate, my role was to win. But today I can sit back with some perspective. Too many peremptories hurt the system badly by allowing lawyers to eliminate ethnically diverse, educated, and smart jurors from the panel. Trials are turned into contests of who can select the stupidest, most bigoted jury. Citizens who are performing an important duty by serving on our juries find the process tedious, time-consuming, and objectionable.

My first recommendation for reforming the jury selection process is, therefore, that peremptories should be limited to three for each side for a twelve-person jury. Three peremptories are not enough to stack a twelve-person jury. If the peremptories are limited, then the lawyers will have less reason to abuse voir dire, to conduct surveys, and to hire jury consultants. Rather than trying to divine whether peremptories are being exercised for constitutionally impermissible purposes such as race, gender, religion, or some other forbidden group characterization, let them be exercised for any purpose and let's get on with the trial. I would like to say do away with all peremptories, as the English have done. But there are always one or two jurors who lie craftily about their biases and therefore can't be challenged for cause. Or there may be jurors with whom you or your client feel extremely ill at ease. That's my concession as a former trial lawyer and advocate. The exercise of three peremptories (fewer, if we go to eight-person juries) should not be unduly time-consuming. The possibility that these remaining peremptories can eliminate a juror with a gross bias, unreachable by a challenge for cause, serves the ends of justice.

Shrink the Size of the Juries to Eight

While some state constitutions specifically guarantee twelve-person juries, the federal Constitution and the Bill of Rights are silent on the magic number of jurors required. The United States Supreme Court has permitted juries as small as six in noncapital cases. More than thirty states permit juries of fewer than twelve persons. Frankly, there is no magic to the number twelve, and I have seen no indication that smaller juries are less fair or more bigoted than larger ones.

I believe eight-person juries would improve the system substantially, saving enormous amounts of money, expediting jury selection, extending the jury pool, and promoting the lasting health of our jury system. The important point is that a group of citizens, representative of the community, are the important buffer between the might of the state and the accused—not a particular *number* of citizens. Like our venerable constitution, the jury system, in order to survive, must reflect contemporary needs. If we hang on to the accident of "twelve tried and true," we may lose the jury system in its entirety. And that is something we cannot afford to do.

Fire the Jury Consultants

I would go further than merely discouraging the distasteful practice of surveys and jury consultants who foster the ugliness of group stereotypes. I would bar entirely the use of jury consultants and surveys that are designed to determine juror biases, tendencies, and inclinations. Jury consultants are expensive, and are used only by the rich and the powerful. Lawyers misuse them to skew jury selection to their side. If nothing else, this creates bad impressions of our system. The *appearance* of fairness is just as important as the *fact* of fairness, since people will judge the system on what it appears to be.

Improve the Jury Pool

The way we select the jury pool guarantees that the quality and education level of jurors will be relatively low. F. Lee Bailey says,

> [The jury system is a] startling weakness in our legal machinery. You never get a jury of your peers. In most states you get a jury of elderly and retired, telephone company

employees, civil servants, and so forth. The rest either duck
jury duty or are eliminated in trial selection.

Think back on it. When was the last time *you* served on a
jury? If you are reading this book, you are probably well educated, have a lot of responsibility at your job, read the newspaper daily, read at least one weekly magazine like *Time* or
Newsweek, and are frustrated with our judicial system. It would be
personally tough for you to be a juror because your small company won't be able to pay your salary while you are on jury duty,
and besides, you have all those projects sitting on your desk you
just haven't gotten to quite yet. Or you have important family-
related responsibilities. Odds are, each time you have received
the notice to serve on the jury, you have ignored it or returned
it requesting an exemption.

Or maybe you have gone to the courthouse for jury duty and
encountered something even more frustrating. You may find
that as a practical matter, the system will not allow you to serve
on a jury precisely because you are well educated and responsible, and have read the newspaper. Take, for example, the following jury selection practice used by some judges in federal
court. If a case is notorious, the judge may ask the entire panel
of prospective jurors to raise their hands if they have heard *anything* about the case. The judge then excuses *any* juror who raises
his or her hand. Something is terribly wrong here. We have just
eliminated most of the jurors who read the newspaper daily and
who stay informed and interested in community affairs. Well-
informed people are as much a part of our community as those
who do not stay abreast of current affairs. Alternatively, you
spend the bulk of your jury service reading a book, because you
have run into the very common practice among defense attorneys to excuse all intelligent or well-educated people from the
juries. What that says is we are eliminating our most intelligent,
best-informed, and best-educated people from juries either in
the process of jury selection *or before the process of jury selection even
starts!* Over a century ago, Mark Twain lamented:

> When the peremptory challenges were all exhausted, a
> jury of twelve men were impaneled—a jury who swore that
> they had neither heard, read, talked about nor expressed
> an opinion concerning a murder which the very cattle in

the corrals, the Indians in the sagebrush and the stones in the street were cognizant of!

—Mark Twain, *Roughing It* (Edited by Franklin Rogers, 1972), p. 307.

Conscription of Jurors

Our society should choose its jury pool from the widest possible cross-section of our community. We should draft jurors, and we should do it with teeth. The draft should draw the jury pool out of the entire population. We need to get serious about it and enforce it. One nice thing about having a much larger pool of jurors is that most jurors would not have to serve nearly as long or as often. A typical term of jury service today in some jurisdictions is thirty days. We can use less onerous assignment systems; for example, we could require that jurors serve for no more than one week or one case, whichever is longer. Having more jurors in the pool means less hardship for everyone.

Of course, if we're going to conscript productive citizens to serve, we must be realistic. We must pay for it. In the next chapter I will tell you how we can do it, without hurting the jurors or their employers financially.

You may not like this recommendation. You may not really want to serve on a jury. But if you do not like what you see in the criminal justice system, and you have not sat on a jury in the past five years, then you are part of the problem. Legislation was recently implemented in New York allowing no exemptions for lawyers, doctors, professional people, journalists, teachers, blue-collar workers, and so on. We need all of you.

Let the Lawyers Choose Better Jurors Through Limited Voir Dire

Once peremptories are limited and we have banished the consultants, voir dire must then be expanded to fulfill its proper role—to ferret out challenges for cause and to reveal whether a juror has the mental tools to deal with the issues that are coming in the case. The judge should set aside a realistic time for voir dire, allowing the lawyers to ask virtually anything that is probative and does not unduly embarrass or humiliate a juror. The judge must control the time, and stick to it. When the time is up, it is up.

Conclusion

Do we want a justice system in which the facts are decided by the stupidest, least educated, and most bigoted people the lawyers can find? Do we want a system that makes it easy for those lawyers to ply their trade? Obviously we don't. Mark Twain thought about the same issues in 1872:

> I desire to tamper with the jury law. I wish to so alter it as to put a premium on intelligence and character, and close the jury box against idiots . . . and people who do not read newspapers. But no doubt, I shall be defeated.

> —Mark Twain, *Roughing It* (Edited by Franklin Rogers, 1972), p. 307.

He was right. Since 1872, few steps have been taken to improve the quality of our jurors. Maybe it's time we started.

NINE

Unhappy Campers

BORED, UNINVOLVED, AND FRUSTRATED

Oh, give me a break. Just a ten-minute break.
When I don't have to sit and take this shit.
Oh, give me a chance to get up and dance.
I long for the door. It is such a bore.
—*poem written by a juror*
  (courtesy of Dr. Elizabeth F. Loftus)

For those who have served on juries, what I have to say in this chapter is no big secret. *We treat jurors terribly.* Sometimes it seems to me that many years ago we surely must have hired some evil sorcerer to design our jury rooms, our jury procedures, our jury instructions, even the chairs the jurors sit in. When we hired this wizard, we told him it was crucial that the experience be as uncomfortable, boring, and frustrating for jurors as possible; we should condescend to them or treat them like children at every opportunity; and they should feel completely uninvolved during the trial. At all costs, we insisted, the sorcerer should encourage jurors to fall asleep during the presentation of evidence.

We give a huge amount of responsibility and power to jurors. Then what do we do? We make them sit passively and listen during trial as the lawyers ask questions, the witnesses give answers, and the judge intervenes occasionally from on high with a ruling. The operative word here is *passively*. About the only thing jurors are allowed to do is listen and take notes. Some judges do not even allow the taking of notes. As the proceedings drone on, and lengthy sidebars take place, jurors often sneak a catnap or two or three, just to relieve the tedium. On some long afternoons in trial, I have seen a medley of heavy eyelids in the jury box. Then, one by one, chins begin dropping to chests. Suddenly they jerk up, awakened by their own sudden snoring or the paw of the bailiff. Of course, this never happened when *I* was examining a witness. (Sure. In my dreams.) They look around, hoping no one has noticed. Everyone has noticed. It's just that no one cares. They quickly figure that out.

We also insist that jurors be passive when they are not in court. Before each recess, the judge sternly admonishes the jurors not to talk about the case or to form any opinions. What sophistry. Who among us just watched the Menendez and Simpson trials and formed no opinions until the end? Who among us was able to resist talking about the cases? Why do we expect the jurors to be any different? In fact, they are not. In defending their two-and-a-half-hour deliberation in the Simpson murder case, the jurors pointed out that they'd had nine months to think about the case. Even worse, suppose the jurors are so passive they actually follow the court's admonition. Suppose they do not even think about the evidence as it is being presented. Is that really what we want?

By the time the jury starts deliberating, they are usually bored and irritated. We make sure the deliberations will grind on forever as one stupid juror, or one with an agenda, holds out on the rest of them. It should therefore come as no surprise that, time and again, jurors have told me their experience was different from what they had expected and, frankly, they were disappointed.

There are a lot of things we can do to get jurors involved, to make their experience less painful and more engaging, and to help them render better decisions.

Encourage Jurors to Talk About the Evidence and Ask Their Own Questions

Juries in England and America in colonial times were encouraged to ask questions of the parties directly. In fact, the jurors were expected to investigate the facts themselves. Today we frown upon jurors asking questions, even though technically there is no rule against it. Today, if a juror investigates the facts personally, we throw out the entire verdict.

After every case I tried, I made it a practice to talk with the jury, to help me learn where I could improve as an attorney. So I have talked with a lot of jurors over the years. Over and over, I've heard jurors tell me how frustrated they were that they could not influence the presentation of evidence the tiniest little bit. Often they would ask me such questions as, "For God's sake, why didn't you ask 'Joey the Juice' about where he left the car?" The simple answer is I would have asked the question if I had thought about it or if I had known the juror was interested or confused. Frequently the jurors wanted the answers to some damn good questions. But I had just never thought about the case that way.

How many of us watched the William Kennedy Smith, Menendez, and Simpson trials and got frustrated when lawyers did not ask what seemed like obvious and important follow-up questions. Were they hiding something, or did they just not think about the questions? Was it just accidental, or were they deliberately misleading the jurors?

I recommend that before each witness is released, we allow the jury a very brief recess. At that point any juror, or the jury as a whole, can submit written questions for the witness, which will be screened by the court. If the court decides the questions would elicit inadmissible responses (for example, if the question asks for hearsay), it will rephrase the question if possible to get to the gist of what the juror is asking. That shouldn't be too hard. Then the court will ask the questions, as well as any follow-ups that are needed. Finally, if the court refuses to ask a question, the jurors are entitled to know why. No more "It's a judge thing, you wouldn't understand."

If we did this, the jurors would immediately become a part of the truth-seeking process. Look what this accomplishes. First, the jurors will know the case better because they have a chance to clear up confusion right then and there. More important, the jurors will be actively involved in the process from the first witness. Not only that, but I guarantee you they will ask questions that will actually elicit answers that are important contributions to the truth-seeking process. I suspect this innovation will be loudly opposed by the attorneys. After all, they control the presentation of evidence; why should they let the jurors muck things up? I suspect it will be especially opposed by defense attorneys. Criminal defendants usually benefit when a jury is confused. Why would they want to encourage the jury to clarify the facts? We should ignore the lawyers' complaints. An involved juror is happier and more attentive, and understands the case better. By any measure, that is a better juror.

Give the Jury Simple Instructions in Plain English

Every one of us with kids has bought a present for them that must be assembled. So we dutifully pull out the parts and then the instruction manual. Every one of us has battled his or her way through at least one instruction manual that might as well have been written in some foreign tongue. Well, welcome to jury instructions. We ask jurors to do something much more important than assembling a toy. They are making decisions about who goes to jail and who does not. We ask them to do so under the "guidance" of jury instructions that contain archaic language, drawn from rituals that are hundreds of years old. I assure you, these instructions do not translate well to modern juries. They might as well be written in Sanskrit.

I know why the jury instructions read this way. Certain ideas have been expressed in a certain way for so long they are regarded as having stood the test of time. The courts are therefore loath to deviate from those tried-and-true instructions for fear of reversal. Listen, for a moment, to a part of the most important instruction given in a criminal case—the definition of reasonable doubt:

> Reasonable doubt is defined as follows: It is not a mere possible doubt; because everything relating to human affairs, and depending on moral evidence, is open to some possible or imaginary doubt. It is that state of the case which, after the entire comparison and consideration of all the evidence, leaves the minds of the jurors in that condition that they cannot say they feel an abiding conviction, to a moral certainty, of the truth of the charge.

What does "abiding conviction" or "moral certainty" mean? And what is moral evidence? If jurors ask a judge for a clarification of any of these terms, they're likely to receive a stern admonishment that they have been given all of the instructions necessary to arrive at a verdict, and to go back and deliberate. Is the judge being disagreeable? Not really. One of the most common reasons verdicts get reversed is the wording of jury instructions. After a criminal defendant is convicted, the lawyers go over the instructions with a very fine-toothed comb. Instructions can and do form the basis of an appeal, so judges are afraid to change even *one word* of an instruction that has previously been approved on appeal, for fear of being reversed. "Approved on appeal" means that an instruction has been previously reviewed word for word by an appellate court, and found to be a proper instruction. Each word and phrase of an approved instruction is regarded as sacrosanct.

For years, when I was a judge, jurors would ask me, "What does 'moral certainty' mean?" I didn't hear this question just once or twice, but over and over. I could not offer an example or even a simpler definition, for fear of creating reversible error. Defense attorneys would jump on any change I made, or explanation I offered, as a way to get a reversal of a conviction. Ironically, the use of the phrase "moral certainty" was recently disapproved by the same appellate courts I was so afraid of. Why? It turns out that the appellate court finally agreed with generations of jurors that the phrase "moral certainty" is confusing and unclear because it has a different meaning to each juror.

We need jury instructions that are crafted in simple, straightforward, modern language. If necessary, examples should be given to illustrate what a particular instruction is about. To do nothing is to make jurors feel stupid and inadequate. It also encourages them to guess about the meaning of genuinely important ideas that really should guide the jurors' deliberations. Suppose I had been able to help the jurors with the following explanation of the terms *abiding conviction* and *circumstantial evidence:* Johnny's mother is baking cookies in the kitchen, when the phone rings in the den. She answers the phone. Five minutes later Mom returns to the kitchen, where she discovers that her cookies are missing. She sees Johnny standing near the place where the cookies used to be. He denies having taken the cookies. His mouth and hands are covered with cookie crumbs. At this point Johnny's mom has an abiding conviction that Johnny is guilty of eating the cookies based wholly upon circumstantial evidence, since no one actually saw Johnny take the cookies! On the basis of what she has observed, she decides to punish Johnny. Isn't that example easier to understand than the formal instruction about reasonable doubt or circumstantial evidence (proof of one fact from which you can draw an inference as to the existence of another fact)? Why shouldn't I have been able to give that example to the confused jurors?

Just Compensation for Jurors—Jury Insurance

For widespread citizen participation in juries to become a reality, jurors need to be paid. You would want it, I would want it. If necessary, just as in public health, we can find a mechanism for funding. Tax credits and other creative devices can be used to compensate corporations for the loss of their employees' services. David Tunno, a jury analyst, has suggested "jury insurance" be provided to the public at large, just as disability and accidental death insurance is now available. The cost of the premium would be based on the amount of compensation needed during jury service. Since the frequency of jury service would be small, because of the greater participation of all of our qualified citizens, the premium costs would be minimal. This is achievable. Employers would pay small premiums on behalf of employees, and professionals and self-employed citizens could choose likewise to pay such premiums. The amount of the premium would be based on the amount of compensation a juror would require during the period of jury service—much like a disability policy that kicks in to protect one's mortgage payments or to provide income during disability. Millions of people paying small premiums to ensure against infrequent jury service is cost-effective and can be administered by major private insurance companies. Its time has come.

What is important is that jurors are compensated fairly for their services. If sequestration is required, additional compensation should be offered, just as we provide overtime for extended work. Additional "hazard" policies could cover extended sequestration costs.

Improve the Physical Condition of Jury Rooms

We often ask jurors to serve under wretched physical handicaps. The facilities provided to citizens who serve their country are important, as they signify our appreciation and respect for their sacrifices and our commitment to justice. Jurors spend much of their time sitting and waiting in ugly rooms filled with uncomfortable chairs. Buildings in decay are a metaphor for a troubled and dispirited system. The facilities must be up to date, spotless, uplifting, comfortable, and attractive. And, for God's sake, give the jurors comfortable chairs to sit in—that's what they spend most of their time doing.

Don't Waste the Jurors' Time

Valuable time should not be spent sitting endlessly, waiting, waiting, waiting for the judge to finish another matter, or to be dispatched belatedly to a courtroom for service. The judges and the attorneys need to learn how to work their schedules around the jurors' needs. If a judge knows there are a lot of motions to be heard outside the presence of the jury, every effort must be made to hear such motions when they do not interfere with jurors' time. If that means early-morning hearings, early-evening hearings, or even weekend hearings, so be it. (We must, of course, pay for it.)

Jurors also have a right to expect that when they arrive at court, their job will begin without delay. Of course, that is not always possible. When delay is absolutely unavoidable, jurors should have access to a library lounge outfitted with computers, library reference materials, entertainment, and other services. Jurors would not resent the inevitable delays, since their time could be more resourcefully or pleasantly spent. Private enterprise would also benefit from providing such amenities, and a portion of the proceeds could be earmarked for a jury fund, which would be used for the constant maintenance and upgrading of jury facilities.

Sequester the Jury Only as a Last Resort

Although sequestration does not happen very often, it probably occurs more often than necessary. As law professor Erwin Chemerinsky has noted, "If we trust twelve people to decide life and liberty, we should be able to trust them not to watch TV." In a case such as the Simpson trial, there were compelling reasons for sequestration and equally compelling reasons against it. Putting strangers together for months at a time, in a strange and unnatural setting, away from their family and loved ones, is highly stressful. When they have nothing in common and they are forbidden to discuss the case, boredom, frustration, anger, and hostility can set in. Factions can develop, making calm and rational debate among the jurors impossible. Cost is also a major consideration. In the absence of physical threats to the jurors or attempts to intimidate or influence a verdict, sequestration should not be permitted. We must trust our jurors to consider only the evidence adduced at the trial. Some will probably sneak a look at the paper or TV, but we must have confidence that the verdict will be based on the trial evidence and instructions of law. If we can't trust the jury, then we might as well get rid of it. Let's try trusting them first.

Non-unanimous Verdicts

Our system also encourages jurors who have a political agenda to lie to get on a jury. Because we require unanimous verdicts, one juror can hold up a verdict and the valuable time of the other eleven jurors. This happens more than you might think.

Let me tell you about the trial of Wendel Gregory Morris in which a lying juror allowed a rapist-murderer to get away almost scot-free. A young woman was raped and then fatally stabbed some twenty-seven times. The rapist left a deep bite mark on her wrist. There were no eyewitnesses. The defendant, who had a record of rapes and aggravated assaults at knifepoint, was connected to the offense by the bite mark and other strong physical evidence including his fingerprint and blood found in the victim's room. Evidence established that the defendant had committed a burglary at knifepoint a short time before the rape-murder, climbing through a window of an apartment located just down the street from the rape-murder crime scene.

When selecting the jury, my co-prosecutor Steve Plumer and I carefully asked each potential juror if he or she had any problems in returning a first-degree-murder verdict if the evidence warranted it. Each juror said no. Each was asked if he or she could find the existence of "special circumstances," that is, that the murder was willful, premeditated, deliberate, and committed in the course of a burglary or rape if the evidence so warranted, knowing that such a finding would automatically trigger the death penalty. All the jurors solemnly assured us they could. Eleven jurors were telling the truth. One was lying. At first the jury hung eleven to one in favor of conviction. The holdout was the woman who had lied to us: she refused to vote for a conviction because it turned out she couldn't stand to see anyone locked or caged up, including fish in an aquarium! She also lied about her views regarding the death penalty. The judge instructed the hung jury to deliberate some more. He instructed the jurors, in accordance with California appellate court decisions adopting such language (so called the Allen instruction) approved in 1896 by the U.S. Supreme Court in *Allen vs. United States* and used since then to extract verdicts from otherwise deadlocked juries: go back and deliberate some more; that the case must at some time be decided and they were as likely as anyone to arrive at a correct decision; that a minority number of jurors should reexamine his or her beliefs in light of the other jurors' arguments, however such juror(s) should not be forced or compelled to change his or her opinion unless convinced by reason and logic; and that such verdict must remain the individual juror's honest conviction. The dishonest juror refused at first to deliberate. Finally she relented and the jury returned first-degree murder, burglary, and rape verdicts.

In the penalty phase the juror held out again, refusing to find special circumstances even though the jury's verdicts of first-degree murder, burglary, and rape compelled them to do so. Finally the jury hung, eleven jurors voting for special circumstances and the one lone hold out juror voting against it. The Rose Bird–led California Supreme Court, deciding that they didn't like the U.S. Supreme Court–approved Allen instruction, caused case after case in which such an instruction was given to be reversed. The California appellate court, following the lead of the Supreme Court, reversed the murder conviction, holding that the instruction was coercive and prejudicial. This same appellate court also criticized us for showing the jury pictures of this once beautiful and vibrant victim in life with her mother sitting near a Christmas tree, the court saying that "the family photographs served only to arouse in the jury a sympathy toward the victim, as being a loving daughter and family member." Incredible! Showing at least one picture of a corpse on a coroner's slab with 27 stab wounds and a bite mark is not prejudicial, but a picture of a human being alive and well is! This is beyond legal sophistry, beyond artifice, and beyond redemption. The case came back for retrial. Another deputy DA handled the case on retrial and took a plea to second-degree murder.

A few years later the defense attorney in that rape-murder case came into my court. I was now a sitting judge. I asked him how his client was doing in state prison. He looked at me with puzzlement and said, "He's been out on the streets for a couple of years." He'd served only a few years for raping and murdering a young woman. I was so upset I had to recess the case before me and spend a little solitary time in chambers.

The dishonest juror was the spark that ignited the injustice. Maybe she thought that by lying she was serving some higher cause. It is hard for me to understand that, when I think about what the defendant did to the victim and her family. I hope this juror knows what her dishonesty did. I hope she has lost at least a little sleep thinking about it.

Two steps can be taken to discourage lying jurors.

The first is to prosecute them for perjury when they give false information or willfully omit facts, which, if known, materially affect their ability to be fair. The second is to draft a special statute that would permit such a prosecution. Today we see jurors lying so often we just sort of ignore it. If we took it seriously, maybe the jurors would also.

Of course, a single rogue juror would not be a problem if juries did not have to be unanimous to reach a verdict. The Constitution does not require that jury verdicts be unanimous. But the strength of the jury system, some argue, rests on unanimous verdicts forged from debate. If one juror is in the minority and the rest agree to a verdict, there is no necessity to engage in a reasoned and careful analysis of the evidence the sole juror thinks is important. The majority are deprived of the perspective of the minority jurors. The majority may have missed something important. Or they may only have missed the political agenda of a dishonest juror. Some balance needs to be struck.

Our nation is becoming more ethnically diverse. Not too long ago, African Americans could not vote or qualify for jury duty. Japanese and Chinese could not be citizens. Women had no right to vote. Eliminating unanimous verdicts would be to remove the voice of the minority. We cannot afford to make the great minorities in our nation feel disenfranchised from the jury system. If they feel they have no effective voice, they will become increasingly disaffected. From a moral perspective, that would be intolerable and unacceptable. From a practical and political standpoint we cannot allow such a perception. Perception is reality. It can cause a city to burn, a society to crumble.

The rogue juror is becoming more of a reality in an increasingly polarized society where frustration and dissatisfaction suffocate reason. If, however, two jurors disagree with the rest, then it is at least possible the majority has failed to consider something important. So I recommend that our eight-member juries be allowed to return either an acquittal or a guilty verdict with a vote of seven to one (or eleven to one, if twelve-person juries are retained). The only exception would be in the penalty phase of capital cases. There, because of the solemnity of the decision, unanimity is absolutely necessary.

Blue-Ribbon Juries

Many complex cases today last months, if not years. They require sophisticated and detailed analysis of esoteric evidence offered by conflicting experts. The DNA testimony in the Simpson case is but one example. What about sophisticated white-collar crime? Securities fraud? The Iran/Contra prosecutions? Money laundering? The trial of Michael Milken or Charles Keating? Cases such as these turn on sophisticated knowledge about subjects like savings-and-loan management and economics, financial markets, junk bonds, securities regulation and markets, electronic transfers, international exchange rates, and perhaps contracts drawn by multimillion-dollar law firms, purporting to define the contract rights in fields of endeavor yet discovered or defined. We need specialists to make sense of these cases. This is not trivial. Many of the Iran/Contra defendants pled guilty to lesser charges out of fear that a Washington, D.C., jury would be completely incapable of understanding their defense.

If you were a defendant in a complex case, would you be comfortable with "twelve tried and true" jurors from the normal pool? Would you be concerned that the average juror would be ill-equipped to understand the nuances and the complexities of finance, economics, patent, and unfair competition laws? Would you be concerned that a verdict based purely on emotion could be returned by this "common jury"?

These questions are legitimate, but they smack of elitism. How, then, do we strike a balance between a representative jury and our need to have competent and knowledgeable jurors in highly complex cases? We already require a potential juror to have a sufficient understanding of the English language to understand the trial proceedings and process the evidence. It is not, therefore, unreasonable in complex criminal cases to require a basic level of understanding and knowledge relevant to the issues expected to arise. This can be achieved by narrowing the jury pool to those who have demonstrated in their answers to a detailed written questionnaire that they possess a level of intellectual functioning and knowledge, however gained, that will allow them to process the expert testimony and concepts to be presented at the trial. If this had been a requirement of the Simpson jury, regardless of their ultimate verdict, no one would have seriously questioned the legitimacy of the verdict. Such a "blue ribbon" jury pool would be similar to the practice in some states of having prominent citizens nominated by trial judges serve on grand juries. Trial judges should be authorized to impanel blue-ribbon juries on a showing of good cause by either the prosecution or the defense.

Summary

Participating on a jury is one of the most important experiences most citizens can have in our government's affairs. Jurors reflecting their individual judgment, unfiltered by representatives, are the essence of democracy and community conscience. This is our buffer against excessive and tyrannical government, overzealous prosecutors, and corrupt judges. Finally, when used appropriately, as in Bushell's case and *Zenger,* the jury can do what no other body can do, namely refuse to follow a bad, stupid, or oppressive law, or to show mercy where unwise and mean-spirited people have not. That is our legacy. Long live the legacy.

T E N

Stop Me Before
I Hurt Someone!

LAWYERS: THE ADVERSARIES

And what a profession it [the law] is! . . . Every calling is great when greatly pursued. But what other gives such a scope to realize the spontaneous energy of one's soul? In what other does one plunge so deep in the stream of life, so share its passions, its battles, its despair, its triumphs, both as witness and actor?
—*Justice Oliver Wendell Holmes*

This chapter is a tough one for me. I am a lawyer. I like being a lawyer. In fact, I am proud I was privileged to practice law for so many interesting years. I number among my best friends defense attorneys and prosecutors. Oddly, however, I find I have the same strange love-hate feelings about lawyers as the public.

From *To Kill a Mockingbird* to *L.A. Law* to Scott Turow's and John Grisham's novels, we love stories about lawyers as good guys, heroes even. We revere historic figures like Thomas Jefferson, Benjamin Franklin, and James Madison. All lawyers. A backwoods lawyer from Illinois named Abraham Lincoln guided our nation through its darkest hours with a wisdom matched by few leaders of any time, or of any nation. Most of our presidents, men we elected, have been lawyers. So we love lawyers, right?

No, actually we hate them. In poll after poll, lawyers rank somewhere below used-car salesmen and just above politicians in public trust. (But since most politicians are lawyers, the second-to-last finish probably doesn't mean much.) Here's a snippet of elegant but vicious doggerel about lawyers, found on a bathroom wall in the criminal courthouse during the Simpson double murder trial:

Bold, hasty and wise, a concocter of lies,
A rattler to speak, a dodger, a sneak
A regular claw of the tables of law
A shuffler complete, well worn in deceit,
A supple, unprincipled, troublesome cheat.

Who wrote it? A frustrated journalist, perhaps. Plenty of Americans saw that trial and would agree this says it all about some members of the Dream Team. Well, I cheated a little bit. The verse wasn't found on a bathroom wall. I found it in a book. The author was the Greek satirical playwright Aristophanes, who wrote it in the fourth century B.C.E. Aristophanes was writing about the Greek version of the modern lawyer. So hating lawyers is nothing new.

Lawyers and the Adversary System

The main reason we hate lawyers is the role they play in our criminal justice system. In an adversary system, each side is entitled to a skillful presentation of the best case that can be made for it. Out of that clash of adversaries, so the theory goes, the truth will emerge. Of course, the lawyers are the adversaries. The theory works pretty well. Think of how many times cross-examination has completely changed your opinion of a witness. Cross-examination is the crucible through which the "truth" is tested.

Our adversary system was forged from centuries of governmental excesses: centuries of innocent blood flowing from the wounds of baseless accusations, staged trials, witch hunts, trials by ordeal, and trials by torture. I am not exaggerating here. Criminal justice used to be unimaginably worse than it is today. Much of the improvement in our justice system is due to the adversary system. So let's begin by looking at the ideal role both prosecutors and defense attorneys should play in a properly functioning criminal justice system.

The Defense Attorneys

The power to arrest and jail citizens is an awesome one, altogether too easy to abuse. For that reason we have learned there *must* be a buffer between the government and the accused. Our imperfect tool of justice—the buffer, if you will—is defense lawyers. They make the state prove up or shut up. They test the mettle of the government's case. They make our government play by the rules of accepted civility and of the Constitution. Defense counsel *must* vigorously assert their client's constitutional rights and aggressively cross-examine witnesses, even if a guilty client goes free as a consequence. In 1820, Lord Brougham defended Queen Caroline, the estranged wife of King George IV, against adultery charges. His defense was no doubt controversial, because here is what he said about the duties of an attorney:

> An advocate, in the discharge of his duty, knows but one person in all the world, and that person is his client. To save that client by all means and expedients, and at all hazards and costs to other persons, and, among them, to himself, is his first and only duty; and in performing this duty he must not regard the alarm, the torments, the destruction which he may bring upon others. Separating the duty of a patriot from that of an advocate, he must go on reckless of consequences, though it should be his unhappy fate to involve his country in confusion.

And so it is today. Defense counsel is *supposed* to use every legal trick and find any loophole that might help its client. That is its job. It is more than just a job. If the defense fails to give sufficiently aggressive representation to its client, it can be sued, disciplined by the bar association, or disbarred. So our society's concept of the adversary system is built right into our job description for defense attorneys.

Do you remember what Robert Shapiro said about the truth? He minces no words. *The truth is irrelevant to defense counsel.* I am going to say it again. *The truth is irrelevant to defense counsel.* I know. It sounds terrible. Some holier-than-thou defense attorneys will scream at my emphasis on this point, insisting they are as interested in the truth as anyone else. Balderdash. No competent defense attorney, including many of my good friends, would refuse to bring a motion to suppress a murder weapon or ten kilos of cocaine. Never. If they did, they would be incompetent and would have violated their duty of fealty to their client. If they succeed? *Voilà*, a guilty person walks free. My friends, that has nothing to do with the truth.

I believe defense attorneys have a much more difficult job than prosecutors do. For one thing, most of their clients are slam-dunk guilty. That was my experience as a defense attorney and as a prosecutor. A friend of mine, Frank Francone, a civil attorney, relates a conversation he had with Eugene Salmonsen, an experienced criminal defense attorney. Gene had represented more than a thousand criminal defendants, and Frank was curious. He asked Gene how many, of all the defendants Gene had represented, were innocent. Gene leaned back in his chair, thought for a minute, and said something like this:

> Altogether? Two of 'em. But one doesn't really count. The police arrested him for robbing a liquor store on the Westside. The client was innocent—he even had an alibi. But the alibi didn't help me much. At the very moment the police thought he was robbing a liquor store on the Westside, he was actually robbing a different liquor store on the other side of town.

So being a criminal defense lawyer is tough. You usually start in a deep hole—your client is guilty. If you are ethical, like my defense attorney friends, including those dedicated public defenders, you look for small victories. It's bad for the ego to lose all the time. But there are victories of a kind: like saving a man's life when the state is seeking the death penalty, or getting a defendant off on a lesser charge, as in the Damien "Football" Williams case or when the DA clearly overcharges and is being mean-spirited, or getting a judge to give a client "one last chance" on probation.

I suppose the most difficult thing a defense attorney must do is to suppress evidence in cases where a dangerous criminal will be released as a result. While evidence-suppression motions are easy in bookmaking and prostitution cases, I have no doubt my colleagues on the defense side of the bar must surely suffer some sleepless nights when a felon who is certain to prey again upon innocent people is released on a technicality. A felon who will hurt people. A felon who will rape and kill—again. The stock answer I get when I ask them about this is, "There is a higher principle than truth at stake. It's called the Constitution. Yours and mine. And it should work for all of us in the same way." It is a noble theory, and they are absolutely correct. But I still believe the good ones have spent some sleepless nights.

So we agree that the role of defense attorney is essential. Someone has to keep the government honest when it arrests and jails citizens. Like most of us, defense attorneys want to do a good job. But when they do a really good job, everyone hates them. Why? To begin with, it usually means a bad guy has gone free or gotten a lot less time in jail than seems right. It seems that what society really wants defense lawyers to do is *pretend* to test the government's case, not go after it with a baseball bat. Alternatively, maybe it seems to us they have done their job with just a little treachery. Guides to misleading a jury have been around for a long time. Longer than, perhaps, attorneys wish to acknowledge. In *Devil's Advocate: The Unnatural History of Lawyers*, Andrew and Jonathan Roth quote the following guide to deceit, addressed to students of law in the first century B.C.E.

> Now I must explain the subtle approach. There are three occasions on which we cannot use the direct opening, and these we must consider carefully: (1) when our cause is discreditable, that is when the subject itself alienates the hearer from us; (2) when the hearer has apparently been won over by the previous speakers of the opposition; (3) or when the hearer has become wearied by listening to the previous speakers.
>
> If the cause has a discernible character, we can make our introduction with the following points: that the agent, not the action, ought to be considered. . . . The defendant's counsel will first show his client's upright life if he can; if he cannot, he will have recourse to thoughtlessness, folly,

youth, force or undue influence. On these matters . . . censure ought not to be imposed for conduct extraneous to the present charge. If the speaker is seriously handicapped by the man's baseness and notoriety, he will first take care to say that false rumors have been spread about an innocent man, and will use the commonplace that rumors ought not to be believed. If none of these pleas are practicable, let him say that he is not discussing the man's morals before censors, but the charges of his opponents before jurors.

Or maybe people hate defense lawyers for taking advantage of the excessive rights we think have been granted to criminal defendants by the Warren Court. The defense attorneys didn't make the rules, the Court did. They are just doing their job when they suppress the murder weapon under the exclusionary rule. And a tough job it is.

The Prosecutors

Prosecutors represent the entire society in criminal proceedings. They represent society's interest in peace, tranquillity, and order. Prosecutors must therefore wear two hats. One hat requires that they vigorously prosecute a defendant charged with a criminal offense. The other hat mandates that prosecutors seek justice. Justice requires that they play fair, that they do not needlessly entangle defendants in unsustainable charges. DAs are not supposed to force defendants into plea bargains by filing greater charges than they can ultimately prove—such as filing a murder case when the facts only support manslaughter, or an aggravated assault when a simple assault only has been committed. Nor should the DA use the great power of his office by using untrustworthy witnesses or by failing to disclose exculpatory evidence to the defense. As H. L. Mencken mused, there is always the present danger that a prosecutor, aspiring to higher office, will assault and destroy a man with the ease and grace worthy of a congressman scuttling his way across the Potomac to Washington. Wryly, Mencken notes that a DA is "seldom promoted [to higher office] because he is jealous of the liberties of the citizen." So, as with defense attorneys, there is both the capacity for greatness and honor as well as mischief.

One thing is certain: prosecutors have the power over life and liberty. They have the power to save or destroy a life. They have the power to charge. They charge a "third strike" against a prior felon and send a person to prison for twenty-five years to life on the crumbs of a stolen pizza—to demonstrate toughness on crime. Or they refuse to send a person to prison for life for stealing some underwear in a store. This is also a great power: the power *not* to charge. In fact there is a whole category of arrests so common they have a nickname: they are called *DA rejects*. The police bring in a suspect. The evidence against the suspect goes to the DA's office. If the DA looks at it and decides there isn't enough evidence to establish guilt, the prosecutor will refuse to file charges against the defendant. This is an enormous power exercised thousands of times each year in L.A. alone. Justice should not be a game in which the dirty business of criminals is outwitted by the dirty business of prosecutors.

As we've said, the prosecution is charged with seeking the truth, but only if it is consistent with justice. The defense is not. That means justice is given a higher value than simple truth. It means the prosecution has to play by the rules, the trial must be fair, and the evidence legally secured. So truth, even for the prosecution, is problematic, because the exclusionary rule and concepts of fundamental fairness override even the naked truth of an accusation.

Why Don't Lawyers Behave Themselves?

Lawyers are only human. They have a job to do. Prosecutors feel that their principal job is to put bad guys in jail. Defense feels that its job is to prevent criminal defendants from going to jail, or to minimize their jail time. For the defense, it's okay to trick people and to conceal the truth from the jury. To an extent, the same is true for prosecutors. There *are* DAs who use questionable criminal informants, questionable expert testimony, and bogus probable cause. Now add normal human failings to that equation. We are not talking about all attorneys, but too many lawyers are seduced by greed, fame, political ambition, or just the fact that the courts have consistently let them get away with misconduct. Suppose you are a defense attorney. You conceal evidence from the prosecution. The judge bawls you out, but nothing else happens. Well, that's okay, you have a big strategic advantage. So you conceal more evidence. This time the judge lets the prosecution give a little extra opening statement. That's okay too. The strategic advantage is still there. So you withhold a report that contains damning evidence about one of your key witnesses and then tell the court that, oops, you forgot about it. The court sternly levies nine hundred dollars in sanctions against you. You are a millionaire. So is your client. You can afford it. So that's okay too. You know what case I'm talking about. We all saw it on TV. Is there any wonder attorneys keep misbehaving? They do it because it works.

Extreme behavior by defense counsel is nothing new. As I said before, *some* defense counsel will do whatever they can get away with. Some will push the envelope to its outermost limits, but stay just within the limits.

Did He Really Rape You, Dearie?

Imagine, for a moment, that you are an attractive twenty-five-year-old female secretary. You are single. You are gregarious, and you love life. Your boss suggests you join him and other employees for a quick drink. Thinking nothing of it, and wishing to be part of the social event, you accept. You laugh, you flirt a little, you kick back. Your boss puts his arms around you from behind, and nuzzles up to you. You try to laugh it off, gently disengaging from his embrace. The boss tells anyone who will listen that you and he are a perfect match. You disengage and politely bid everyone good night. A half hour later he shows up at your apartment, uninvited and drunk. He insists on coming in for a moment. Not wishing to offend him or to jeopardize your job, you allow him to come in "just for a minute." He rapes you.

Before the California Legislature passed the Rape Shield Law, here is what defense attorneys were allowed to do on cross-examination. One of the best at it was Gladys Root, a defense attorney who wrapped herself tightly from head to toe in clinging clothes resembling elegant draperies. She wore a flowered hat and white gloves. Though I saw her first when she was in her six-ties, she still displayed the hourglass figure of a screen siren. She reminded me of Gloria Swanson in *Sunset Boulevard*. All young lawyers, when they had the chance, ran to the courtroom where Gladys Root was performing. Here is a typical Gladys Root–style cross-examination of the rape victim.

Q.: Let me see if I can get this straight, dearie. [The rape victim was always "dearie."] You say that my client, Mr. Jones, forcibly had sex with you, is that what you're saying? [Root would hold a lorgnette to her eyes, as if looking at a specimen under the microscope.]

A.: Yes, ma'am, that's what I'm saying.

Q.: I see. So you must have put up quite a struggle, dearie?

A.: Well, I did what I could. But I was overpowered.

Q.: So you screamed at the top of your lungs so your next-door neighbors could hear you, is that right?

A.: It wouldn't have made any difference. They weren't home. They were—

Q.: So what you're telling us is that you didn't scream, is that what you are telling us, dearie?

A.: Well, there was no point. I told him to stop. "Stop it," I said.

Q.: I see. You told him to "stop it." Did you whisper that to him, dearie?

A.: No. I just told him to stop.

Q.: Now, you're a nice girl, are you not? You wouldn't just go to bed with anyone, now would you?

A.: Of course not.

Q.: Of course you wouldn't. But you didn't scream to let Mr. Jones know you didn't want any, did you, dearie?

A.: No . . . it wouldn't have done any good.

Q.: Oh, are you telling the jury that Mr. Jones is hard of hearing?

A.: I didn't say that.

Q.: So he just tore your clothes off and forced his penis into your vagina, dearie? Just like that?

A.: He raped me, if that's what you mean. Yes, that's what he did.

Q.: You would agree that a good girl would fight him off. Struggle with him. Bite him, kick him, slap him, do anything?

A.: He was too powerful. I tried to get away from his grasp. But I couldn't.

Q.: I see. So you twisted your body and you moved your legs so that he could not penetrate you, dearie, is that what you are telling these people?

A.: I did what I could. I didn't want to be beaten. But I did struggle, yes, I did.

Q.: So what you're telling this jury is that while you were struggling and moving your hips to defeat his advances, he penetrated you with his penis, is that right, dearie?

A.: I'm telling you that he had sex with me against my will.

Q.: I see. Perhaps you can show the ladies and gentlemen of the jury just how hard you fought to resist the advances of Mr. Jones.

At this point, Root produces a doughnut! She has tied a string around the doughnut. She begins to swing the doughnut in an arc. The jury and the witness look at the moving doughnut with fascination.

A.: I don't know what you mean. . . .

Q.: You see this doughnut swinging? Well, if the doughnut represents your vagina, and it is "moooving," would it not be extremely unlikely that a penis could penetrate it, dearie? [The jurors are riveted on the moving doughnut.]

A.: I don't know about doughnuts. I only know that he raped me.

Q.: I see. He raped you. Now, you're not telling this jury that you are a virgin, are you, dearie?

A.: I never said I was.

Q.: How many different men have you had sex with, dearie?

A.: I don't know, a few.

Q.: You don't keep track? More than a hundred?

A.: Absolutely not!

Q.: All right. How about fifty? Have you had more than fifty men?

A.: No!

Q.: Well, all right. More than one?

A.: Yes.

Q.: More than five?

A.: More than five.

Q.: How about twenty-five . . . twenty-five [she spells it out] d-i-f-f-e-r-e-n-t men?

A.: I don't know . . . yeah, maybe . . . I just—

Q.: Is this the first time you say you've been raped?

A.: That's right.

Q.: Well, now, on these other occasions when you had sex with these other men, did you tell them you wanted sex, or did they just assume you wanted sex?

A.: I don't know how to answer that question. We both—

Q.: You can answer that question, dearie, by telling us the truth. Didn't your boyfriends sometimes want to have sex when you didn't feel like it?

A.: I'm sure there were times when one of us felt like it but the other didn't.

Q.: So that when you didn't feel like it, nevertheless you submitted to your lover's advances, correct, dearie?

A.: I know what you're driving at. They did not rape me, counsel!

Q.: You would agree that sometimes you'd have sex with them when you didn't feel like it—you know, to accommodate their desires?

A.: Sometimes I would accede to their wishes. But it was never forced upon me.

Q.: Did you flirt with Mr. Jones that evening?

A.: No. I was just trying to be pleasant.

Q.: I see. So you weren't flirting with Mr. Jones. He just normally puts his arms around you and whispers sweet nothings in your ear?

A.: I wasn't doing anything. He was the one who—

Q.: Yes, who put his arms around you. We know that. Had he ever tried to do this to you before this evening you were drinking with him?

A.: Absolutely not.

Q.: So, then. Something was different that evening when you were relaxing with your boss and your fellow employees and enjoying a few drinks, correct?

If your blood is boiling at this point, well, so is mine. How could she do that? Well, it was her job. The system allowed her to engage in an assault on a truthful witness for the purpose of discrediting the witness before the jury. Critics say this conduct is unethical when the attorney, knowing a witness is telling the truth, deliberately confuses and discredits the witness's testimony. And yet her client was entitled to the most aggressive and effective defense possible. As long as the courts let it happen— and they did—Root was behaving according to the rules. If you don't like it, change the rules. Eventually the people of California did change the rules; rape victims are no longer asked about sex with other men unless it is relevant to the instant case. But as to alleged prior acts of consensual sex with the same defendant, anything goes. And it often does.

Bullheaded, Mulish, and Kind of Lovable

Then there are characters like defense attorney Irving Kanerak. Kanerak was Charles Manson's attorney. Manson wanted to act as his own attorney, but the court would not allow him to do so. Manson said that if he could not represent himself, he was going to get the worst lawyer he could find. He chose Kanerak. Kanerak was not a bad lawyer. He was a notorious obstructionist who would wear anyone down with his pit-bull tenacity, intimidating witnesses with outrageous questions after being warned by the court to desist. He gave judges and even fellow defense attorneys fits. He was known to take a half-day theft case with one eyewitness and drag it out for six weeks. Let me tell you about some of my encounters with Kanerak.

Bill Littlefield, one of Kanerak's fellow defense attorneys and the former public defender of Los Angeles County, delighted in teasing Kanerak. Kanerak was easy to lead on. He resembled Norman Mailer, right down to his curly mop of gray hair and fireplug build. He would often come into the public defender's lunch room to eat. Littlefield, noting Kanerak's presence and fully aware of which case Kanerak was trying, would casually mention a *nonexistent* case as authority for a legal proposition Kanerak was arguing. Invariably, Kanerak would go back to the courtroom citing the case without checking it. When the judge and the DA were unable to find the case, they would explode at Kanerak, who would repel their wrath like an armadillo spurning water. He did not even seem to notice.

I recall a pimping and pandering case, in which Kanerak was on his third week of cross-examination of a witness, one of the prostitutes. There was no reason for him to have prolonged the case for anything close to this long, except that he was Irving Kanerak. Before the jury reconvened, Kanerak complained to the judge, "She [the witness] called me an SOB."

Turning to the witness, the judge inquired, "Did you call Mr. Kanerak an SOB?"

KANERAK: Yes, she did, I heard it!

WITNESS: No, I didn't call him an SOB.

JUDGE: What did you call him?

WITNESS: A dirty, rotten SOB!

But in his own mulish way, Kanerak did his job, and frequently did it well. It was not elegant or pretty. He was invariably aggravating and annoying. He did whatever he thought was necessary to obtain an acquittal for his client. And if the court let him get away with it—well . . .

Lawyer, Seamstress, Tailor—Weaving the Lie

In most states, defendants are entitled to find out all of the prosecution's case against them before they are required to disclose any of their defense to the other side, if at all. This is true even in states providing for reciprocal discovery—a fancy name for requiring the prosecution and the defense to reveal their respective cases. Defendants never have to reveal witnesses who incriminate them, as long as they do not intend to call them to testify, nor do they have to turn over inculpatory evidence. On the other hand, the prosecution is obligated to reveal to the defense all evidence, including any that may tend to exonerate a defendant. In reality, the defendant gets a good look at the prosecutor's case before having to decide on a defense. From a constitutional standpoint this seems only fair, since the burden is always on the prosecution to prove a case against a defendant beyond a reasonable doubt without help from the defense.

Herein lies the dilemma. The majority of lawyers are ethical and committed to their clients. Unfortunately, a minority are equally intent on prevailing at any cost. The law is not in their heart; winning is. Ethical lawyers know the moral line between testing the mettle of an alibi witness's or defendant's story and weaving a defense from whole cloth; the knaves do not. Commenting on a pending legislative bill to form a bar association to regulate lawyers' conduct, Will Rogers said, "Personally, I don't think you can make a lawyer honest by an act of the legislature.

You've got to work on his conscience. And his lack of conscience is what makes him a lawyer." Unfortunately, Rogers's opinion is embraced by a large segment of the public. Robert Traver captured the essence of a lawyer's dilemma in his novel *Anatomy of a Murder:*

> The lecture is an ancient device that lawyers use to coach their clients so that the client won't quite know he has been coached and his lawyer can still preserve the face-saving illusion that he hasn't done any coaching. . . . "Who, me? I didn't tell him what to say," the lawyer can later comfort himself. "I merely explained the law, see."

It's easy to condemn lawyers who sew the fabric of a story, handing the finished product to their client or witness. But what about lawyers who diligently prepare their client or witness for testimony? How far do you go in retelling the story, reshaping its essence?

Suppose a defendant is charged with murder. The lawyer receives a police report that is vague and sketchy. The client says he wasn't at the crime scene and did not commit the murder. The lawyer tells him that there are witnesses who put him there. The defendant responds that he might have been in the area earlier, but definitely was not there at the time of the murder and he can prove it because he was with Scott Gordon, who can vouch for him. The lawyer asks where she might find Scott. Defendant says he doesn't know. The lawyer tells him that a witness saw a partial license plate number corresponding to the first three digits of defendant's car. Defendant "remembers" that he loaned his car to a friend, but doesn't know where he is or how to locate him. Defendant denies knowing the victim.

Needless to say, the lawyer is highly skeptical. Two weeks later, pursuant to mandatory discovery, the DA turns over a supplemental report containing a witness's account of an argument between the victim and the defendant a week before the killing. The lawyer confronts her client, who now recalls having met the victim at a party and having some words with him. He denies having made any threats, however. The lawyer's investigator locates a witness at the party who contradicts the defendant, stating that the defendant brandished a gun and threatened the victims. This witness is unknown to the prosecution. The investigator also finds Scott Gordon, who denies having seen the defendant on the night of the murder. The lawyer tells the defendant that his story is not believable and asks whether there is possibly another account of what happened. Defendant reluctantly admits that he killed the victim, who came at him with a knife, in self-defense. The lawyer tells the client to shut up and listen as she reads from a coroner's report stating that the victim was shot in his side and back as he attempted to move away from his killer. The lawyer instructs her client to sleep on it, and tell her what happened the next time they meet. At the next meeting the defendant tells the story that the victim and his unknown friends had him surrounded; that the victim appeared to be reaching for a weapon and he feared for his life; as he fired in panic, the victim seemed to twist his body away from the defendant.

At the trial the lawyer calls the defendant, who testifies to the last story in a narrative form. No mention is made of the fight at the party, nor is any evidence presented that the defendant knew the victim. Needless to say, Scott Gordon is never called as a witness. The jury returns an involuntary manslaughter verdict, stating that there was no apparent motive for the killing, that all they had to go on was the defendant's claim of self-defense.

Do you think the lawyer crossed the ethical boundaries? Did she put words in her client's mouth? Did she retailor the story to conform to the evidence? Does the fact that the lawyer permitted the defendant to tell his story in the narrative form—without prompting or questioning—relieve her of her ethical responsibilities? Did the lawyer have reason to believe that the information and advice given to the defendant would result in a "new" story being given? Is that a euphemism for subornation of perjury? Is this the face-saving illusion that she hasn't done any of the coaching of which Robert Traver speaks?

On the other hand, you can have too little witness preparation. Failure to prepare a witness properly can result in disastrous mistakes. In the O.J. civil trial, Sergeant David Rossi was asked to identify blood spots observed on the Bundy Drive rear gate by him and other officers on the night of the murders. The defense team claimed these blood spots were planted some three weeks after the murders. Rossi, who was asked to point to the blood spots in the picture taken just a few hours after the discovery of the murders, erroneously pointed to some spots that turned out to be rust spots and berry stains.

Because the defense claimed police had planted the evidence, it was critical for Rossi to identify the blood spots correctly, and to differentiate them from the rust spots and berry stains depicted in the photos. Did the plaintiff's lawyer prepare him enough? Should the lawyer have made sure that Rossi could accurately ID the blood on the rear gate before testifying? Absolutely. Once the lawyer determines that the witness did see what he said he saw, in this case the blood on the rear gate, the lawyer must properly prepare the witness. Reference to the officer's crime-scene notes and other crime-scene reports can assist the lawyer in refreshing the memory of the witness. There is nothing wrong with familiarizing Rossi with the crime-scene photos before he takes the stand. Indeed, a lawyer is derelict in failing to do so—with the caveat that the lawyer cannot tell witnesses what to say, or instruct them to identify something that they can't recognize. There is a very fine line between overzealousness and underpreparation.

Judge Harold J. Rothwax says it all: "If the truth is the goal—and it is where discovery is concerned—there is no reason in law, morality, or common sense why a defendant's access to the People's case should not be conditioned on his willingness to give up any right to misuse that evidence."

In his book *Guilty*, Judge Rothwax offers the "Sealed Envelope Proposal" as a way to mitigate the abuse. Following the filing of criminal charges, a defendant who requests discovery of the prosecution's case must file a written account of what happened and place it in a sealed envelope that is filed with the court. This device would go a long way toward preventing the defense from offering a newly contrived story tailored to conform to the prosecution's information. In fairness to the defendant, the sealed statement could not be opened *unless* the defendant testified. While Judge Rothwax suggests that the statement be used only to impeach the defendant's inconsistent testimony, I suggest that it be used *both* for discrediting a defendant's inconsistent testimony and as substantive evidence that can be used against the defendant in proving the People's case. As always, the jury can choose which story it believes. Because discovery is not covered under the Constitution, individual states are free to set their own rules and conditions under which discovery is granted.

Stop Me Before I Hurt Someone!

Many defense lawyers feel that their job is to be as aggressive as necessary, and to do whatever is necessary. A certain portion of the bar will inevitably behave in an execrable manner. As long as our law and judges do not stop the behavior, it will continue. It is as simple as that. It is a little like testi-lying by the police; our system encourages it. Sure, we disapprove of it, but we don't do anything. So it continues. Here are some suggestions about how to get back control of our courtrooms:

1. Judges have to take control of their courtrooms. They are in charge—not the attorneys.

2. Our good judges have to stop being afraid to hold lawyers in contempt of court and assessing real fines and jail sentences. Judges are often pretty weak in this area. Do you know why Judge Ito imposed fines of under one thousand dollars against the defense and the prosecution in the Simpson case, even though he found all of them in contempt of court despite several warnings? Well, here is a dirty little secret. The attorneys would have had to report sanctions in excess of one thousand dollars to the state bar. The bar would have had to launch a disciplinary proceeding against the attorneys. How delicate of Judge Ito to make sure these attorneys did not have to explain their behavior to the state bar! He should have assessed sanctions that *bit*—a stay overnight in jail and substantial monetary sanctions. And he should have written a letter to the state bar, demanding a formal investigation.

3. Each year the state bar disbars relatively few attorneys while disciplining a lot more, although rarely prominent and wealthy attorneys. Have you ever wondered if any members of the state bar disciplinary committee were watching the Simpson trial? Have you ever wondered why disciplinary proceedings have not been started against at least *some* of the lawyers in the Simpson trial? Well, I have.

The bar association must change its policies. It can easily take steps that really have a bite. Disbarment of an attorney is a huge sanction. This drastic sanction should not be reserved, as it is today, only for those who misappropriate clients' funds. At a time when the public holds lawyers in low regard, it is imperative that *repeated* conduct that brings shame and disrepute to an otherwise noble profession should result in censure and removal. Period. Only then can we begin to rebuild public confidence and raise the standards of our profession. Another option is temporary suspension. It is also a drastic remedy because it prevents an attorney from earning a living—sometimes for a suspension period of years. If the bar does not start to take control over this process, the public should demand that the legislature empower public (non-attorney) members to control the disciplinary procedures.

To an extent, overly zealous attorneys will always be with us; this situation is built into the adversary system. But we should not have to tolerate the nonsense we have seen on our TVs over the past five years. There is a way to change this behavior. The key to doing so is our judges. In the next few chapters we'll climb up on the bench, peek under the bench blotter, pick up the gavel, and take a look around.

ELEVEN

The Principal in
a Reform School

JUDGES AND THE COURTROOM

We need a new kind of courage—the courage to face
unconquerable imperfections in the solution of human
problems.
—*Jerome N. Frank, 1949*

The trial judge is the glue that holds the whole adversary system together. The role is cluttered with perks and obstacles. You see, it is easy for a trial judge to become arrogant, insensitive, and judgmental. Attorneys, witnesses, and the press usually pander to the judge, often shamelessly. Even if they don't like the judge, even if they think he or she is stupid or dishonest, they pretend otherwise in the courtroom. An old Arab proverb overstates the case only a little: "When the judge's mule dies, everybody goes to the funeral; when the judge himself dies, nobody goes." It's easy to believe that the people who appear before you actually mean it when they appear solicitous, forgetting it is neither the mule nor you they care about. At the same time, being a trial judge is truly a humbling experience. I know. I sometimes felt completely helpless in trying to control the often ridiculous flow of events in my courtroom, helpless to make justice happen in what was sometimes a crazy system.

So the judge *seems* all-powerful in the courtroom. And there is some truth to the appearance of power. Trial judges control (or should control) the big decisions and the little ones. They decide what instructions will be read to the jury, what witnesses the jury may hear, and what evidence is so inflammatory a jury should not hear it. On the other hand, they must also field complaints from sequestered jurors about the program on their TV in the jury recreation room.

Judges work within an elaborate set of rules and must apply them quickly and fairly in a way that keeps the trial moving along. An entire verdict may be overturned if the judge fails in that task. Even worse, trial judges often have to make rulings they think are wrong or just silly, because of decisions made by higher courts. So the judge's power is perhaps not as great as it appears. Using that limited power, judges must maintain control in their courtroom and give the defendant a fair trial. If it sounds easy, it isn't.

A Judge Must Maintain Control of the Courtroom

An important function of a judge is to maintain control over the trial. Failure in this task makes a fair trial unlikely. Certainly, if the judge loses control over the courtroom, it is very unlikely the trial will *appear* to be fair. In trials held in the public eye, the *appearance* of fairness is as important as actual fairness. If a trial does not appear to be fair, cities can burn, and the justice system is reduced to shambles.

Keeping control is often not an easy task. The lawyers will try to get away with anything they can; they think that is their job. So perhaps the most important job of the judge is to draw clear lines for the attorneys. But attorneys are not the only problem. Witnesses and defendants can and do engage in outrageous behavior. Jurors lie to get on the jury. The media is, well, the media. As a group, the media observes no bounds or limits whatsoever that are not forced on them. They have the mighty First Amendment on their side. At times, as a judge, I felt like a principal in a reform school that was reserved for only very naughty children.

Control over a courtroom comes from one of two sources. Sometimes judges are so respected by the attorneys who appear before them that control is automatic. Subtle but very effective.

Alternatively, judges may, on a moment's notice, hold anyone in court in contempt. They can also sanction counsel and/or the parties. That can mean anything up to and including fines or a night in jail. Judiciously administered, a little contempt of court goes a long way toward controlling a trial that is about to get out of hand, a trial where the attorneys are pushing the envelope a little too hard.

Judge Laurence Rittenband, a brilliant jurist who graduated from Harvard Law School before he was old enough to be admitted to the bar, was so well respected he seldom had difficulty controlling his courtroom. As an attorney, I wanted to do well in front of him, because I wanted him to think well of me. Most attorneys I knew felt the same way. He was also a little cantankerous—which added a little fear to the respect. A potent combination.

I always waited for his critique after I had tried a case in front of him. He would start with a list of words I had misused. I would be crestfallen. He would then laugh and tell me it isn't about perfect English, but about *communicating* with a jury. More than once he told me a story about Clarence Darrow. After a particularly brilliant victory in a murder case, Darrow turned to his young Ivy League assistant for the expected praise due him. The lad said he found Darrow's argument very effective, quite good in fact. However, he noted Darrow's lapses in proper English grammar and syntax sprinkled throughout his colorful argument. The great lawyer, looking as if he were about to swallow a soft, succulent mushroom, eyed the young man and bellowed, "Son, when the English language gets in my way, it don't got no chance!" The point being that Rittenband shared his wisdom and counsel with lawyers who, in return, respected him enormously.

Rittenband actively controlled his trials. He let the jurors know exactly what he thought of each witness. All he had to do was raise one of his prominent white eyebrows and cock his head at ever so slight an angle, and the jury knew the good judge thought a witness was as believable as life on Venus. Or his eyes would twinkle and the jury would adopt a witness as if he or she were "family." Or he might ask "just one or two questions for point of clarification," to clear up the "confusion" in his mind.

Defense lawyers, though they enjoyed the judge's strong intellect, dreaded trying a weak case before him. He was especially tough when the defendant had dredged up a dubious alibi witness—not an uncommon event. I shudder to think what would have happened had Johnnie Cochran argued time of death on the basis of melting yogurt and burning candles, or had the prosecution called Kato Kaelin as a witness before the good Judge Rittenband. Or, for that matter, had Cochran implored the jury to "send a message."

While raw judicial power is a powerful tool, it works like a sledgehammer and not a scalpel. It is hard to get it just right. Too little, and the Dream Team owns your courtroom. Too much, and you make the justice system look ridiculous. Look at what happens when it is overused.

It is Chicago, 1968. Members of the Black Panther Party and political protestors are arrested for inciting riots outside the Democratic National Convention. Judge Julius Hoffman presides over the infamous Chicago Seven trial. To be sure, the attorneys and defendants were unruly. But the judge was completely unable to control his courtroom with ordinary measures. You may recall the extreme measures to which Judge Hoffman went to maintain order. Defendants were gagged and shackled, attorneys repeatedly held in contempt. Although a judge has the power of contempt, when it has to be used that often and in that way, the judge has lost control of his courtroom and justice fails.

On the other hand, it is my opinion that recent trials, such as the Simpson criminal trial, would have benefited from a sterner hand. It has been twenty-nine years since the Chicago Seven trial. Judge Lance Ito is a very different kind of judge from Julius Hoffman—a decent, caring, and sensitive person, a judge with infinite patience at times, a short fuse at other times, and possessed of a strong intellect. Ito, unlike Hoffman, was as concerned with the *appearance* of justice as he was with the *fact* of justice. Hoffman had to deal with attorney William Kunstler, a formidable trial advocate and presence in a courtroom. Ito had to deal with Cochran, Bailey, and the rest of the Dream Team, as well as contentious prosecutors.

Ito is a well-respected jurist—respected by prosecutors and the defense bar alike. But the public pressure of the trial appeared to remove all the restraints the trial attorneys normally feel in Ito's courtroom. Every argument was made as if the future of the nation depended upon it. Every cross-examination was five times longer than it would have been in a normal trial. Unlike Hoffman, Ito gave enormous leeway to the attorneys—allowing arguments and cross-examination to continue for what seemed forever, treating serious attorney misconduct with what appeared to be wrist slaps.

Remember when Christopher Darden was cross-examining defense witness Robert Heidstra? Heidstra testified on direct having heard two voices at about 10:40 P.M. on the night of the murders. He said he heard a voice say "Hey, hey, hey," and another voice, a very angry voice of an older man, screaming. This was right around the time of the murder. It was possible the angry voice was Simpson's. Darden asked Heidstra whether he had told anyone the voice of the angry older man had sounded black. This was a perfectly proper question under the circumstances. It was utterly unobjectionable.

But Cochran exploded, shouting in front of the jury, "Your Honor! This is offensive." Ito, fuming, excused the jury. Cochran, digging deep into the race-card issue, said, "I resent that statement. You can't tell by somebody's voice whether they sounded black . . . that's a racist statement!" Darden, in his book, *In Contempt,* confesses "to having an urge to beat his [Cochran's] ass right there in the courtroom." Darden explains he turned to Cochran, "ignoring Judge Ito and talking to the man who really controlled this courtroom," saying: "That's what has created a lot of problems for my family and myself, statements that you make about me and race." Cochran stood by his guns, insisting the question "is racist and I resent it, and that is why I stood and objected and I think it is totally improper in America at this time that we have to hear this and endure this."

How disingenuous. Cochran, the author of the race card, was playing it cynically and magnificently to the whole world by accusing another black man of being a racist. Everyone knows some voices have a very distinct character and can be the basis for identifying Irish, Jews, Scots, southerners, or any group that can be distinguished by an ethnic dialect. Linguists, phoneticists, and comedians know this. We know it too. So does Cochran.

So why did Cochran jump up in mock horror in front of the jury? Cochran needed to paint Darden as an Uncle Tom doing the evil white man's bidding to the predominantly black jury. Cochran's conduct was reprehensible and should have been dealt with summarily. All Ito did was lose his cool and storm off the bench without taking proper and decisive action.

Worse, Ito permitted lawyers to make intemperate remarks to TV reporters about the fairness and correctness of his rulings. Remember Cochran's angry statement, made outside his office at a TV press conference, regarding Ito's limitation on what would be admissible in the Fuhrman tapes? Cochran said, "This inexplicable, indefensible ruling lends credence to all those who say the criminal justice system is *corrupt.* This is unspeakable." Such remarks bring the court into disrepute and constitute a clear violation of the canons of ethics guiding lawyer conduct. No sanctions were assessed. Cochran should have been held in contempt, fined, and sent to jail, and the matter referred to the state bar. Period.

It is easy to second-guess Judge Ito, and, of course, that is exactly what I am doing. But he had a courtroom full of first-grade rebels who were behaving as if they had just arrived at his reform school. And they were testing him. Instead of enforcing discipline, he let the kids do pretty much what they wanted, including the prosecution, to preserve the *appearance* of a fair trial. Maybe I could have done better. Maybe not. Good or bad, a judge is often criticized by persons who have little understanding or compassion for his or her job.

Justice William O. Douglas wrote that "judges are supposed to be men of fortitude, able to survive in a hardy climate." Yet we judges want so very much to be appreciated for our self-perceived intelligence, wit, and charm. When a lawyer objects to our hearing a case, we are offended, since we know we are quite fair and evenhanded—and besides, we're just plain good guys. Truth is, we like being liked. We like the collegial nature of our profession, and we want that to continue when we take the bench. It's lonely sitting up there on that raised bench, the one we sometimes think is one step closer to God. It's difficult to come down hard on our former lawyer colleagues who practice before us. If we do that, we're not going to be popular. We're not going to be liked. The toughest thing in the world for most judges is to impose a tough sanction against a lawyer—especially one whom he has known for a long time, and maybe even has gone fishing with, even though the lawyer's conduct warrants such action. I know how hard it was for me. But one can't worship at two altars. The conflict is too great. Justice demands that judges, who hold the public trust, have the fortitude to do what is right, regardless of the personal consequences. That's the price of being a judge.

Judge Ito, like me, has known Johnnie Cochran for years. Cochran is likable, friendly, and always entertaining. We've been friends since our law-school days. No matter. Ito should have levied effective sanctions against Cochran and the other kids in his courtroom. Perhaps Ito was too concerned with his relationships to rein in the adversarial excesses that threw the Simpson trial into orbit. As Victor Hugo noted, "Popularity? It is glory's small change."

A Judge Must Conduct a Fair Trial

I could talk all day about the elements of a fair trial, but the difficulties faced by a judge are better illustrated by examples. Often my idea of a fair trial was much different from those of the appellate courts. My duty was to follow the higher court rulings, no matter how silly or poorly reasoned they seemed. Even when I bent the rules a little to achieve what I thought would be justice (and on occasion I did), the goals of fairness and justice proved more elusive than I thought. So I want to tell you about two of my cases as a judge: you be the judge of how I did.

One of these cases, the John Sweeney murder case, was highly publicized. I was widely criticized for some of my rulings in that case. To the father of the victim, it probably seemed I callously excluded evidence of Sweeney's murderous past. I felt I had no choice but to apply unsensible appellate decisions rendered by the California Supreme Court. The victim's father and I agreed on one thing: a vicious murderer had gotten away with murder. Even when you are a judge, with all the power that seems to imply, things do not always work out the way they should.

No one has ever heard of the other case I am going to talk about. I bent the rules a little in trying to help a fifteen-year-old runaway named Jenny—I'll call her Jenny X—to turn her life around. And as I said before, even when you are a judge, things do not always work out the way they should.

The John Sweeney Murder Case

John Sweeney, a star chef at the fabled Ma Maison restaurant, a place where celebrities "did lunch," strangled actress Dominique Dunne in a fit of rage. The reason? She had broken off their relationship. Sound familiar? That Sweeney killed Dunne was never much in doubt. What made the case troublesome to the jury (but not to me) was whether Sweeney had the state of mind to have committed second-degree murder.

Sweeney had a violent, brutal past. Twice in a three-year period he had hospitalized Lillian Pierce, his previous girlfriend. During those three years he had broken her nose, perforated her eardrum, and collapsed her lung. Needless to say, the prosecutor wanted to introduce evidence of how Sweeney had brutalized Pierce. Just as obviously, Sweeney's attorney did not want the jury to hear this evidence.

In 1983, decisions by the California Supreme Court prevented me from allowing the prosecutor to introduce this evidence. The reason was that evidence about Sweeney's having brutalized his previous girlfriend was evidence of other crimes he had committed in the past, for which he was not on trial. The California Supreme Court decisions at that time did not allow such evidence to be admitted. For example, in *People v. Sam,* the California Supreme Court reversed a murder conviction arising out of a barroom assault. The victim of the assault died of injuries from multiple kicks. The trial court had admitted evidence of Sam's prior acts of violence—evidence that the defendant had viciously kicked his mistress during a drunken quarrel a month before, and had similarly kicked a man during a brawl more than two years earlier.

Listen to what the California Supreme Court said in *People v. Sam* about admitting evidence of the previous kicking incidents:

> This case is a dramatic illustration of the prejudice that can be injected into a trial through the device of demonstrating prior criminal acts. By use of this stratagem, the

prosecution was able to place before the jury the largely irrelevant but manifestly harmful information that defendant was a man who often drank to excess and was
frequently drunk; that he was often belligerent and fought
with others; that he had been living with a married woman
not his wife; that he had struck that same woman with sufficient force to hospitalize her; that he had helped to assault his good friend Tubby so severely that an ambulance
and the police had to be called; that he had admitted to
one assault and battery and had been charged with another. In short, defendant was made to appear to be an anti-
social individual [which he was] of generally bad character
[which he had], an immoral person unworthy of the jury's
belief or consideration [which was true]. . . . (Bracketed
text added by author.)

Exactly. The defendant in *People v. Sam* appeared to be precisely the kind of guy who regularly assaulted and hospitalized
people by kicking them. He was accused in that case of assault-
ing, kicking, and killing someone. The California Supreme
Court held that it was not fair to the defendant to be made to appear to be exactly the kind of guy he was. Whew.

It would seem to a layperson, and indeed to me, that the
other crime evidence in *People v. Sam*, while damning, gave the
trier of fact great insight into the violent nature of the defendant. It was clear evidence of the defendant's willingness to use
extreme force, clear evidence that, at the slightest provocation,
his violent nature would explode, clear evidence that he knew of
his ability to hurt people with his feet.

As a prosecutor I had always pushed the envelope, always trying to get the judge to admit other acts of violence, other crime
evidence. Why? Because I thought it was highly relevant to establish a defendant's bad character, which I believe gives a trier
of fact great insight into that defendant's probable behavior. His
violent behavior is predictable by virtue of his disposition toward
violence—his patterned use of lethal force. There are legal ways
to admit such evidence. For example, if previous crimes show an
MO or a motive, they can be admitted. I would use whatever theory I could. After all, I was an advocate; my job was to get the evidence in. The defense's job was to keep it out. And the judge's

job was to make the difficult decision on whether to admit or exclude the evidence, trying to balance what the jury should know with what would unduly inflame them, rendering the trial unfair.

I well remember the hearings at which Lillian Pierce, Sweeney's previous girlfriend, testified about the vicious beatings she had received at his hands: her hospitalization, her broken nose, her perforated eardrum, her collapsed lung. I was more than upset. I'm supposed to be a neutral judge, and I was outraged, inflamed! This Sweeney was a son of a bitch. The attorneys argued and I read the cases.

You know, it is easier being an advocate than being the judge. As an advocate, you just present the strongest case you can. You try to win. You do what the adversary system allows you to do. You push the envelope and hope justice is served. Things were different. I was a judge. But what kind of judge? Should I take the easy way out? Let the evidence in? Certainly the public wouldn't criticize me for siding with the victims. If I am reversed, should I shrug my shoulders and blame it on a "soft-headed," liberal court led by Chief Justice Rose Bird? The public, held hostage to violent criminals, certainly would have sided with me. But it's funny what a judicial oath can do to you. I had taken an oath to uphold the law, even laws I thought stupid or unwise, for we are a government of laws, not of men. I wrestled with what was right. I did not like where it was leading me. I wanted to let this evidence in. I wanted the jury to hear it.

The night before I ruled, I could not look at myself in the mirror. I was afraid I would see the face of dishonesty, feel its shame. That I would do the wrong thing for the wrong reasons. I felt alone. I could not talk to my wife or family. I reread the cases. Uneasy about sharing my conflict with other judges, I sat in a darkened room, my mind racing. The next day I ruled, in accordance with *People v. Sam,* that the beatings of Sweeney's previous girlfriend could not be admitted in evidence. In this case, I refused to bend the law even a little. A law I detested.

The jury still heard about Sweeney's previous beatings of Dominique Dunne. They also heard that Sweeney continued to strangle Dunne for upwards of four minutes. This evidence was more than sufficient to establish murder with malice. Yet the jury returned verdicts of only voluntary manslaughter and simple assault. I will never understand the jury's verdict in the John

Sweeney case. The upshot of the verdict was that Sweeney was incarcerated for only a couple of years beyond the conclusion of the trial. He was out of jail, it seemed, before one could blink. I will never know for sure whether the evidence I excluded would have made the difference. As the great Benjamin Cardozo said, in 1924:

> Judges march at times to pitiless conclusions under the prod of a remorseless logic which is supposed to leave them no alternative. They deplore the sacrificial rite. They perform it, nonetheless, with averted gaze, convinced as they plunge the knife that they obey the bidding of their office. The victim is offered up to the gods of jurisprudence on the altar of regularity.

That is some comfort. Some. Nevertheless, my enthusiasm for being a judge crumbled at the moment I heard the jury return its verdict in the Sweeney case.

A Judge's Right to Comment on the Evidence

The Constitution does not prohibit trial judges from commenting on the evidence. In years past, judges occasionally would speak to the jury about the evidence, being careful to remind the jurors that they, not the judge, were the sole and exclusive finders of fact. Unfortunately, our appellate courts were not warm to this practice. They reversed some convictions, chilling the efforts of trial judges to clarify the evidence for the jury. I do not know of any judges who comment on the evidence today; and that is a shame. We should encourage trial judges to do so. The jurors would, of course, remain completely free to reject the judge's interpretation of the evidence, or of a witness's testimony.

Had Judge Ito been able to comment on the DNA and the alleged conspiracy evidence, bringing the force of his analytical skills to the task, the jury might have come to a different conclusion. When lawyers mislead jurors, when they twist an honest witness's testimony, when they misinterpret evidence, the truth is served by impartial commentary by an unbiased observer. If I could have given the Sweeney jury the benefit of my analysis of the evidence or of how the evidence fit into the strange language of the jury instructions, I think they would have arrived at a better verdict. That jury did ask for an explanation of the complex jury instructions mandated by law. I could not, as a judge, change or embellish the wording of those obtuse instructions. But in commentary, I could have illustrated how they applied to the facts. Perhaps that would have made a difference.

Judges must return to a more proactive role in seeing that justice is done. One of the ways they can do that is to comment on the evidence in complex or confusing cases or in cases where there is danger of a jury being misled by the attorneys. Commentary, when used fairly, can level the adversarial playing field, leaving the jurors free to focus on finding the truth and doing justice. But the attorneys, ever jealous of their playing field, will fight any such intrusion by "judicial interlopers." A judge might discredit their effective but specious arguments.

The Jenny X Case

I frequently sat by special assignment as a Juvenile Court judge. One day a girl named Jenny appeared before me. She was barely fifteen, going on thirty. She was first brought into my court before they had cleaned her up. Her face was heavily made up, her eyes lined with purple mascara. She wore a micro-miniskirt that exposed her very white thighs. Jenny had been picked up on Sunset Boulevard in Hollywood, doing a bad imitation of a hooker, not far from where Hugh Grant was arrested some years later. Her attorney, Jerry Fogelman, was a dedicated and highly principled defense attorney in Los Angeles. A few days later Fogelman came to my court. I asked where his client was. He looked at me in puzzlement as he nodded toward a freshly scrubbed little girl nestled into the crook of a chair. She looked like Tatum O'Neal in the movie *Paper Moon*. Only lost. Very lost.

Jenny had been living in crash pads and hanging with pimps, first in New York, then later in Los Angeles. I stole another glance over the reports at Jenny. She sat there, refusing to utter a word, content to curl in the chair's folds, as if hiding in her own secret world. What cruelty in her life had caused her to become so lost? How had we failed her as a society? How many more were there out there just like her? Black, brown, yellow, white? Color didn't matter. Only the children; they matter.

In Juvenile Court, guilt is supposed to be irrelevant. It is the behavior that must be modified before the character hardens into a predatory crust. I tried to elicit a response from Jenny. She twisted into a tighter ball and looked at me with contempt. I ordered counseling and tutoring for her in Juvenile Hall. This is juvy. Here, a judge has much more power over a child than over an adult; more options in dealing with emergent criminal behavior. As a judge, you act more parental, trying to reach them before it's too late. So you shout, scream, swear—whatever gets their attention. You become the big brother they never had. You take off your robe, you come down from the bench, you do all the things you can't do in adult court. Before I knew it, I heard my voice. It didn't sound like mine. Here was no neutral, passive judge—just my voice, trembling and angry:

"You think this is just a lotta bullshit. No big deal, right?" I paused for a long time. I couldn't believe I had used that word in court. "No big deal. Ya ain't in any trouble. Just a bunch of dumb sucks gettin' in your face, right?" She furrowed her brow. Her lips tightened. "I bet you're having a great time. Living on the street. Going from crash pad to crash pad. You're not gonna see sixteen. Because you're gonna die."

A glint of a reaction flashed before she turned it off. Was she listening?

"Hey, that's cool," I went on. "No one cares. Why should they? You don't. You think it's okay to crash in Watts. You're a survivor. You'll make it, right?"

I paused again, looking for some sign. There was none. She was withdrawing further.

"You're going back into the Hall. I'm not. Think about whether you want to live or die. I'm not wasting my time on you, if you're gonna throw your life away. What pisses me off about you is that you are so pretty that other girls would die to have your looks. You don't have a clubfoot. You're not scarred. You haven't been shot or stabbed—yet." I softened my approach. "If you want some real help, we're here to give it to you. We're here for you. And some of us even listen to heavy metal—like Judas Priest. So does your attorney. So talk to him."

I don't know if I was imagining it, but I thought I saw a faint glimmer in her eyes. Jenny wanted out. She wanted to be with her pimp. Feeling he had no other legal option, Fogelman decided he was ethically bound to move for her release from detention. He had pretty solid grounds. She probably should have been released, because the probable cause for the initial arrest was pretty thin. Fogelman cited case law justifying the suppression of her admission that she was "hooking for her pimp." But I winked at the sufficiency of the probable cause, denied his motion to dismiss, and declared her a ward of the court. I did it so we could try to save her.

Yes, I was playing God. But I didn't have enough time against her for this minor offense to place her in a very special facility called the Dorothy Kirby Center, which provided intensive psychiatric counseling for girls like Jenny. Although there was a waiting list, I was determined to get Jenny X into Kirby any way I could. I just needed some more time.

Jenny was starting to respond in Juvenile Hall, losing the hard edge, losing the gangsta rap. She even smiled occasionally. But I still didn't have the time I needed to place her in Kirby. She just shrugged, gamely trying to give the impression that it wasn't any big deal anyway.

Fogelman admonished me, "Judge, you just can't put her away because you think it's good for her." Then Jenny gave me a gift—an odd gift, but a gift nevertheless. She had a temper tantrum in Juvenile Hall and threw a book at a juvenile staff officer. We now had a new "assault" charge. Yes, I probably bent the rules to keep Jenny in detention long enough so she could be admitted to the Dorothy Kirby Center. Her attorney vehemently protested my bending of the rules. I told him to do what he had to do. "I'm going to do what I think is right. If you don't like my ruling, appeal it." He did.

Although Fogelman vehemently disagreed with me on the law and vigorously represented Jenny in her desire to be released, he later wrote me about Jenny,

> We, all of us, would like to make an impact in our lifetime. Some of us are in professions where that can happen. Ours is such a profession. So let there be no doubt whatsoever, you do have an impact. You should be very proud.

Along with his letter were a letter and a Halloween card from Jenny. It looked as if she might just make it.

Hi Mr. Katz.

How're you doing? Its been a while since we last saw each other. . . . As for me I'm doing O.K. I've been waiting for the write [sic] time to write you, because I didn't want to write to you when I was messing up!

I saw Mr. Fogelman today! He has been coming to see me here often. I like him coming to visit with me. He is a great person.

I think it was a good decision to send me to "Kirby center." Were [sic] going to have a contest tomorrow, to see who has the best cottage. (The cottages are going to be decorated for Halloween.) Hopefully our cottage will win. We're going to have a haunted house! Its going to be great. You know what you guys should decorate the courtroom. I could just see people walking in to Department 277, and you have decorations everywhere!

I hope you have a nice Halloween! I'm going too. My birthday is the next day (November 1), so I'm going to have a good time! I'll be *sixteen*. Just think pretty soon I'll be twenty, then thirty, then forty and then fifty and so on. . . . But no matter how old I am, I'll always remember the things you have done for me!

I'll write you back soon! Bye, Bye.

P.S. tell everyone in department "277" that I said "Hello" and Happy Halloween! Hopefully I'll see everyone in department 277 again!

Jenny wrote on her handmade Halloween card:

I would like to say I really appreciate all the things you have been doing for me. I [sic] glad that I had you for a judge, because you've helped me out so much I only wish that there were more people like yourself and Mr. Fogelman around when I needed someone to support me and try to help me out the best they can. I hope I'll get a chance to see you again. But for now "stay cool" Ha! Ha! And happy Halloween!

On the card Jenny drew a picture of Casper the Ghost, above which she wrote, "Its only me wishing you a happy Halloween." On the back she drew a picture of a smiling round face with one hair growing out of its head. I thought that maybe, just maybe, we were going to save one of the kids from the street.

At the conclusion of the Kirby program, Jerry gave Jenny the money to travel by bus to go back to her mother. Her mother, a waitress at a greasy truck stop, was now living in a trailer in Wyoming. She had no phone and offered no amenities or necessities to Jenny. Within a couple of weeks, Jenny went back to the gangs and the pimps. Jerry last heard from Jenny when she was eighteen and pregnant, having been busted for prostitution. There was nothing more the juvenile system could do, since she was now regarded as an adult.

Somehow this child had touched both Jerry and me. Both of us saved her letters and her file for years after her juvenile case had long been closed. There is a lot of pain in life. There is even more in the justice system. We lost her, and that hurt—real bad.

Conclusion

I do not know what recommendations I could make that would change the Sweeney case and the agony Dominique Dunne's family felt over the result in that case. Maybe all prior acts of violence should be admissible in murder cases where issues of intent, MO, and identity are contested. That would be a start. Commenting on the evidence would undoubtedly also have helped. I encourage trial judges to give an impartial analysis of evidence and witness credibility where it is appropriate to do so.

Likewise, I do not know how the system could be changed so Jenny X would have had a fair chance in life. Maybe there was nothing to be done, but I don't really believe that. We could have done something. We should have done more—we just failed. The judicial system is imperfect. I have said that before and I will say it again.

Regarding control of the courtroom, I have more advice for judges than policy recommendations. Do not become jaded to unethical attorneys, lying witnesses, and lying jurors. Keep your sense of outrage about outrageous behavior. Take back control of your courtrooms. Use your powers of contempt. Notify the state bar about attorneys who behave unethically or unprofessionally. Use your power to sanction miscreant attorneys. Recommend prejury trials for lying witnesses, cops, and jurors.

The perception among attorneys, jurors, cops, and witnesses is that they can misbehave in your courts and suffer no serious consequences. By and large, they are right. They may be scolded, but they are unlikely to receive punishments that hurt. As trial judges, we see misbehavior so often we stop being outraged or even upset. We really expect it. So we just scold and move on. That breeds contempt for our judges and our judicial system. You, the trial judges, should be on the cutting edge of winning back respect for the bench and for our judicial system.

The various participants in our judicial system often do behave like children. Like children, they will benefit from clear lines of discipline, consistently enforced. Popularity, collegiality, and friendship aside, justice requires action. Sometimes that is excruciatingly painful.

T W E L V E

Did You Bring
Your Toothbrush?

PROBLEM JUDGES

The greatest scourge an angry Heaven ever inflicted
upon an ungrateful and a sinning people, was an ignorant,
a corrupt, or a dependent judiciary.
—*Chief Justice John Marshall*

We confer tremendous power on the judiciary. Judges
have the intrusive power to let the police invade your
home, have you arrested and thrown in jail, keep
you in jail without bail, and stain your reputation, all without a
shot being fired. That is power. So it is entirely appropriate that
we demand high qualifications, high performance, and high
ethics from those who serve as judges. One of the secrets of our
judicial system is the existence of some *very* bad judges. Furthermore, because of their personal weaknesses, many judges
do not have the will to make the difficult decisions that come
with being a judge. My first judge in the "Shorty" Shea murder
case was such a man. He was manipulated shamelessly by the
Manson family, and was incapable of completing his judicial duties in that case. Finally, some judges are bigoted, imperious
and arrogant. In this chapter we are going to take a long look,
from inside the courtroom, at all three types of "problem"
judges.

Bad Judges

When I was a young DA, a few judges worked hard to put the fear of God into everyone who came into their courtroom. These judges weren't just stern; we could have handled that. Rather, they displayed explosive or bizarre behavior. It happens, believe me. Even young DAs and public defenders who professed atheism often muttered prayers just before entering into these particular hallowed courtrooms. Let's look at the careers of two of the more colorful former members of the California bench, Leland Geiler and Nancy Noel Cannon.

Leland Geiler regarded public defenders as obstacles to the efficient operation of his court. He demonstrated a degree of tastelessness, vulgarity, and willful misconduct toward the PDs that was, at times, almost unbelievable. One morning the judge invited a PD and the DA into his chambers. Emerging from the vicinity of a file cabinet, the judge thrust a buzzing, battery-operated dildo into the PD's buttocks. The judge laughed and thought it was hilarious. But that was only the setup. Later that morning, in the course of a preliminary hearing, the judge began to interrupt the same PD on cross-examination. This is what transpired:

PD: One or two questions, Your Honor, then I won't take any more of your time on this case.

GEILER (to his clerk): Get the machine [the dildo] out.

CLERK: The battery?

GEILER: The battery.

PD: I have no further questions, Your Honor.

The dildo treatment continued that afternoon. The PD persisted in a line of questioning, even though the DA had objected. The judge's response was almost gibberish—but what is clear is that he continued to threaten the PD in open court with the dildo:

GEILER: Ha, ha, ha. Shove it. That's what you're thinking about. You're convincing me more every moment [to get out the dildo]. [To his clerk.] Did you get those batteries?

CLERK: I'm charging it [the dildo] up. I've got a bigger one. Fifteen volts.

GEILER (to the PD): John, we've got a fifteen-volter in there now.

CLERK: With a longer handle. [The judge obviously had planned out a routine with his clerk. This was not just a spur-of-the-moment indiscretion.]

GEILER: Hurry, John. We got a fifteen-volt battery for you.

PD: Okay. We're referring to that incident this morning, Your Honor?

GEILER: No, the one that you're going to take home tonight. Go ahead.

PD: I have no further questions of this officer, Your Honor.

Clearly the judge accomplished exactly what he wanted. He cut short the cross-examination of the PD—depriving the defendant of the right of effective representation.

This same judge, on another occasion, approached a traffic court commissioner from behind in a public corridor of the Hall of Justice, and grabbed his testicles. This conduct, together with numerous offensive, abusive, and salacious comments to women and employees of the court, resulted in the California Supreme Court removing the judge from office. Eventually.

If you think Geiler's conduct was boorish and outrageous, let me tell you of another judge, Nancy Noel Cannon. I shuddered when I entered her courtroom. Anything could happen, and often did. This judge once had her chambers painted pink for a press conference at which she advocated that "women should arm themselves against attack with derringers and hatpins." She also had a mechanical canary that she kept in chambers. That canary sure knew how to chirp. She left open the door to her chambers during hearings, trials, whatever. The mechanical canary was loudly audible in the courtroom through the partially opened chamber door. It was terribly difficult to concentrate on doing your job while that stupid canary chirped away. We attorneys wondered if the purpose of the canary was to keep her dog company. Oh yes, she also had a dog she brought to court and kept under the bench or in her lap.

A dog, a canary, pink chambers, hatpins, and derringers. All this was going on at a time when the job of the judge and the attorneys was to determine whether people should or should not go to jail. Accordingly, full concentration was mandated. Despite many complaints, she refused to close the door to her chambers or to turn off the damn canary. So far, what I have told you is odd, eccentric. Now listen to some of the really strange things this judge did.

On one occasion, a PD made an entirely appropriate motion to exclude a police officer from the courtroom while another witness was testifying:

PD: I would like him excluded, well, if not under 867, then perhaps the court would permit me to clear the courtroom under 868. [If that motion is made under 868, the judge *must* grant it. It's the law.] I may wish to call him.

CANNON: You know you are not going to call him. Please don't lie to me.

PD: I may wish to call him.

CANNON: Please don't make those phony motions, and don't lie to me in open court. Now, Paul James did that to me, and he had better not do that again, and none of you had better do that to me again, lying to me in open court. Do you still want to clear the courtroom? [Paul James, to whom she refers, was later to become the chief public defender. He is a softspoken and humble PD whose integrity is beyond reproach.]

PD: Yes I do, Your Honor.

CANNON: The courtroom is cleared. I am tired of these obstructionist tactics. You have no intention whatsoever of calling that person. I have had this practiced on me by PD after PD, and in particular participated in by Paul James of your office who lies to me in open court. I am tired of this practice. All right, the court is in recess for five minutes. *Nobody is to leave the courtroom* [an interesting way to clear the courtroom, no?], and nobody is to use the phone.

After the "recess," Judge Cannon escalated her odd behavior.

CANNON: Mr. Defender, you are held in contempt of court. Mr. Bailiff, will you please take Mr. Defender into custody. [The judge then turned to another PD.] Will you please prepare the case forthwith. I should advice you in advance that I will not put up with any more obstructionist policies. [The second PD stands up to take the case. The DA begins questioning.]

DA: Officer Jones, . . . would you state for the court your occupation and assignment on that date?

JONES: Police officer for the City of Los Angeles . . .

PD No. 2: Your Honor, at this time I really do intend to call the other officer.

CANNON: All right Mr. [PD No. 2], you are held in contempt of court. [To the bailiff.] Take Mr. [PD No. 2] into custody.

Not only lawyers tiptoed around Judge Cannon's court, but the police were terrified of her too. The judge was on her way to court one morning when she was stopped by one of LAPD's finest for excessive use of her horn. This is how the cop saw the encounter, according to the official record:

> She rolled down her window when I pulled up alongside her, at which time I said, "Ma'am, there is no reason to honk your horn. The gentleman was just waiting for a pedestrian, like he should have." At which time she told me that she would honk her horn any time she "damn well pleased." At that time I said, "Ma'am, there is a Vehicle Code Section that covers excessive use of the horn." At which she told me, "You go to hell, Officer."

When she got to court, she ordered her bailiff to "find the son of a bitch; I want him found and brought in right away. Give me a gun; I am going to shoot his balls off and give him a .38 vasectomy."

The judge then went to the police officers' waiting room at court with her bailiffs. There she told a police officer, "God damn it, find him, find that son of a bitch for me. I am not going to take the bench until you find that male chauvinist pig." Other police officers came to her chambers to pacify the judge, but to no avail. Finally the cop who had warned her about blowing her horn came into chambers. Upon arrival, he sat there in silence while she brooded. Then she said, "You've been a very naughty boy." He replied, "Well, if you say so, Your Honor." She then started talking about how public defenders ask stupid questions, and about a recent religious seminar she had attended. She gave the cop a couple of her own dogeared religious pamphlets. Incredibly, two weeks later she wrote the chief of police that "LAPD was the finest police department in the world, and the T.E.D. motor squad was the finest of L.A. and the cop [the "very naughty boy"] was the finest of the fine!"

Needless to say, Judge Cannon was censored and removed from the bench for willful misconduct.

Today, supervising judges are more on top of things, as are the Commissions on Judicial Performance, than they were in the era of Leland Geiler and Nancy Noel Cannon. As a consequence, their conduct would not continue today in state courts as long as it did then without effective intervention. Federal courts are an entirely different matter.

Scared Off by the Manson Family

In many ways, the worst judges are not the corrupt or crazy ones. The worst are decent, well-meaning judges who just are not up to the job. The first time I tried Steve Grogan for the murder of Donald "Shorty" Shea, the case ended in a mistrial because Judge Joseph Call could not keep going when things got rough. When you were dealing with the Manson family, things could get rough.

Judge Call had been appointed to the bench over thirty years before the Grogan trial. Few lawyers were willing to risk a complicated case before Judge Call. As luck would have it, we drew him for Grogan. We were having difficulty finding a judge who could try a case that was going to take as long as Grogan. We reluctantly agreed to Judge Call. It was to prove a costly mistake for both the defense and the prosecution.

During the trial, Nancy Pitman (a.k.a. Brenda McCann), "Squeaky" Fromme, Mary Brunner, Sandra Good, and other Manson family members slept out and "held court" on the corner of Temple and Broadway, just outside the Hall of Justice. Each morning, outside my office, I would encounter the family huddled together picnic-style, looking like innocent suffragettes bonding together for the cause. The Manson girls were as schizophrenic and enigmatic as Charlie himself. Sometimes they were pleasant, even coyly flirtatious. They would invite me to go camping with them at Spahn Ranch so they could reindoctrinate my misguided and corrupt establishmentarian ways of thinking. When things were going poorly for Charlie, they were menacing and dark-spirited, rubbing the sheath knives they kept lashed to their hips. They were always strangely entertaining, shrouded in mystery, myth, and rumor.

During the Grogan trial, a fierce rumor floated about that the Manson family was going to free Manson, Steve Grogan (the defendant in my trial), and Tex Watson. Death threats had been directed at Judge Call and everyone else involved in the trial— even at the defense attorneys. Security was beefed up. Undercover cops were sprinkled throughout the courtroom audience. I was told I was to dive under the counsel table if a shootout started, because I was (as they delicately put it) "expendable" in any court shootout. The cops' priority was to protect the judge. The DA's bureau assigned a personal bodyguard to protect me and my family, and armed me with a snub-nosed .38, which I carried strapped under my arm. We were all edgy. But Judge Joseph Call came completely unglued. It started in the judge's own chambers.

Fearful that Grogan would accuse him of something sinister if a chambers hearing occurred outside Grogan's presence, Judge Call allowed the defendant to be present in chambers during a discussion with counsel. The judge sat there nervously, jiggling some coins. Grogan sat only a few feet away. As the judge attempted to reassure Grogan he was doing everything he could do to provide a fair trial, Grogan suddenly moved. He knelt in front of the startled judge, his hand on the judge's knee—like a supplicant with a beatific smile, kneeling before Christ. We all stared, transfixed. At that moment, Grogan could have killed him. The judge's face was ashen; his hands shook. Before the bailiff could help, the judge looked at Grogan for reassurance and said in a quivering voice, as if to convince himself: "Steve doesn't mean anything by it." Grogan, looking up at the judge and still smiling, gently replied: "It's okay, Joe, I know you're just trying to be fair . . . you'll do the right thing." From that moment on, the judge began to unravel. All he wanted was to get out of trying this case. The only way he could do that was to declare a mistrial. You will probably not be surprised that he found a way to do precisely that.

Things might have settled down, had there been no further incidents. But it was not to be. Several Manson family members, including Mary Brunner and Catherine Share (a.k.a. Gypsy) tried to rob a gun store. In the ensuing gun battle with the people, over fifty rounds of ammunition were fired, but miraculously no one was seriously hurt. Manson family lore has it that Gypsy's bra was shot right off her by police gunfire ripping through the getaway van in which she was waiting. The police did find a bloody bra in the bullet-riddled van, which amazed me. To my knowledge, Gypsy had never previously been sighted wearing a bra. Following their arrest, an additional cache of weapons was recovered—weapons that were to be used in freeing Charlie Manson and his faithful followers.

Needless to say, we were all on edge as we began the third month of trial. The stage was now set for the showdown on the stand with Brenda McCann. McCann was an important witness because she was present during a conversation between Grogan and Paul Watkins, a Manson family member and close confidant of Charles Manson. After surviving a mysterious trailer fire that nearly took his life, Watkins turned state's evidence. He believed Manson was behind the fire, and he was probably right. As a government witness, he had testified to a stunning confession made by Grogan in that conversation. You have read part of it earlier:

> Charlie told me to cut his [Shorty Shea's] head off. So I had this big machete and I chopped his head off and it went, bloop, bloop, bloop and rolled over out of the way . . . it was real groovy. . . .

Grogan told Watkins that he had blood splattered all over him, and it was all warm, and he had it all up his arm.

Watkins then asked Grogan if he felt guilty. Grogan replied,

> Any guilt that I have is my changes [a term used in scientology] because in reality one baby should be able to kill another baby and then reach over and eat his shit . . . any guilt that I have is something I have to work out with myself.

Defense attorney Charles Weedman called Brenda McCann as a witness in an effort to refute the damning confession. She claimed she had heard the same conversation, and denied that Grogan had ever confessed to the murder of Shorty Shea. In an effort to discredit Watkins, she claimed he boasted that he was avoiding the draft by feigning mental instability, epilepsy, and seizures. Further, she said that Watkins claimed he had learned to mock up cancer in his lungs so that an X ray would reveal a black spot! She also added that he claimed to be a homosexual. The last point was hilarious inasmuch as the jury had just observed the extremely handsome and youthful Watkins on the stand for several days, regaling them and the court with his tales of lust for the family females, who, like honey attracting bees, had induced this adventuresome youth to join the family. Watkins testified,

> Well, when I first met Charlie, I was all alone and I wandered into a house and then there was Charlie and a couple of other guys and ten girls, and that was what I had been looking for. I knocked on the door and three girls met me at the door, and right away I recognized the smell of marijuana, and they asked me to come in. And so then

when I went in, it was [*sic*] some people didn't have their
clothes on, and so right away I felt the free atmosphere,
and I was overcome by a feeling of this is what I was looking for.

Watkins was as homosexual as John F. Kennedy. I began my
cross-examination. I wanted to show the jury this witness was
completely untrustworthy because of her Manson family affilia-
tion. The attitude of the "family" toward conventional values was
summed up as follows in their own words:

> Whatever is necessary, you do it. When somebody needs
> to be killed, there's no wrong. You do it, and then you move
> on. And you pick up a child and you move him to the
> desert. You pick up as many children as you can and you kill
> whoever gets in our way. That is us.

Virtually from my first question, I knew it was not going to be
easy, as Charles Weedman and the court kept jumping in. I
began to focus on the subject of her being a member of the Manson family, and her obvious loyalties and biases. Here is some of
that testimony:

KATZ: [Y]ou understand at this time Mr. Grogan is on trial for
his life, don't you?

McCANN: Yes.

KATZ: You understand the significance of your testimony, don't
you?

McCANN: Yes.

KATZ: You understand . . . if the jury believes you they might
acquit the defendant; isn't that right?

McCANN: Yes.

Manson and his followers had disavowed society's rules and
laws; they X'd themselves out of society. I explained to the
judge that, during the Tate-LaBianca trials, Charles Manson,
Susan Atkins, Katie Krenwinkle, and Leslie Van Houton had

carved X's on their foreheads. Other family members quickly
followed suit, symbolizing the family's rejection of society's
rules and conventions. Hence I felt it was appropriate to ask
whether Brenda recognized her duty to tell the truth under
oath.

KATZ: [Y]ou would do anything you could, you would lay down
    your life for Clem [Grogan]; wouldn't you?

McCANN: Yes.

KATZ: As a matter of fact, Brenda, with respect to the so-called
    establishment and society as we know it, you have X'd
    yourself out from society, haven't you?

WEEDMAN: Oh, Your Honor, for heaven's sakes. How long is this
    going to go on?

The court said it was not proper cross. I then asked her if
she believed in the law against perjury. More objections were
sustained by the court. I now turned my attention to the actual
conversation between Grogan and Watkins. On direct, I had
deliberately refrained from asking Watkins about the entire
conversation in which Grogan and McCann had talked also
about killing Frank Retz, who owned property next to Spahn
Ranch. Retz had physically thrown Manson off his property
and advised George Spahn strongly to kick the family off
Spahn Ranch. He was regarded as an enemy of Manson. I believed that this information was irrelevant to the confession
and arguably too prejudicial. However, when Weedman made
a tactical mistake in asking Brenda McCann on direct whether
she had described the *whole* conversation, to which she replied
yes, the door was open wide enough to accommodate two ele-
phants and a rhino. The law allowed me to elicit the *entire* conversation, which included the damning death threats to Retz. I
asked McCann whether she and Grogan had talked about
killing Frank Retz. Of course, I expected her to lie about it, and
she did. Before I could ask a follow-up question, Weedman
jumped up and asked to go into chambers. The testimony was
reread. Weedman argued that this was impeachment on a col-
lateral matter and highly prejudicial. He then made a brief ar-

gument and a halfhearted motion for a mistrial. Judge Call had been terrorized with the news of the gun-store shootout just five days earlier. Weedman's mistrial motion was just what the judge had been waiting for—a way to get himself out of this case.

The judge started talking about a whole series of small matters he claimed were prejudicial, things that had not even come up as objectionable at the time of the testimony, things that were not even the basis of Weedman's motion. What is absolutely amazing is that he was ignoring virtually indestructible, well-settled rules of evidence. I then asked for a recess so I could prepare a brief on the law permitting such questions to be asked. This was summarily denied. It was clear where Judge Call was going, and he wanted no impediment to his decision to jettison the case by declaring a mistrial. The judge said, "I am serious on the question of a mistrial. I am serious about it. I think it is highly prejudicial, highly inflammatory, and it can't be otherwise."

Dejected, I went home. The next morning I appeared in court. Weedman and I were locked out of chambers for two hours. I had case citations with me establishing that my cross-examination about Retz had been entirely proper. But Judge Call never heard about those citations because he did not want to hear anything that interfered with his decision to get out of the case. At 10:50 A.M. we were ushered into chambers. The judge immediately started picking over the entire transcript of the previous day's proceedings. He read into the record minor points having nothing to do with the subject of Weedman's mistrial motion, and even alluded to questions asked of a witness other than McCann. This nitpicking went on for nearly three hours. Then the judge stated, "This is my final summation. I do grant the motion for mistrial."

As the old saying goes, you should be careful what you wish for, because it may come true. Weedman was horrified. I know he had moved for a mistrial. The judge had just granted his motion. Why was he upset? In truth, a mistrial was the last thing he wanted. All he was trying to do was set up an issue on appeal. Basically, he had moved for the mistrial so he could argue to an appellate court later that he should have gotten a mistrial he did not really want. Defense lawyers do this all the time. This was nothing different. What was different was having such a weak motion granted by the court.

Weedman frantically tried to backpedal. First he asked the court if he could confer with his client before the jury was dismissed. The judge was ready to discharge the jury, but Weedman asked for another chambers discussion in which Grogan was present. Craftily, Weedman then told the judge that while he did not necessarily agree with his client's assessment, Grogan had expressed a "feeling that some of these matters could be sufficiently cured so as to insure [*sic*] him of a fair trial in this matter." Weedman mentioned that this had been a long trial, and it had been a considerable strain on Grogan; that while he believed the errors could not be cured, he needed more time to discuss the ramifications of a mistrial with Grogan, who might disagree that a mistrial was necessary. Weedman had cleverly placed the court in a vise, on the one hand suggesting his client might object to a mistrial, even though he, as his lawyer, believed it was warranted. A declaration of mistrial over the strenuous objection of the defendant can result in double jeopardy, barring a retrial. The trap was being set.

Judge Call quickly began to reiterate, apparently for the benefit of Grogan, how devastating the supposed prosecutorial error had been:

> Your jury is prejudiced. I'm telling you my opinion again. It is deadly. I think it has created irreversible prejudice in the minds of those folks. *You should go out and get a new jury on this and a new judge; let somebody else rule on it. I'm out of it. I mean, in a new trial, they should get somebody else in.* (Emphasis added.)

Note Judge Call's insistence that he personally should be removed from the trial. The usual rule is that the trial judge at the first trial also presides over the second. Because he is already familiar with the evidence and the law pertaining to that case, the rule saves time and makes good sense. But Judge Call was the senior judge. He was not worried about anyone junior to him telling him he had to retry this case. Not on your life.

Weedman took one last stab. First he told the judge he had no objection to his continuing in this trial. Then he was allowed to confer once again with Grogan. Upon returning, he asked that the court delay the discharge of the jury until the following Monday (it was Friday) with a view toward *withdrawing* his mistrial motion. The judge refused. The jury was dismissed. The case was over, as far as Judge Call was concerned. The jurors were confused, shocked. Not one juror understood the reason for the mistrial. Not one thought the question about Frank Retz was that important. Fortunately the case was quickly reassigned to the very competent Judge James Kolts. He conducted a fair and expeditious trial. The case was tried swiftly and without incident to a conviction and a death-penalty verdict which Kolts reduced to life in lieu of granting a motion for a new trial.

The Arrogance of the Life Appointees

Federal judges present a special problem. Most are highly qualified, overworked, and extremely dedicated to the law. Federal judges derive their authority from Article III of the United States Constitution, which provides for lifetime appointments. The only way they can be removed is by an elaborate impeachment process. First, the House of Representatives brings the charges and the Senate tries the judge. If two-thirds of the Senate votes for removal, the judge is removed and may be barred from holding any federal office in the future. Hence, federal judges are, practically speaking, judges for life. No one can touch them. They are sometimes derisively called "Article III judges" because their behavior is frequently autocratic, capricious, and grandiose.

In our two hundred–plus years as a nation, only a very few federal judges have been formally impeached. The impeachment process itself, because it is unwieldy, divisive, and time-consuming, is rarely invoked. Instead, the Department of Justice usually brings criminal charges against a judge, or threatens to do so, which usually effects a voluntary resignation. Fewer than two hundred judges have resigned from federal office because of misbehavior. Negotiated compromises are struck whereby a judge may be allowed to keep his or her pension upon resignation.

Some Article III judges are so arrogant they refuse to resign from the bench even though they have been convicted of a crime and sent to prison. Judge Harry Claiborne defiantly continued to draw his federal judicial salary as he languished in jail for some two years, vowing to return to his Federal District Court seat in Nevada, before Congress removed him from office through a 1986 impeachment process. Robert Collins continued to accept his judicial salary, while in prison, until his resignation in 1993.

T H I R T E E N

Taking Charge

You Get What You Pay For

Never buy what you do not want because
it is cheap; it will be dear to you.
—*Thomas Jefferson, 1825*

The bad news is that there are some terrible judges, just
as there are terrible doctors, scientists, and teachers.
Additional bad news is that the good judges are so
overworked they cannot possibly keep up with the workload.
The good news is that we are well equipped to do something
about our judiciary. It's time for some real changes. To begin
with, we can first admit that we will never have a perfect system
and that no judge will be without faults. Then we can get on
with the following suggested steps, as a program of improvement.

Fund the Judicial System Properly

Our judicial system is woefully underfunded, and the problem gets worse every year. It's not too hard to figure out why. In
the past thirty years, crime—especially violent crime—has skyrocketed. From the 1960s to the 1990s the reported violent
crime rate has trebled. The actual number of violent crimes
committed, including those unreported, is five times today what
it was in 1960. The number of arrests has, not surprisingly, sky-

rocketed. *But the numbers of judges and courtrooms have stayed pretty much the same.*

We are pushing an ever-increasing number of criminals through a court system that was designed and staffed for better, more civilized times. As if that were not bad enough, because of the Warren Court's criminal rights revolution, the amount of time spent on each case is immeasurably greater today than it was in 1960. Evidence-suppression hearings are enormously costly. Still, we have about the same number of judges and courtrooms.

Conducting a criminal court calendar has become one of the most depressing and tedious experiences one can imagine. A tidal wave of guilty humanity washes through the court system every day—one young man after another. Assault, murder, rape, sale of crack or heroin. One young man after another. One more plea bargain to keep the system from collapsing altogether under the weight of one more guilty defendant. I do not exaggerate one bit. Tom Wolfe wrote eloquently of the Bronx Criminal Courts in *The Bonfire of the Vanities,* but he might as well have been writing about the criminal courts in any major city in the United States. This is what it's really like:

> Every year forty thousand people, forty thousand incompetents, dimwits, alcoholics, psychopaths, knockabouts, good souls driven to some terrible terminal anger, and people who could only be described as stone evil, were arrested in the Bronx. Seven thousand of them were indicted and arraigned and then they entered the maw of the criminal justice system. . . . And to what end? The same stupid, dismal, pathetic horrifying crimes were committed day in and day out, all the same. What was accomplished by assistant DAs, by any of them, through all this relentless stirring of the muck? The Bronx crumbled and decayed a little more, and a little more blood dried in the cracks.

Wolfe wrote that passage over ten years ago. Today things are ten years worse. This part of the problem is simple to define: There are far too many criminal (and civil) cases, and not nearly enough judges, courtrooms, bailiffs, or clerks. Judges' caseloads are far too heavy and their pay is far too low.

I know my saying this will irritate and perhaps even infuriate some of you who may feel that judges are overpaid and underworked. If you believe this, listen up for a moment. We want to have good judges. We need them. Successful private attorneys earn from three to ten times what a judge earns. That's a fact. There is also a rapidly expanding private judges' market. A retired judge can earn two to five times his salary as a judge by leaving the bench and going into private dispute resolution, while still keeping his retirement benefits. That's a fact. The numbing workload before every trial judge makes the job a terrible burden; we have raised the price of serving as a judge hugely over the past thirty years. That's a fact. When I began as a young lawyer, I was privileged to appear before many veteran judges with years of experience—wise judges who guided and taught young attorneys. Today those same judges have taken early retirement so they can do private judging. Why? So they can put their sons and daughters through college and provide for their families in these increasingly difficult times—just like you and me. And that, too, is a fact. As a consequence, the judiciary is suffering a major loss of experience and talent. We, the public, are being shortchanged.

We must improve working conditions and pay for our good judges. Criminal justice is no different from anything else; we get exactly what we pay for. If we want to get tough on crime, we must have the capability to process the criminals through our court system in a way that guarantees them due process. We must have good judges to supervise the process. We cannot get tough on crime without paying for the facilities to do so, and the criminal courts are a crucial part of those facilities.

You, your friends, your city council members, your county supervisors, your state assemblymen, your congressmen and senators all need to bite the bullet and realize criminal justice is not free. We have to demand that our politicians stop the "get tough" charade. You want to get tough on crime? Make the politicians allot your tax money for more courtrooms, more judges, more clerks, more bailiffs (and, yes, more prisons). With enough courtrooms, we could stop criminals from plea-bargaining to far lesser crimes than they actually committed. We could try them and let them serve the terms they deserve. We can either support these types of measures or sit back and let our politicians *pretend* they are getting tough by passing legislation like the "three strikes" law.

Continuing Judicial Education

Even if we were to fund the judicial system properly, that would still not take care of the problem of bad or poorly trained judges. Let me tell you a little secret. When I became a judge, I had years of daily courtroom experience as a trial lawyer. I discovered to my shock that I was not "born" a judge. It's hard. Judging is a craft. Judging is something you learn how to do. In most states there are judicial education programs, as well as "trial colleges" for judges. All judges should be encouraged and given the opportunity to attend these, which should include mandatory, public-oriented courses that train judges in *creating the appearance of courtroom fairness and ethics, and relating to the public in an effective and positive role.* Such programs should be improved and expanded—some tailored to new judges and some tailored to the continuing education of our existing judges. I know this is not a really "sexy" recommendation, but my experience tells me such programs are tremendously useful.

Judicial Elections

Judicial elections are another way to hold our judges accountable to the people. If our judges are bad, we can throw them out, or so the theory goes. Let's take a step back for a moment. When we became a nation we created a legislative branch of government, which was to be directly answerable to the electorate. If we want tougher laws against criminal recidivists, we tell our legislators to enact a "three strikes" law for our protection. If our congressional representatives say to us, "I don't think it's really such a good idea," we can refuse to vote for them in the next election. In fact, we can and do vigorously campaign to defeat them if we feel strongly enough. They're our representatives, and we are entitled to have our values and desires reflected in our laws. Legislators can either go against our wishes and risk defeat in the next election, or thus yield to our pressures and enact such legislation. The same is true for our executives—the governors and our president. We're tired of crime. So sign the damn bill! Heavy-handed, yes. Appropriate, yes. All is fair in the give-and-take of politics.

Now suppose the governor has signed the bill, and a criminal defendant, convicted under the new "three strikes" law, challenges its constitutionality. Can we go to the trial judge and say, "Look here, we told our legislators to pass the law, we told our governor to sign the law, and now we want you to leave it alone and uphold our will. If you declare this law to be unconstitutional against our will, we will vote against you in the next judicial election and give lots of money to your opponent." As you might imagine, to try to influence a judicial decision in this manner is totally improper. It is wrong to threaten a judge with defeat at the polls, were he or she not to rule in accordance with public sentiment. In fact, depending on the circumstances, it is a crime. Why? The judiciary is our buffer, if you will, against the tyranny of a runaway majority. It is a crucial part of the checks and balances between the legitimate will of the people and constitutionally impermissible majoritarian mob rule.

So, if the judiciary is supposed to act as a buffer against majoritarian mob rule, why do we have judicial elections? Doesn't it seem contradictory to have judges come back to the angry people to seek reelection for doing their job? How can judges be independent if they have to campaign? Historically, judicial elections are something of an anomaly in the United States. Right after the American Revolution, judges were appointed. Slowly various states began to provide for judicial elections, some authorizing them only for the lower courts, others permitting elections for the highest courts. In California, for example, the municipal and superior courts, which comprise the trial courts, are subject to contested judicial elections. That is, one person can try to unseat another person for judge. You run for judge in California. The appellate courts in California, including the Supreme Court, are subject to periodic retention elections in which a simple majority yes vote will keep them in office for another term, while a simple no vote will send them back to obscurity. The people of California exercised this "retention election" right resoundingly with former California Supreme Court justice Rose Bird and several other members of her court, who were not retained for another term. Variants on this California election system exist in many states.

Look at the consequences of contested elections for trial judges. If a trial judge makes an unpopular ruling (such as ordering school desegregation as *mandated* by the higher courts), he or she will likely be defeated in the next election. That happened to us in Los Angeles. Judge Gittleson desegregated the L.A. schools. He had no choice under the orders and rulings of higher courts. Yet Judge Gittleson got the blame, and we lost a very fine trial judge, one with unimpeachable integrity, intelligence, and experience. Contested judicial elections tend to encourage judges to compromise their rulings, lest they encourage the wrath of the public, ensuring their defeat at the polls. Legislators, governors, and presidents can take polls to see what the public wants. But a judge should not take public opinion into consideration, no matter how strong it is, unless it is directly relevant to ascertaining the *legitimate* will of the people where that itself is an *issue* in the case before him. Do we want judges to vote the will of special interests so they will contribute to costly reelection campaigns? Do we want an ignorant, corrupt, and dependent judiciary? Or must we insist on a "complete independence of the courts of justice," which, as Alexander Hamilton said, "is peculiarly essential in a limited constitution"?

While judicial independence is great in theory, there is another side to this problem. If trial judges are too independent and untouchable, they often become arrogant and imperious. Our two-hundred-year experiment with Article III federal judges is not encouraging. Horror stories abound from the darkened chambers of the federal courts. When judges become lifetime appointees, it seems that at times they think they are in lockstep with God.

I wish there were an easy solution. There isn't. There is only a balancing of the need for simultaneous independence and accountability. I recommend that, except for the United States Supreme Court and the highest courts of each state, we should eliminate life appointments. All other judges, federal and state alike, should be subject to retention elections every ten to fifteen years. In this way, the judges would not be subjected to the whims and caprice of public sentiment, but rather have a chance to establish a track record of valued performance and service in the judiciary. In essence, they would run on the merits of their own performance over a period of years. The costs of most retention elections, being a fraction of the costs of contested elections, consequently require little if any economic assistance from parties who have the potential to influence a judge's decision. Thus the appearance of impropriety is avoided. The period of ten to fifteen years between elections is necessary to attract qualified judges, who, after giving up an established law practice, deserve a sufficient degree of stability for a reasonable period of time.

Judicial Review Commissions

So many pressures are brought to bear on a judge that I sometimes wonder why anyone who is sane and has *other* interests in life would want to be one. Judicial review commissions sometimes seem to accomplish nothing more than to make the life of a judge completely impossible.

Clearly, being a judge has its rewards and privileges. But the rewards are fewer and fewer as the caseload becomes more and more numbing by the year. The toll rises higher and higher as we have become much more cynical, militant, and vociferous about the performance of our judges. Unfortunately, much of this militancy is fueled by the media, which give us only sound bites of information or misinformation with which to assess the integrity and competency of a judge. The media are far more aggressive today in seeking out sensational stories that seemingly demonstrate judicial impropriety. The media do not seem to care that most of the charges of impropriety are proven wrong after a long and arduous process, a process that leaves the judge compromised, burned out, and bitter. Having appeared before many judges, I have had my doubts about some of them. But, unlike the public, who was kept at bay, I had a basis in fact for concluding that a particular judge was not up to snuff. I am not smarter than the public, nor do I have superior judgment. I simply had the information—information rarely made public.

Sometimes the lines are blurred between the needs for judicial *independence* and judicial *accountability.* Under the guise of independence, the judiciary has sometimes wrapped itself in a cocoon of impenetrable secrecy. While state constitutions generally provide for an impeachment mechanism for corrupt and incompetent judges, impeachment is so unwieldy it remains unused. The burden of removing incompetent or corrupt judges, or those guilty of willful misconduct in office, defaults to the state commissions on judicial performance (or whatever euphemism is used to describe the self-monitoring mechanisms in each state).

Again we have a balancing act. Judicial oversight programs should let us get rid of bad judges and change the behavior of others. But judicial oversight programs cannot be so public and so Orwellian that they drive off the good judges. The danger of more openness is that the media would pounce on routine announcements of an investigation, fueling the fires of discontent, bringing even more disrespect to an already embattled judiciary. If we make the life of our good judges even more unpleasant by confronting them with aggressive media and aggressive judicial oversight bodies that publicize every complaint, regardless of merit, our good judges will just quit. Private alternate dispute-resolution programs that offer arbitration, mediation, and trials—outside the regular public court system—to those who can afford them are already sucking up the reservoir of experienced sitting judges whose salaries we paid while they acquired the expertise and skills of judging. Instead of giving us more of their productive years on the bench, when they are performing at their peak levels of achievement, they opt to retire, take a deferred or immediate pension, and reap the rewards of private judging.

Certainly, public trust in the judiciary would be enhanced if the commissions were permitted to release more information about judicial investigations. Not only would the public benefit, but so would the judge, who may be a victim of a groundless and specious attack. But if all commission proceedings were to be public, witnesses, including lawyers and judicial colleagues, might be more reluctant to testify against an errant judge for fear that the "dirty laundry" would bring the judiciary into greater disrepute, or that groundless allegations would sully an otherwise unblemished career.

Once again, a balance is absolutely necessary. Here is what I recommend:

1. The judicial oversight commission should be allowed to release explanatory statements about investigations it undertakes.

2. All complaints about judicial misconduct should be subject to a preliminary investigation that is private. The purpose of the preliminary investigation would be to determine whether there is sufficient validity to the claims of misconduct to justify further proceedings.

3. Any conduct amounting to a crime or moral turpitude must be addressed in public hearings once a preliminary investigation has determined good cause. Until then, it shall remain private.

4. Housekeeping hearings relating to minor behavioral problems, such as rudeness to court staff, witnesses, parties to a lawsuit, or lawyers, should remain private so that corrective measures can be taken without staining the judge's character or career.

5. Any behavior not amounting to a crime or involving moral turpitude or serious character flaws should be privately redressed with an emphasis on abating the offensive conduct through education, therapy, and training. In this way, the public benefits by a swift and effective intervention. If the conduct continues, it should be grounds for removal, since it would bring the judiciary into disrepute.

Summary

To my judicial colleagues, I say: You've been there before. Judging is like being a referee. It's not about popularity, it's about being effective, fair, and evenhanded. It's about respect for yourself, for those who appear before you (including lawyers), and for your special position of public trust. It is human nature to want to be loved and appreciated and admired. Sometimes that is not possible when you are a judge. It is lonely and difficult at times, and painful to do what is right: to stop misbehavior, to sanction a colleague—perhaps even a friend. We, the public, expect no less. No deals. No steals. Take full control of your courtroom, set clear standards and rules for the conduct of trials, rein in adversarial excesses, and impart a reverence for the law. Then you will be entitled to, and will receive, the appreciation and esteem of a grateful public.

Witnesses—Part I

Ah, witnesses. They come in all sizes and forms. Some God-fearing, others defiant; killers, pimps, hucksters, snitches, coconspirators . . . victims, children, senior citizens, experts—all kinds, all colors. The witnesses are the cables of communication . . . if we only strain to listen. Even when they're lying, if we try really hard, we can hear the truth in the spaces of their testimony. Let's look at a few different witnesses and see what was done and how we could have done it better.

Coconspirators

Mary Brunner

Many times it is very difficult to prove a crime against one or more individuals because of the absence of independent eyewitnesses. Resorting to the use of coconspirator witnesses is sometimes required. Coconspirators present unique challenges. By definition, conspirators contrive to commit crimes in secrecy. Establishing guilt is especially difficult where the only proof against a defendant consists of the observations by a coconspirator (accomplice) of statements made and actions performed by the other in the planning and preparation stages of the crime. Indeed, statements or conduct, standing alone, may be perfectly legal and, when observed by a non-criminal witness, without more information, may be unremarkable and meaningless. Here is an example: Suppose George Washington conspired to overthrow British colonial rule in America. In secret, he told Alexander Hamilton and Thomas Jefferson that they should publish a paper exhorting the colonists to "break the shackles of their servitude" to imperialist England, and to demand autonomy for the colonies. To that end, Jefferson and Hamilton proceed to legally purchase printing supplies consisting of paper and ink. Further, they arrange for the use of a printing press.

Those legal acts, standing alone, prove nothing without evidence of the unlawful purpose. Thus the testimony of Jefferson or Hamilton would be required to establish the fact of a conspiracy, implicating Washington. Then those acts committed in furtherance of the conspiracy, such as the purchase of the ink and paper, *even if legal when standing alone,* can be used against all members of the conspiracy as evidence of the crime.

There is a catch, however. The law, in its wisdom, requires that the accomplice's testimony be corroborated because of the inherent "untrustworthiness" of its source! Because an accomplice has an obvious motive to fabricate, the jury is instructed to view an accomplice's testimony with caution.

Problems are compounded when the accomplice is reluctant to testify and has an abiding allegiance to the defendant coconspirator. Such was the case with Mary Brunner, one of the most troubling witnesses I ever had. Mary was well on her way to earning a master's degree at the University of Wisconsin, engaged to a "professional student," when she decided that being a faculty wife and giving tea parties was not what she wanted out of life. So she quit and moved to California, acquiring a job as a librarian at the prestigious University of California Berkeley. She met and fell in love with Charles Manson, a charismatic iconoclast, spiritually light-years from her comfortable world of academia and books. She came from a stable and supportive family, though her parents were distant, displaying little outward affection. Mary was to become the first of the Manson family women, moving into an old, ratty school bus with Charlie in 1967. Manson sired her son, "Pooh Bear," legally named Michael Manson. She was attracted to what Manson seemingly had to offer: freedom to be a child, to be oneself, to love, to experience the warmth, sense of belonging, and adventure of communal living. This seductive lifestyle was later to transmigrate into "Charlie's death trip," culminating in her willing participation in the murder of Gary Hinman.

In return for an immunity agreement fashioned over several

months of difficult negotiations with Mary and her attorney, veteran civil rights lawyer Hugh Manis, she reluctantly agreed to testify. The immunity was conditioned on Mary testifying *truthfully* in *all* of the Manson family cases involving the murder of musician Gary Hinman, including any Hinman murder testimony to be presented in the penalty phase of the Tate-LaBianca murder trial. In addition to Bobby Beausoleil, who was already charged, we were in the process of seeking murder indictments against Charles Manson, Bruce Davis, and Susan Atkins for the Hinman murder.

Mary, in fact, testified truthfully before the grand jury and in the guilt phase of the Bobby Beausoleil trial. Beausoleil, nicknamed "Cupid," was drop-dead handsome, and the alleged procurer for Manson, bringing new female blood to the family's quarters at Spahn Ranch. After the jury returned a verdict of first-degree murder, a death verdict was imposed by the same jury in the penalty phase. This so shook up Brunner, who felt enormous guilt over Beausoleil's plight and her perceived betrayal of Manson and the family, that she seriously contemplated suicide.

Following her guilt-phase testimony, Mary had returned to her mother's home in Wisconsin. Between the time of the rendering of the death verdict and the formal sentencing hearing, Squeaky Fromme, Sandy Good, and Brenda McCann paid Mary a goodwill visit. Shortly thereafter, we heard she was going to recant her testimony, alleging that sheriffs Charlie Guenther and Paul Whitely and the DA (me) forced her to testify against her will, falsely. The integrity of the jury's verdict rested on our discrediting her allegations. Our dilemma was not to undermine her credibility so much that her testimony before the grand jury and the Beausoleil jury was rendered useless. At times that seemed to be impossible.

When we originally struck a deal with Brunner, we were unaware of the true extent of her involvement in the Hinman killing. We had been led to believe that she was passively present while Bobby Beausoleil and Susan Atkins (a.k.a. Sadie Glutz) did Manson's bidding. After she agreed to cooperate, with the encouragement and support of her biological family, we were to learn disturbing additional facts. By then it was too late to withdraw our offer of immunity. I was heartsick that we had to give Brunner immunity, knowing the things she had done.

Now we were at the Beausoleil sentencing hearing, where a motion for new trial was being sought. Beausoleil, having dismissed his public defender and acting as his own counsel, recalled Mary Brunner. He conducted a very credible and competent examination of Brunner. And here was Brunner, trying to wiggle out of her commitment. Before she testified for Beausoleil, I reminded her that the immunity agreement was off if she stuck to her recantation story. Secretly, I was glad she was recanting her testimony; we would now be free to bring charges against her for her remorseless participation in a torture-murder in which Gary Hinman was told he should get ready to die. A murder in which he was given his religious beads so that he could chant to his God, after being stabbed in the chest. A murder in which he was told by Beausoleil "that he was a pig and that society did not need him . . . this was the best way for him to go. . . ." Beausoleil had told Hinman that he was just doing him a favor! A day earlier, Manson himself had slashed Hinman's face with a sword, viciously cutting his left ear in half, before leaving his victim in the deathwatch of Sadie, Mary, and Bobby, to suffer another day of indignity and abuse before Manson ordered Beausoleil to kill him. No, I wanted all deals to be off. To this day, I still think of Hinman, a gentle soul, being tortured, debased, and snuffed; his blood used to write the words "Political Piggy" on the wall above his body. Tears still come to my eyes. I wanted to charge her with murder.

Brunner was obviously torn between her loyalty to Manson and Beausoleil and her own well-being. It was incredible to think that after being handed her life back, she was going to throw it all away—including her son, whose custody she was desperately trying to regain. Her son, fathered by Charles Manson!

Judge William B. Keene presided over the Beausoleil case. Keene was an imposing judge who commanded respect. He was later to become the TV judge in *Divorce Court* and other TV judge-oriented shows, aided by his telegenic appearance and very droll wit. Keene began the hearing with a stern admonition to Brunner:

KEENE: It's previously been established . . . in consideration of your testifying . . . in front of the grand jury and in front of the jury in the case of Mr. Beausoleil, both of which you have done, and in any *future* criminal trial that may arise out of the death of Gary Hinman, that you personally were to be granted immunity. . . . You have fulfilled only a portion of that agreement with the office of the district attorney. Now, in the event that you testify here in this case, it is my belief that you will be arrested upon leaving this courtroom and charged with the crime of murder in connection with the death of Gary Hinman. . . . In the event that does occur and you testify here today, anything that you say here . . . can and undoubtedly will be used against you at any trial in which you are charged with the crime of murder. Do you understand what I've told you?

BRUNNER: Yes, sir.

KEENE: Do you understand the serious ramifications to you personally by your giving any testimony in this court this morning?

BRUNNER: Yes, sir.

KEENE: I might also suggest and point out to you, Miss Brunner, that if you do testify . . . in response to any questions asked you by Mr. Beausoleil, this court will ask you to answer all questions directed to you not only by Mr. Beausoleil but by Mr. Katz; do you understand that?

BRUNNER: Yeah, I understand that.

Brunner prepared to lay down her life for Beausoleil as he began his coolly delivered examination.

BEAUSOLEIL: Are you also aware of the fact that beyond being charged with murder that you could be charged with perjury?

BRUNNER: Yeah, that occurred to me.

BEAUSOLEIL: And very probably violation of probation, isn't that correct?

This was important, because this would affect her ability to get her baby back. Beausoleil began to focus on Paul Whitely and Charlie Guenther's first visit to Madison, Wisconsin, in December 1969. He probed into the alleged threats and attempts used to induce her to testify against him and Manson. I was impressed with his ability to frame a comprehensible question and ask appropriate follow-up questions. He also interposed objections, and while they fell on deaf ears, they were quite well done. I couldn't help thinking about Beausoleil's natural gifts. He was handsome, articulate, intelligent, a quick study and a gifted poet, artist, and musician who had his own rock group in Berkeley, competing favorably with the emerging but still relatively unknown Credence Clearwater Revival band. What seed or gene had distorted an otherwise almost perfect genetic blueprint, allowing him to execute another human being, a friend with whom he had lived? He had mortgaged his life on "Charlie's death trip"! What a waste!

His questions were deceptively simple, demonstrating a skill far beyond many lawyers' reach. Brunner and Beausoleil were rocking to each other's rhythm. Yet Beausoleil was given virtually no time alone with Brunner for preparation. His communication was limited to his Manson family visitors, such as Sandy and Squeaky, who were his conduits.

BEAUSOLEIL: In reference to how you feel about your child, how do you feel about your child? Let me rephrase the question. You love your child very much, don't you?

BRUNNER: Yes.

BEAUSOLEIL: I would imagine that he probably means more to you than anything else in the world—isn't that correct?

BRUNNER: Than most anything else.

BEAUSOLEIL: Anything means more to you?

BRUNNER: Yeah.

BEAUSOLEIL: Could you tell the court what it is?

BRUNNER: It means more to me, Bobby, that I undo what I did to you.

BEAUSOLEIL: When you say that—to undo what you did, did you not tell the truth at that time?

BRUNNER: That's right.

He's done it. She has recanted her testimony, and now Judge Keene is saddled with a real problem. There is not a chance in the world that a death verdict in 1970 will stand the scrutiny of the California Supreme Court on that record. Just two years later, that court was to declare California's death penalty law unconstitutional. The ruling was retroactively applied to all on death row, including Sirhan Sirhan, Manson, and serial killer Juan Corona, who slaughtered twenty-six victims.

On top of this, the guilty verdict was also in grave jeopardy as Beausoleil returned to the theme of Guenther's alleged undue influence. She told the court of Guenther's approach: "He got very soft-voiced and very earnest and very, you know, look you real deep in the eye . . . type emotion." Evidently, Charlie Guenther had met his match with this young woman, who was indeed very, very hard.

Judge Keene, over the protestations of Beausoleil, now took over the questioning.

KEENE: What did he [Guenther] say?

BRUNNER: He was telling me how wonderful they were being to me, and how everybody out here was ratting on me and bad-mouthing me and how if I felt anything for my son that I owed it to him to give a statement against Bobby.

KEENE: Did that end the conversation then, between you and Deputy Guenther?

BRUNNER: Around this time I got to crying and Whitely came back into the room.

KEENE: Now tell us what was said.

BEAUSOLEIL: Your Honor, I object to the court questioning the witness. I am completely capable. She is my witness. I'd like to question her now, if I may.

The court refused, but I've always thought that Beausoleil
was right. He was addressing issues relevant to this hearing—
namely, what were the pressures brought to bear on Brunner?
Had such pressures caused her to testify falsely because she
feared she would lose her child, be imprisoned and charged
with murder? In fact, she was warned repeatedly of the consequence of a capital charge if she failed to cooperate. These are
tough questions. While it is not unlawful to spell out to a coconspirator what her options are, and the consequences of failure to
cooperate, there is a point where the onerous consequences
might influence testimony. Judge Keene had the unhappy task
of trying to sort it out, to determine whether these factors over-
came free will *and* caused her to give false testimony. I was not
envious of the judge's position. He overruled Beausoleil's objection and pursued the witness, pressing her to repeat what she
had told Guenther and Whitely about the Hinman killing. I
watched with fascination as Beausoleil fought Keene, toe to toe,
for his life.

KEENE: All right, tell us what you said, what you told the
officers.

BEAUSOLEIL: Your Honor, she's given this information already.
She told the court that it was the same as what she testified
to, or at least basically. There's a forty-page written
statement, Your Honor, of a conversation that happened
later after she gave her original statement and it has been
testified to by Sergeant Whitely that the questions that he
asked were based on statements given—

KEENE: Just a minute, Mr. Beausoleil. Your objection is
overruled. Tell us what you told the officers.

BRUNNER: I told the officers that Bobby killed Gary. That is the
main thing—I told the officers.

KEENE: What else did you tell them?

BRUNNER: I told them that Bobby and Gary had a fight. I told
them that Charlie cut Gary with a sword. I told them we
had been in that house for a couple of days, Bobby and
Sadie and I.

KEENE: Was that statement true?

BRUNNER: Parts of it.

KEENE: All right, what parts were true and what parts were not true?

BRUNNER: Bobby didn't kill Gary.

Now the confrontation is focused. If Bobby didn't, who did? Brunner is backed into a corner. She can't selectively pick and choose which questions she will answer. And the judge goes for the jugular.

KEENE: Who killed Gary?

BRUNNER: I don't have to answer that.

KEENE: Yes, you do have to answer that and—

Beausoleil quickly jumps in—to save Brunner's testimonial recantation!

BEAUSOLEIL: Your Honor, I object—Your Honor—

KEENE: —you are ordered to answer that by this court.

BRUNNER: I'll take the Fifth Amendment on that.

KEENE: You may not take the Fifth Amendment. As I indicated to you, you could not pick and choose what questions you were going to answer.

BRUNNER: I have the right not to incriminate myself.

Bobby and Mary had anticipated everything. Or so they thought. But *this* judge was not to be intimidated by a claim of self-incrimination—even in a capital case. Contrast this with the Simpson case, where Judge Ito let Mark Furhman take the Fifth on the issue of having used a racial epithet in the last ten years— after fully testifying before a jury just weeks before. Judge Keene was an exceptionally strong judge who did not look over his shoulder in anticipation of an adverse appellate ruling. The O.J. team would have fared quite differently under Keene's iron fist.

BEAUSOLEIL: May I be heard?

KEENE: Mr. Beausoleil, you may not. Your objection is
overruled.

BEAUSOLEIL: You haven't heard my objection, how can it be
overruled?

KEENE: Just a minute, Mr. Beausoleil. [To Brunner.] I've
ordered you to answer that question as to who killed Gary
Hinman.

BRUNNER: I'm telling you that I don't have to incriminate
myself, as you advised me.

The courtroom was packed to standing-room capacity, filled
with media from all over the world, including the Soviet bloc na-
tions. The tension was so palpable you could skate on it. I wondered how we were playing in the Iron Curtain countries, whose
correspondents were feverishly scribbling in their pads, eager to
show the "disintegration of a corrupt capitalistic society."

KEENE: . . . you tell me in your own words truthfully what
occurred in that Hinman house to the best of your
knowledge, and I want the truth.

BEAUSOLEIL: Judge Keene, you are denying this woman a fair
trial according to *Miranda v. Arizona,* according to the
Fourteenth Amendment of the Constitution, the due
process clause, according to the rights under the Fifth
Amendment, according to her rights to have an attorney
present.

KEENE: Mr. Beausoleil, your objections, all of them, are
overruled.

BEAUSOLEIL: All of my objections are overruled, even the ones
I'm going to make?

Pretty quick thinking for a non-lawyer, unschooled in trial
tactics.

KEENE (to the witness): Go ahead and tell me what happened.

BEAUSOLEIL: In other words—

KEENE: Mr. Beausoleil, this is the last time I am going to tell you. When I am finished talking to this witness, I will tell you so, and you may ask her some questions. I do not want you to interrupt me.

Bobby stayed a steady course, cool and deliberate. No anger. Just control. It made me wonder how cool he must have been when he ended Hinman's life!

BEAUSOLEIL: Your Honor, I have a duty to interrupt you. I have a duty to make my objections.

Judge Keene continues to sidestep Beausoleil. But Brunner won't budge. She tells Judge Keene she will not answer the question because of self-incrimination.

KEENE: You refuse to answer any questions as to what occurred in that house?

BRUNNER: You've told me—your question was that I tell you everything that went on. That was your question?

KEENE: Yes, that's what I want.

BRUNNER: And if that is your question, I can't answer that because it would be self-incriminating.

KEENE: I am instructing you to answer the question.

BRUNNER (defiantly): I've answered it.

We had reached an impasse. Judge Keene could proceed no further. The record was a shambles. The court had the option of striking her testimony of recantation because of her refusal to answer all questions on the issue. But, as noted, this was a capital case that must stand the scrutiny of a strongly anti-capital-punishment California Supreme Court—and it was unlikely to pass constitutional muster. Judge Keene found Brunner in contempt of court, and ordered her remanded until she answered the questions. But first he allowed Beausoleil to continue his questioning of Brunner.

Again, Beausoleil's facileness surprised me. Beausoleil was sharp enough to ask her if there was a tape recorder at the sheriff's office when she claimed they told her that if she didn't "bring Charlie into it now that this whole business of immunity would be dropped . . . that her probation would be violated and she would not be able to see her baby when she was charged with murder." Beausoleil pressed further, asking her whether anyone had turned the tape recorder on. He then got her to say that it wasn't in any written statement she had seen! Not bad. He also wanted to know if anyone had turned the tape recorder off for any interval. Shades of Nixon's secretary, Rosemary Woods, and the infamous "eighteen-minute gap" of Watergate fame. I'd say that was damn good lawyering for a twenty-two-year-old man with little formal education.

Judge Keene stopped the proceedings again, telling Brunner that she had filed an affidavit stating that her testimony before the grand jury and before the Beausoleil jury was false. He now wanted her entire statement. She refused, and was remanded to the custody of the sheriff over the lunch hour. Over her initial objection, attorney Ernest Graves was appointed by the court to represent her, owing to Manis's unavailability. Beausoleil was permitted to have a short meeting with Graves and Brunner.

In the afternoon session, she appeared with Graves. This time Brunner appeared tired and confused. Graves asked for a clarification of Brunner's status, if she were to testify fully and truthfully at this hearing. The immunity agreement was reiterated, with emphasis that she was obligated, as jointly agreed, to testify in future proceedings against Charlie Manson and other family members. Judge Keene, sensing a change, immediately withdrew the contempt charge, making it clear that he would not use this to compel her testimony, and emphasizing that what she was about to do must be totally free and voluntary.

Brunner wanted to know if she was free to go back to Wisconsin, "if I testify for the prosecution."

We were at a critical point, and Beausoleil looked pale and scared as he sensed what was coming.

BRUNNER: If I testify today, then I can just walk out of the courtroom and go back to Wisconsin?

The court told her she could, as long as she remained available for the other trials.

BRUNNER: Is that the DA's contention, too?

She was told it was. Present in the packed courtroom were Squeaky, Sandy, Catherine Share, and Kitty Lutesinger (Bobby's girlfriend), among others. Brunner was obviously highly stressed. She appeared to be communicating nonverbally with Squeaky and the others. We were all standing on earthen clods, crumbling into a sinkhole of unknown depth. Would Mary turn on Bobby in front of the girls, in front of her "sisters"? Unknown to me at that time was the enormously powerful pull of the family women—these women were the eyes, ears, and legs of Charlie. They also carried buck knives openly displayed on their hips while they camped out at the corner of the Hall of Justice, proudly exhibiting the X's carved on their foreheads, just like Charlie Manson, Sadie, Leslie, and Katie. All, X'd out of society. And those knives were virtually identical to the ones used in the Tate-LaBianca massacres. Sandy, Squeaky, Brenda, and Gypsy were fond of rubbing their hands up and down the handles of the knives as I passed them each day on my way to court. Graves, sensing he was losing Mary, asked for some time to confer with her. I began to wonder: What's this justice system all about? Does the foreign press have contempt for all of this nonsense, for our way of justice? I was lost in thought when Graves's voice suddenly startled me.

GRAVES: Your Honor, I believe the witness is again prepared to meet the question whether she is prepared to testify in this case.

KEENE: What's your decision, now, Miss Brunner?

BRUNNER: I'll testify.

KEENE: . . . Do I have your assurance that anything that you are going to testify to at this time is going to be the truth and nothing but the truth, so help you God?

BRUNNER: Yes.

KEENE: In its entirety, without question—is that correct?

BRUNNER: That's right.

Mary told the court why she filed the false affidavit.

BRUNNER: Bobby got the gas chamber, and that to me, is the same—you're doing the same thing to him as he did to Gary, and you made me a part of the second one, too. . . . So I filed it hoping that Bobby could get a retrial and not get the death penalty.

The court again asked who had stabbed Gary, and who had sliced Gary's face with the sword, to which she replied it was Bobby and Charlie.

Keene turned over the examination to me. I wanted to nail down her testimony against Charlie, Bruce Davis, and Susan Atkins, to give her less wiggle room when she was called to testify at their trials. She confirmed her earlier testimony. I had her confirm that she *and* Susan put the pillow over the dying Gary's face to silence his death rattle. I also wanted to pin her down on her alleged reason for filing the false affidavit.

KATZ: You contrived the fact that you would execute a false affidavit to secure a new trial for Mr. Beausoleil in the hopes that he would not receive the death penalty; is that correct, as you told Judge Keene?

Her pithy "Yeah" locked her in, or so I thought.

I then directed a series of short questions on key points to forever lay to rest the accuracy of her testimony: Did she have any doubt that Beausoleil stabbed Hinman? any doubt that she and Susan Atkins put a pillow over Gary's head? any doubt that she drove to Hinman's house with Susan Atkins and Bobby Beausoleil? any doubt that Charlie Manson and Bruce Davis arrived together at Hinman's house? any doubt that Manson struck Hinman with a sword, severing his left ear? Finally she admitted that the affidavit she had filed was false.

A disheartened Beausoleil gamely tried to come back, but Mary wouldn't look at him. "Mary, look at me, please. . . ." He suggested that she was testifying this way because of the same fear she had felt before, with Guenther and Whitely, that she would be charged with a capital murder and would lose her baby. Bobby decided to go for it.

BEAUSOLEIL: Okay, I'll ask one question and hope that I do get the truth. You testified in my trial previously in April that you saw me standing over Gary's body, but you didn't actually see me stab Gary, but you saw me standing over Gary's body with the knife. Was that statement correct or incorrect?

BRUNNER: That I saw you standing over—it's like one of those questions, Bobby, that the DA feeds me, you know, and it comes out, well, could it have happened this way, you know, but I can't say that it did happen that way. Right now what happened at Gary's house, you know—like—well—did I actually see you standing over him? I can't recall right now. I can't picture it right now.

Mary was at the point of emotional collapse, and Bobby took a final shot at her.

BEAUSOLEIL: Would you lie to save your child? Would you please tell me the truth?

BRUNNER: It's a hard question to answer.

BEAUSOLEIL: That isn't an answer.

BRUNNER: What did you say?

BEAUSOLEIL: That isn't an answer.

BRUNNER: You're right, it isn't an answer.

BEAUSOLEIL: Would you give me the answer to the question? Mary, look at me. Would you give me the answer to the question and give me the truth. You know the truth, and you know that I know the truth.

BRUNNER: Bobby, you know I'd do anything.

BEAUSOLEIL: Anything for the child?

BRUNNER: Uh-huh.

BEAUSOLEIL: Including lying for him—isn't that correct? Is your answer yes?

BRUNNER: Yes.

Bobby, having nothing to lose, takes another stab at it:

BEAUSOLEIL: I want the truth. Did I kill Gary Hinman? And please look at me when you answer me.

We all waited for the answer. Then Mary's lawyer made an objection. The court jumped in, over Beausoleil's protest. Beausoleil was forced to surrender his witness to the court for the last time. The stakes were too high.

KEENE: Did he stab Mr. Hinman?

BRUNNER: Yeah.

For now it was over. But not for Mary Brunner—she was to perjure herself in the penalty phase of the trial of Charles Manson for the Tate and LaBianca killings, and once again in the Hinman prosecutions. And she was to be charged with the murder of Gary Hinman and with perjury, just as Guenther and Whitely and I had promised. Howard Weitzman and James Patterson now represented Brunner. They filed a motion to dismiss the charges, contending that Brunner had fulfilled her obligations under the immunity agreement. To my amazement, the court agreed. We appealed, and the appellate court upheld the trial judge's ruling, likening the conditional offer of immunity to a simple contract in which the people had substantially received what they had bargained for. The appellate court was to note that, even with her false recantation, she had unwittingly helped the prosecution by setting the groundwork for the use of her grand-jury and Beausoleil trial testimony in the subsequent trials. Legal sophistry notwithstanding, we could not prosecute Brunner. To this day I still don't understand why the DA is not free to enter into a voluntary agreement with a witness, who is represented by counsel, and offer immunity conditioned on her *truthful* testimony in *multiple* proceedings, regardless of where it may fall. In such a situation there is no more danger of inducing an untruthful story than there is when someone is offered immunity for her testimony in a single proceeding. But who am I to say?

There are some lessons to be learned from the Brunner experience:

1. Given today's technology, all statements taken by the police should be videotaped. No off-the-record conversations; no softening up of the witness off the record, before the formal tape is started. The entire record should be available for review so that the trier of fact can assess the credibility of the witnesses, based upon the totality of the circumstances in which they give their statements and offer their testimony.

2. The DA and the witness should be allowed to enter into a voluntary agreement in which the DA offers immunity on the basis of the fulfillment of mutually agreed conditions. Those conditions cannot transcend existing public policy against the imposition of requirements that are likely to generate or induce the giving of a false testimony. Thus it must be clear that the DA is not entitled to a particular set of facts without which immunity will not be granted; rather, the DA is only entitled to the truth—wherever that may lie. The only remedy the DA has for diametrically opposed testimony given under oath is to retain the power to charge perjury, if it can be established that the witness gave willfully false testimony about a material fact, with the intent to mislead the trier of fact.

To facilitate proof, a statute should state clearly that a presumption of perjury exists when two diametrically opposed statements are made under oath. This would have the effect of placing the burden on the defendant to explain the inconsistent statement. Failure to do so could be considered by the jury in drawing adverse inferences therefrom. However, the ultimate burden of proof remains, as always, with the People.

3. A clear statement must appear in the record which demonstrates the witness's understanding that if the witness fails to live up to the immunity agreement, all testimony given will be used against the witness in any subsequent proceedings. A waiver of the privilege against self-incrimination as to all testimony must be reflected in the agreement.

4. The DA's agreement with the defendant must be video-taped in the same manner as any statements taken by the police.

5. An attorney must be present at the formalization of the immunity agreement, to represent and to advise witnesses of their rights, and to ensure that witnesses understand their obligations under the immunity agreement. A statement of the attorney's approval must appear on the videotape, including the statement that client-witnesses have knowingly, intelligently, freely, and voluntarily waived their privilege against self-incrimination as to the matters which are the subject of the agreement.

These changes will reduce the likelihood of undue duress and consequential untrustworthiness, and ensure that the witness clearly understands and voluntarily assents to the immunity agreement. They will also make it far more difficult to undermine an immunity agreement, as was done in the Brunner case.

What happened to Mary Brunner after the Beausoleil trial is another story to be told. Suffice it to say she returned to the Manson fold, joining her "sisters" and "brothers" at Temple and Broadway, her head shaved, an X etched into her forehead. Later she was to participate in a bold robbery, discussed in chapter 12, of a gun supply store, in which over fifty rounds of gunfire were exchanged with the police. Her purpose was to steal weapons to "free" Charlie Manson and to protect the family!

Jerry Sartain

Jerry Sartain presented substantial problems for the prosecution in the case of *People v. McKinney and Sartain*, discussed in chapter 2. In the Manson cases I was never concerned with which story Brunner told was the truth. Independent investigation, including numerous interviews with other witnesses, verified which story was true. Physical evidence corroborated the version we ultimately relied upon. This was not the case in *McKinney-Sartain.*

In chapter 2 you met Jerry, the cagey defendant who led us to the recovery of the buried .22 automatic with a silencer and the handcuffs used in a triple murder. He was the one who received a steak dinner and had a .38 police revolver directed at his gut as he ate! There were no independent eyewitnesses to the murders. Never was the old saying "When a crime is committed in hell, you don't have angels for witnesses" more applicable. The case was so weak that other deputy DAs refused to file it. I decided to go ahead after LAPD homicide officers Vinnie Barrett and Mike Maloney convinced me of Sartain and McKinney's involvement, but only after promising me an incredible follow-up investigation, which I outlined. The real test of justice is in the hard cases—where there are no eyewitnesses, just dead victims. Our strategy was to get one of the defendants to break. We needed the leverage of filing the case and some evidence pointing to each of the defendants, which admittedly would be insufficient to gain a conviction, but might be enough to scare one of them into cooperating with us. This is the kind of case that isn't going to get any better by waiting. Your choice is to do nothing and give up on the notion of bringing to justice those responsible for three brutal murders, or to take your best shot, hoping you can build your case as you inch toward the trial, always looking for a break, or just bits and pieces that begin to fill in a puzzle. We'll never get all the pieces, but maybe enough to present a compelling case before a jury.

The investigation was to reveal, as the appellate court said, "a whirligig of plot and counterplot, of perjury, theft and murder."

The information we had at the time of the filing was that Robert Loether, the manager of the NuWay Bar Lounge, owned by victims Herb and Virginia Chance, met with Jerry Sartain to discuss the robbery of the Chances. Chance was reputedly a "juice man" or loan shark, who took custody of syndicate money and loaned it out at exorbitant rates. Loether and Dee Watson, a waitress at the NuWay, were said to be the source for heroin, cocaine, guns, and women. Sartain agreed to contact codefendant McKinney, whom both had met in federal prison. As mentioned in chapter 2, Sartain was a prison writ writer extraordinaire, who got McKinney, Loether, and some thirty other prisoners early releases from Leavenworth. Needless to say, McKinney and Loether were grateful to Sartain.

McKinney agreed to commit the robberies. According to Sartain's story, he was just to finger the Chances and receive five thousand dollars for doing so. Loether was to be out of state when the crimes occurred. McKinney flew to L.A. two times, the second being a couple of days before the slayings in which the Chances were brutally murdered, execution-style, in their home. Three .22-caliber bullets were fired at extremely close range into Herb Chance's head, and two into his wife's. Jewelry and cash in excess of $63,000 were taken.

Dee was found dead in a car, eight bullets fired into her head, including one at point-blank range. The murder weapon was the same silencer-equipped .22 used in the Chance slaying. On the night of her death, Sartain telephoned Dee, who was staying at Loether's apartment, and drove there to kill her. When he saw her small children asleep on the floor, a pang of conscience momentarily seized him. All heart, he decided not to kill her in front of her children, so he had her drive him in Loether's car to a dark street, where he shot her to death. Later we were to learn that McKinney, before flying back to St. Louis after the Chance murders, had instructed Sartain to kill her because she knew too much about the crimes, and to "torch" the gun and cuffs. Instead, he buried them in the desert. The later recovery of those items greatly aided the prosecution. It also gave Sartain a bargaining chip. I can't help thinking it was Sartain's carefully crafted ace in the hole, if he got caught.

At the time of the murders, McKinney was on parole, as was Sartain, who likewise had spent some eighteen years in federal and state prisons. Loether also had served time in prison with Sartain and McKinney.

Loether, in poor health, denied any involvement. We were to indict him, only later to dismiss the case against him, owing to the insufficiency of the evidence. At the time of the murders, he was conspicuously in Florida. He did, however, give us enough information to seek out Sartain.

The cops interviewed Sartain's family while Jerry was on the run. They learned that on the weekend before the killing, a man named George had stayed with the Sartains. This George was later identified as defendant George Patrick McKinney. The cops got a photograph of McKinney from Sartain's stepdaughter. She had fortuitously taken it during his visit to Los Angeles, because she thought George handsome and "neat". The daughter also had observed McKinney carrying a briefcase on the weekend of the killings. She remembered seeing a surgical glove sticking out of the briefcase. Later that evening she saw surgical gloves on McKinney's dresser after his return. Jean Appel, Sartain's common-law wife, whom McKinney also wanted killed, told the cops that she remembered seeing a briefcase, handcuffs, walkie-talkies, a wig, and a silencer-equipped pistol at the house between McKinney's two visits. She also recalled seeing McKinney try on the wig. Sartain married her after the Chance slaying, so she could not be called as a witness to testify against him—or so he thought.

Continuing the investigation, Barrett and Maloney were able to locate airline records showing that McKinney had traveled twice to Los Angeles under a false name, in violation of his parole. At this point we were able to go to the grand jury and secure an indictment on murder and kidnapping-robbery charges against McKinney and Sartain. We were hoping that McKinney would fight extradition. We needed time to develop the case, and a quick trial without Sartain's testimony would have surely resulted in an acquittal. McKinney obliged: it took some five months to get him. By that time we had secured the critical testimony of Sartain's former attorney, whom he and McKinney had kidnapped and robbed on McKinney's first visit to L.A. McKinney had terrorized the attorney by removing the silencer-equipped .22 automatic pistol from his briefcase, donning surgical gloves, and shoving the gun's muzzle inside the quivering attorney's mouth. The attorney, who at first refused to identify McKinney because of his fear of certain death, agreed to testify only after we granted him immunity for soliciting the murder of McKinney. The man the attorney had hired to kill McKinney was none other than Jerry Sartain, who had convinced the attorney that McKinney was going to come back and kill him and his family if he didn't act quickly. While in jail, McKinney put out a separate contract to kill the attorney. Needless to say, the attorney's testimony was also to prove instrumental in dealing with Sartain.

Sartain was arrested within weeks of McKinney's return to L.A. He immediately waived extradition. Things were starting to break for us. The stage was set, and it was now time to deal with Sartain!

The only thing we had to offer a wily career criminal was his life. That he had personally killed the waitress, having fired eight bullets into her brain, was the extent of the concession. Sartain and his attorney, Don Wager, weighed the offer. An ex-DA and a formidable defense attorney, Wager knew we needed Sartain. He also knew that California's death penalty was in jeopardy and in all probability would be overturned by the liberal California Supreme Court. But it's one thing to have an expert opinion on the subject, and another when your life is at stake. And we didn't let Sartain forget that we would vigorously pursue the death penalty against him. His only chance to save his life would be to cooperate with us and testify against McKinney. It was Sartain's life, and he wasn't willing to roll the dice, despite Wager's protestations to the contrary. Personally, I believed that our Supreme Court would never let a capital defendant die. But it was not my decision. I only told Sartain what we were going to do. Sartain cut the deal. We gave him life imprisonment; he gave us McKinney. Or did he?

Shortly after the voir dire began, the California Supreme Court overturned the death penalty. Once again, California was without a death penalty. Sartain could not help feeling he had been snookered. He was sentenced to life imprisonment. But Wager got two concessions. First, his sentence was concurrent with any federal time. Second, he was to be turned over to the feds to serve that time in a federal penitentiary, far away from the reaches of McKinney, to be returned to California only upon completion of the federal sentence, but only if California still desired him to complete his life sentence. Federal time, if you knew your way around the system, was said to be much easier than time served in the gang-infested, out-of-control California prison system.

Sartain's knowledge that his turncoat testimony against McKinney was a death warrant caused him to embark upon a messianic effort to singlehandedly sabotage our case against George Patrick McKinney. Don Wager was the key to Sartain. The only problem was that it might be the wrong key. I was not to know that answer until the end of the trial, when the verdict was rendered.

The first testimony Sartain was to give for the People was before the grand jury. There he corroborated the kidnapping-robbery counts involving his attorney, and his attorney's solicitation to kill McKinney at his behest. He told the attorney he had killed McKinney and promptly extorted more money from the hapless attorney, who now thought he was guilty of the crime of murder for hire, a capital offense. Then he told of McKinney's cold-blooded execution of the Chances, describing with alarming detail how McKinney had killed his victims, afterwards feeling their carotid arteries to verify their deaths. He also told of Loether's involvement. Then he added an explosive element. He testified that Anthony Borsollino, an alleged Chicago gangster, came to California on a certain date and was involved in the murders in an effort to muscle in on the NuWay Bar Lounge racketeering. As a result, Loether and Borsollino were joined in the new indictment with McKinney.

With the assistance of the FBI, we verified Borsollino's alleged Mafia connections. However, Borsollino produced a home video, clearly depicting himself at his son's football game on the date he was supposed to be in Los Angeles. Its authenticity was confirmed by the FBI.

We immediately dismissed the indictment against Borsollino. Sartain was confronted with his perjury. Without missing a beat, he cheerfully admitted it. We had a problem. A big problem. We were going to use an admitted perjurer, and ask the jury to disregard the perjury and consider his testimony at the trial. The problem was compounded by the fact that we did not know what Sartain would actually testify to at the trial. And all through it, Wager was saying, "Trust me."

Meanwhile, our victim-attorney, fearing disbarment, perjured himself when he denied putting out a contract on McKinney's life and denied financing Sartain's criminal enterprise in Florida. Our two key witnesses were proven perjurers.

What to do? What could I say to the jury in my opening statement? I didn't know what Sartain was going to say. I knew he was a pathological liar who could be quite convincing. He sort of took one into his confidence and told it "like it is." Unfortunately, in truth, he told it "like it ain't." So I told the jury I was going to call to the stand a vicious, remorseless killer who had fired eight shots into his victim's head. A killer who matched, step for step, the evil of the defendant. A killer who had watched his crime partner snuff two human beings with the calmness and precision of a skilled surgeon. Crime partners in hell. I told the jury of Sartain's perjury before the grand jury; that he was not to be trusted; and challenged them to reject all of his testimony that I could not corroborate or otherwise convince them of the force of its truthfulness. That challenge was also one I made to myself. I was prepared to tell the jury to reject all of his testimony, if need be.

Sartain had mentioned, after he admitted the Borsollino perjury, that another individual may have been involved, one Paul Hammett or Hammond. He told us that he didn't know whether he was going to testify to this or not. He wanted to think about it. We conducted five polygraphs of Sartain, all of which he failed. While normally they would be inadmissible, we made sure the jury knew about them. I wanted them to know everything I knew about Sartain. After all, their decision as to whether Sartain was worthy of any belief was what counted. Clearly, Jerry was going to try to sabotage the case. My job was to see that he didn't. We played cat-and-mouse with one another. Frankly, I didn't know whether I was the cat or the mouse. He enjoyed the gamesmanship without displaying a pittance of remorse for his crimes. A true sociopath.

Wager could not represent to me whether his client was going to testify about this Paul Hammett or Hammond. Never believing in his story, I went on the assumption he would not, inasmuch as he had retracted that statement to the police. I was wrong. He told the jury, early in his testimony, that he gave Paul Hammett $63,000 in L.A. immediately following the killings. Two days later, as my direct examination began to take on a full-bore cross-examination, he admitted on the stand that he had perjured himself before the jury. Sartain admitted that he was trying to blow the trial sky-high in an effort to gain a hung jury or acquittal for McKinney by leaving a trial of inconsistent statements and tainted testimony—at the same time trying to gain the benefits of his own plea bargain.

His testimony got so ridiculous that defense attorney James Epstein asked Sartain to raise his hand when he was telling the truth. Sartain promised he would do so. Several days later, on cross, Epstein reminded him of his promise, noting that he hadn't raised his hand. Sartain said he hadn't forgotten and would let him know when he was telling the truth! Sartain never raised his hand, but the critical evidence against McKinney that he offered was corroborated by other evidence, including the conduct of McKinney himself.

I couldn't resist asking Sartain some final questions. I wanted the jury to know what kind of human being Sartain was, and, by association, McKinney. So I asked Sartain how he had felt when he fired the first shot into the back of Dee Watson's head. He shrugged. "When you fired the second shot into the back of her head, did you think that was enough?" Sartain wore a blank expression, again shrugging his shoulders. "Jerry, the third shot into her brain, did you think that was enough?" Again he just shrugged his shoulders. "The fifth shot, Jerry, was that enough?" Again no response from Sartain. Exasperated, I asked, "How did you feel when you fired the eighth bullet into her brain, Jerry?" Sartain looked at me with a blend of wonderment and disdain. He paused for a long time, glanced at the jury, then back at me, and said, "I didn't feel anything!" Everyone in that courtroom knew that statement was one of the few that could not be contradicted. Finally, on the tenth day of his testimony, I could not resist closing with these questions:

KATZ: Jerry, there was a great film some years ago, called *Casablanca*. Do you remember it? You know, the one with Ingrid Bergman and Humphrey Bogart. . . . The one with the song "As Time Goes By"?

SARTAIN: Yeah, I think I know it.

KATZ: Remember the scene at the end of the movie where Laslo is talking to Rick, and Laslo says, "Man has a manifest destiny for both good and evil. . . ." Would you agree with that statement?

SARTAIN: Huh?

KATZ: You know. Man has a capacity for both good and evil, that is, he can do both good and evil?

SARTAIN: Yeah.

KATZ: The trouble with you, Jerry, is that you have devoted your life to the pursuit of evil to the exclusion of any good, wouldn't you say that is true?

SARTAIN: You might say that!

And that was how his testimony ended, ten torturous days after it began.

A footnote should be added. In the audience that day were defense attorney Jim Epstein's father and uncle, Academy Award–winning screenwriters Jules and Phillip Epstein, who co-wrote *Casablanca* among other great screenplays. I guess I couldn't resist the irony of their presence.

McKinney was convicted of the Chance murders and some of the kidnapping-robbery counts pertaining to the lawyer. He is still serving a life sentence, protesting his innocence to this day, though you should know that Japanese handcuffs, of the same make as those used in the crimes, were found in a Garland, Texas, apartment rented by McKinney, in violation of parole, several months before the crimes. Sartain had no knowledge of or connection with them.

Sometimes it is necessary to use the testimony of coconspirators. We saw Mary Brunner and Jerry Sartain try to sabotage the proceedings. Each had been offered a benefit—an inducement, if you will. Each had substantial reasons for lying. Each had loyalties to the defendant. In such situations it is imperative that the prosecution and the police provide corroboration wherever possible, corroboration even beyond what is legally required for an accomplice, by conducting an investigation that has as its goal the establishment of guilt virtually independent of the accomplice. It is not always possible to do this. But it must be the goal. And the effort must always be made. The trier of fact must be informed of every factor that impinges on an accomplice's testimony—not just the obvious ones, such as inducements, deals, favors, and the like, but things such as prejudices and biases, personal confrontations, and experiences that color one's testimony for or against a defendant.

For practical and moral reasons, a coconspirator's testimony should be avoided unless a conviction cannot be secured in its absence. Sometimes timing determines whom the prosecution will use. Unfortunately it is not always the least culpable person, just the one who is first to come forward with the evidence. In *Tate-LaBianca*, Susan Atkins was offered a deal first, she having mercilessly stabbed a pregnant Sharon Tate after telling her, "Look, bitch, I don't care if you're having a baby . . . you're

going to die and that's all there is to it." Fortunately, she disavowed the agreement with the DA and was prosecuted. Linda
Kasabian was then offered immunity, she being far less culpable,
having killed no one and exhibiting great remorse for what happened.

In the McKinney case, Sartain is no better than McKinney. If
the latter had come forward and offered to turn state's evidence,
I suppose, in this case, we would have offered him life imprisonment just as we did Sartain. After all, this was a case that had
been rejected when it was first submitted to the DA. Life imprisonment is still better than nothing!

FIFTEEN

Witnesses—Part II

Truth does not always stalk boldly forth naked. . . . She oft hides in nooks and crannies visible only to the mind's eye of the judge who tries the case. To him appears the furtive glance, the blush of conscious shame, the hesitation, the sincere or the flippant or sneering tone, the heat, the calmness, the yawn, the sigh, the candor or lack of it, the scant of full realization of the solemnity of an oath, the carriage and mien. The brazen face of the liar, the glibness of the schooled witness in reciting a lesson or the itching over-eagerness of the swift witness, as well as the honest face of the truthful one, are alone seen by him. In short, one witness may give testimony that reads in print, here, as if falling from the lips of an angel of light and may testify so that it reads brokenly and obscurely in print and yet there was that about the witness that carried conviction of truth to every soul who heard him testify.
—*Henry Lamm,* Creamer v. Bivert *(1908)*

Child Witnesses

The justice system has no greater responsibility than to minimize the horror and fear to which a child witness is subjected when placed in the pincers of the criminal justice system. Any shirking of that obligation can result in the permanent emotional scarring and dysfunction of a child. The difficulty lies in the tension that exists between this responsibility and the need to protect scrupulously a defendant's due-process rights.

No area is more problematic than the area of child abuse. Children are pitted against their parents, torn apart by divided loyalties and separation anxieties, fearful of losing their parents if they testify, fearful that the horrible acts of abuse will continue if they do not! Often the actual physical acts of abuse are secondary to the emotional pain of the child who wonders what she's done wrong, believing that she is at fault, that it must have been something she did to warrant such treatment. Cross-examination is said to be the crucible through which the truth is emitted. And while the process may work with adults, it often can destroy a child who is simply unarmed and ill equipped to fend off the trial lawyers' cavalry charge of counteraccusations, confusing interrogatories, and ridicule.

Young children are highly suggestible. They are often mistaken. Lacking in life experience, they frequently misinterpret people's intentions. So, too, they may say things that are not true to "get even," not realizing the enormity of their charges until it is too late for simple apologies and easy retractions. They can be highly manipulative, saying and doing things to gain acceptance, appreciation, and rewards. These traits, in the hands of adults with a personal agenda, challenge the very underpinnings of justice. No greater danger of manipulation and false accusations exists than in domestic relation cases involving bitterly contested divorce and child custody matters. In the past few years these claims have dramatically increased.

We have all heard horror stories in which adorable tiny tots, perhaps innocently, but falsely, claim that an entire preschool has corrupted the children through the commission of unspeakable acts of child abuse and observance of satanic rites. Such charges, fueled by hysterical parents aided by incompetent, unprofessional, and unscrupulous "experts," with the advice and consent of ambitious police and a high-profile DA, put the justice system to the ultimate test. The way we go about determining what is the truth, before a person's reputation is destroyed forever, in the backwater of sensational and unsubstantiated vulgarity, puts American justice on trial.

It is important, however, to emphasize that most children

testifying in trials are not only truthful and worthy of belief, but are victims of a pandemic social disease known as child abuse.

All of what has been said are just words. What follow are a few examples that illustrate how difficult it sometimes is to divine the truth.

Suppose a four-year-old child is called to testify as to what a defendant allegedly did to him. The first step is to determine whether the child understands the obligation to tell the truth, and the second is to determine whether he can receive accurate impressions of events and correctly relate them. Before the child is permitted to testify, the judge must make a preliminary determination of these facts. Let's eavesdrop on the examination to qualify the child as a witness—as substantially reported by a trial judge:

Q.: What does it mean to tell a lie?

A.: Crackers and things.

Q.: Crackers and things?

A.: Yeah.

Q.: That's what it means to tell a lie?

A.: Yeah, to be bad and eat crackers in bed.

Q.: Do you eat crackers in bed?

A.: Umm, only sometimes.

Q.: Do you tell the truth?

A.: When I drink my milk and Mommy lets me watch TV.

Q.: You only tell the truth when you drink milk and watch TV?

A.: Yeah, and when Daddy makes me tell the truth.

Q.: And when does he make you tell the truth?

A.: When I get out and bird.

Q.: Get out and what?

A.: Bird. You know, when I do something bad.

Q.: "Bird" means to do something bad? Why do you call it "bird"?

A.: Daddy says it's bad to stab the bird.

Q.: Is it bad?

A.: I don't know. . . . it's fun to do that and things and chase the cats and go home and eat.

Q.: Do you ever lie to Mommy or Daddy?

A.: Sometimes to my dad.

Q.: Just to your dad?

A.: Yeah, 'cause he hits me sometimes.

Q.: Will you tell us what happened to you?

A.: Yeah. My mommy told me.

Q.: Your mommy told you what happened?

A.: Yeah. She told me what happened and my Daddy said he'd spank me if I didn't tell.

On a certain level, the child appears to know what happens to him when he tells a lie. He does not, however, appear to understand the moral obligation to tell the truth, nor is it clear whether he regards the truth as he sees it or as his parents see it. Can you imagine sending someone to prison for life, based on this uncertainty? In this scenario, the child would not qualify to testify under oath in most courts. That does not mean, however, that a case could not be brought on the basis of this child's complaints, if there were corroborating circumstances. Such external facts as the following are but a few of the things that can be presented to buttress the case: an independent doctor's examination showing a damaged hymen or an anal tear; a spontaneous statement by the child; a recent complaint of sexual abuse; changes in mood, behavior, and sleep habits of the child; a suspect's opportunity and access to the child; and other witnesses who have knowledge of the crime or facts from which an inference of guilt can be drawn.

Let's take a look at the kind of shocking, horrible allegations that are made in one form or another. Suppose Rachel, now eight and a half years old, has testified to being molested at a preschool nursery when she was five years old. She identifies two of the school's staff as having fondled her and having made her fondle them. She tells of a male teacher exposing himself on several occasions. She tells of being stripped naked, and of animal sacrifices. She is adorable, precocious, and likable. The examination of Rachel reveals that she has been seeing Dr. Judith Summers, a psychotherapist, for over two years. Rachel is very attached to her. The little girl is given anatomically correct dolls during her therapy sessions, with which she is asked to show Dr. Summers what happened to her. The story is repeated often, during which times Rachel's mother is sometimes present. When she forgets something or makes a mistake, her mother corrects her. Sometimes Rachel is shown pictures of the defendants and asked to explain who did what to whom. When Rachel does "well" at her session, her mother takes her for a special yogurt treat.

Rachel's dad takes her to movies and buys her popcorn and candy. She loves her parents and wants to please them. Her father is angry, insisting on criminal proceedings. Several months pass before Rachel tells her mother about the claimed abuse, and only after the mother confronts her with stories about other preschool children being molested. During those interim months, she has gone to preschool every day, never discussing the abuse with anyone, nor have other children discussed their claims of abuse with her.

Rachel claims that she and some other children were taken to an abandoned building in a bus prominently exhibiting the name of the preschool on its exterior. She was never able to locate this building for the police. No building of such a description was ever found. No one ever reported seeing the preschool bus near an abandoned building or under strange circumstances. Rachel says two teachers took them to a basement, where they were made to take off their clothes and sit naked in a circle. It was dark and scary. The teachers took off their clothes, too. The children were told that if they didn't cooperate, the evil spirit would come and get them.

One male teacher lit a candle. He then pulled a squirrel out of a sack and cut off its head with a big knife. He warned them that if they told anyone about this ritual, the same thing would happen to them, their parents, and their brothers and sisters! They were too frightened to scream. The squirrel's head was passed around, and each child held it for a few seconds before passing it to the next child. "Blood and goo" came from its head. A towel was passed around, and the children wiped their hands. The children were told to dress, then were taken back to the school, where they played on the school grounds until their parents picked them up.

When Rachel's mother told her, weeks later, "what happened" to the other kids, she started to have nightmares. It was after this that her mother took her to see Dr. Summers. In her dreams she "saw" her teachers touching her naked body.

This business of justice is not as easy as we think, sitting in our overstuffed chairs, second-guessing the judges, lawyers, and juries. How would you vote, on the basis of Rachel's testimony? Are you satisfied enough with her story, comfortable enough to send two schoolteachers to prison for multiple lifetime sentences? Can we be certain of what Rachel in fact experienced? Beyond a reasonable doubt? How do we separate fact from fantasy in this tumbling tumult? How do we separate her experience from her mother's and her therapist's suggestions?

There is a very real danger when adults with their own agendas, good faith aside, bring pressure to bear on young, suggestible minds. Children naturally want to please adults. They also are armed with vivid imaginations that are constantly fed by strong, memorable visual images. I find myself, even as an adult, wondering sometimes where a bizarre image came from, where I experienced it, only to realize that I saw it in a fifteen- or thirty-second blip on an MTV music video! Haven't we all mixed metaphors; dreams fabricated from touches of a real-life experience colored by dashes of strong images we have seen, stirred and shaken up with our own vivid imaginations?

There are no real winners in this scenario. No one will ever be the same. If the defendants are innocent, they will never be made whole. Though they may have been legally vindicated from the charges, their characters and reputations are despoiled—forever! In crimes of alleged child abuse there is a presumption of guilt, and that never ever entirely goes away even in the face of a unanimous verdict of acquittal. The enor-

mous economic burden shouldered by the defense has bank-
rupted them. No one will hire them, even those who believe
they are innocent, because of the obvious adverse effect on
business. They truly wear the scarlet letters of shame and opprobrium.

And what of the child? If the horrible things she told of
didn't happen but she truly believes they did, will she grow up
a damaged soul, eternally damned by the "nightmare"? If the
child knows that she told a lie, destroying the lives of innocent
persons, how will she deal with that as an adult? How will she
view a justice system that facilitated, if it did not actually con-
spire in, framing an innocent person? How can any of us trust
such a system?

Here are some of the things we can do to mitigate systemic
abuses:

1. Develop an informative educational campaign apprising
the public of child-abuse problems without creating a climate
of hysteria, fear, and suspicion.

2. Encourage healthy relationships between children and
adults, emphasizing the positive points, including the importance of love and appropriate physical touching. Aggressive
child-abuse awareness programs, if not well thought out and
measured, can have a chilling effect on the very important and
essential relationships between children and adults. Grandpar-
ents will be afraid to touch their grandchildren; to pat them on
the back, rub their tummies, tickle their funnybones; to tousle
their hair or hug them tightly, as will some parents, family, and
friends. All will be the losers, for the children will not know the
special warmth and love that will light their souls and bond
them to healthy, loving adults, and the adults will not experience the special gift of innocence and unconditional love that
recharges their souls, stripping away the accumulated layers of
cynicism, giving true meaning to their lives.

3. When it becomes necessary to pursue an investigation,
all efforts should be made to find independent, corroborating
evidence of a child's claim of abuse.

4. Trained professionals must avoid all leading and suggestive questioning and undue influence, and conduct examina-

tions of the child victim in accordance with standards set by the courts and professional associations.

5. All examinations should be unobtrusively videotaped. No repetitious off-camera warm-up sessions. The entire session must be on videotape.

6. A support network should be provided for the children and parents, including appropriate therapy and counseling *after* the criminal proceedings have been resolved. If, however, the child needs ongoing therapy before and during trial, then a special program of support and counseling can be initiated with the approval of the court and in accordance with strict guidelines designed to minimize any coercing and undue influence.

7. To facilitate a frightened child's testimony, if the court deems it appropriate and necessary, a support counselor can remain with the child witness while testifying, and touch the child to reduce anxiety. However, a big caveat here: only in cases where the witness would not otherwise testify, and in which, therefore, such testimony before the jury would be lost, should this be allowed. Excessive demonstrative touching and emoting must be avoided, as this would unfairly bolster the credibility of the witness in violation of the defendant's due-process rights.

Another troubling area in child-abuse cases relates to the use of "rape shield" laws to prevent questioning of child-abuse witnesses about past sexual experiences. The problem arises, for example, when the child describes, in words inappropriate to her age, an act concerning which a normal child would not have knowledge. Most juries would appropriately conclude that the child must be telling the truth, because she would have no way of knowing about these terrible things unless they happened to her! But what if the defense has evidence that another person, sometime in the past, did these things with the child? Can this evidence be introduced to the jury so they may concluded that her knowledge of these sex acts came not from the defendant but from this other experience? All courts should, under these special and limited facts, admit such evidence. In jurisdictions like Texas, the court is given broad latitude to admit evidence of previous sexual conduct of the victim when its probative value outweighs the prejudicial effect. The judge's ruling is as much dependent on his or her own personal sense of values, morality, and justice as on the law of precedent. In those jurisdictions holding that the rape shield laws prevent such inquiries, except in unusually narrow circumstances, the court theorizes that prosecutions for child molestation must be encouraged, and that the introduction of a minor's past sexual history would have a chilling effect on such actions being brought. One thing is absolutely clear: when a child has to explain not only the current claim of abuse, but is forced to remember and relate other past sexual conduct, the ensuing trauma can result in emotional dysfunction for life. The courts have a higher duty to prevent this from happening.

Having said that, Americans still recall, in lore if not in fact, the Salem witch trials, which were said to have arisen out of young girls dancing and playing imaginary games involving the devil, ghosts, and witches. When pressed by the Puritan town elders, under threat of punishment, to explain their activities, they told them that the Salem women had taught them witchcraft! And innocent women swung from the gallows.

Picture this testimony today. A small child, with adorable ringlets, possessing the smooth skin of a polished apple, softly and breathlessly tells an incredible story. Her sparkling blue eyes and Shirley Temple mouth entrance you. You strain to hear. The DA painfully and methodically draws the tale out of this shy, bewitching little girl. You glance at the defendant. He's tense. He sweats. He knows this little girl can reach hearts that have been in a long, deep slumber—hearts that have long forgotten the wonderment of childhood. And he's afraid. Afraid you will believe her. Afraid you won't listen to his side. Will you?

Criminal Informants

Criminal informants present yet another challenge. By definition they have an inherent motive to fabricate. They are offered either money for their information or a "deal" on pending charges. In either case an inducement, rather than altruism, is the mother's milk of a cooperative effort. As with accomplices and gang members, independent corroboration, while not required by law, is a practical necessity, since juries tend to disbelieve such "paid" witnesses.

I have never felt comfortable using a jailhouse informant. You just can't be sure whether the informant is making it up, embellishing, or telling the truth. So, if one must be used, it is important to give the informant *no* information about the crime, if possible. An independent investigation should be conducted to determine what, if any, sources of information about a defendant's case the informant might have had access to. In the past, some clever jail informants have peeked, or had another inmate peek, at a defendant's "papers," which may include a statement of the charges, some police reports, and a preliminary hearing transcript setting out the offense. Or the informant might use the phone provided to inmates and pose as the defendant or even as a lawyer to get information about his case. Yes, it has been done, and not just a few times! If these criminals applied their many talents to legitimate enterprise, they would be quite successful.

Information from an informant should be verified and independently sourced, if at all possible. Informants should sign a statement describing the circumstances under which the defendant's statement was made, where it was made, opportunity to hear, persons present, date and time, and so forth. An informant must be forbidden to pump the defendant for information, as he would then be regarded as an agent for the police, conducting an interrogation in violation of the defendant's Sixth Amendment rights to counsel. If at all possible, a court-sanctioned bug might be appropriate under certain circumstances where probable cause exists and there is no reasonable expectation of privacy. This would go a long way toward imparting credibility to the informant's testimony.

In the Tate-LaBianca murders, cellmate Virginia Graham's explosive revelation of Susan Atkins's tale of atrocities at the Tate home freed the prosecution from having to cut a bad deal with Atkins, allowing them instead to use her boastful confession as damning evidence against her. Atkins had boasted to Virginia Graham that when Voytek Frykowski, who was covered with blood, ran out the front door, she chased him and stabbed him three or four times. She had laughed when describing

Sharon Tate's murder. She was the last to die. Susan said she had held Sharon's arms behind her back as she cried and begged for her life: "Please don't kill me . . . I want to live . . . I want to have my baby. I want to have my baby." Susan said she had told Tate, "Look, bitch, I don't care about you. I don't care if you're going to have a baby. . . . You're going to die, and I don't feel anything about it." Susan bragged about killing Tate a few minutes later, saying what a "trip" it was to taste her blood.

The disclosures of Susan Atkins's active involvement in the Tate murders sickened the DAs and the cops over the prospect of having to give her a deal (which she was balking at) in order to get her to testify against Charles Manson and the other murderers. When family member Linda Kasabian, who had killed no one, agreed to testify in return for immunity, this, together with Virginia Graham's jailhouse revelations, prevented a grave injustice.

Finally, how the prosecutor and the police handle the inducements can be problematic. Two things must always be kept in mind: First, the inducement cannot be given in return for a particular version of the facts to which the DA or police believe the informant should testify. It is okay to point out to informants inconsistencies in their version and the existence of independently proven facts, and to ask them for clarification. It is not okay to suggest to informants what the facts are, or that they are expected to testify in a certain manner. The DA and police have a choice: they can decide to use or reject the testimony. Second, the inducements must not be used as a hammer to secure testimony. Prosecutors sometimes like to be vague about what is being offered in return for testimony. They imply that things will be taken care of, but are unwilling to commit to a particular reward before the witness testifies. This open-ended deal raises questions about the veracity of the informant, since there is an implication that the better the testimony, the better the deal. With today's cynical "show me" juries, this is akin to leaving a barrel of sardines in the hot sun. Something smelly, something that leaves a bad taste.

Gang Witnesses

Gang witnesses present unique challenges. Not only do they come with the baggage of an accomplice, whether legally one or not, but they bring to the playing field a mixed loyalty— a ticking bomb ready to explode in your face. Gangs provide things otherwise missing in a gang member's life: standing, importance, self-worth, values, loyalty, a sense of purpose, acceptance, opportunity, being a part of something, having a special identity, to name a few. Consequently, there are grave risks in using such a witness. Even when gang members know that something intrinsically wrong happened, they still feel an abiding loyalty to a group that has filled a void in their lives. The strongest ethic inculcated in the gang member is that of fealty and loyalty. Prosecutors are constantly beset with the problem of whether the gang member will in fact testify fully, completely, and truthfully, regardless of the consequences. In truth, a vacillating gang member does not even know whether he will do so until the moment he looks at that jury—and maybe not even then, until that question is put to him, and he hears his voice forming words . . . words of betrayal!

In addition to the usual inducement problems we've seen with accomplice testimony, the prosecutor is often beset with insurmountable problems of providing protection against gang retaliation. If the witness is incarcerated, this act of revenge can come from any source, including a rival gang who has agreed to snuff out the turncoat witness.

Prison gangs are highly ingenious and deadly when it comes to penetrating the protective shield, and the DA and the witness know it. Even witnesses who will be relocated or placed in a witness protection program can never be assured that their cover will not be penetrated by the tentacles of reprisal. And those tentacles can and often do reach deep into the innocent families of the witness.

Wendell Hall was such a witness in the McKinney case. Hall claimed to be a member of the White People's Party, an offshoot of the more notorious Aryan Brotherhood, a militant white supremacist organization. He had a known reputation for prison violence. McKinney, a veteran of prison culture and a man who knew how things worked, quickly found out whom to go to for his problem. He accosted Wendell and made arrangements to kill three witnesses on the outside. Unknown to McKinney was that Hall, beset with his own problems with the White People's Party, was looking for a way out of his mess. This was his chance. He purportedly agreed to make the arrangements to kill the attorney for $2,500, and Sartain's stepdaughter and wife for $2,000 each. Hall then notified the cops, who informed me of this break. Evidence of an attempt to kill a witness is powerful evidence of consciousness of guilt, and this provided a strong boost to our troubled case against McKinney, independent of Sartain. We set up an undercover sting in which McKinney's wife was videotaped, delivering a "small down payment to a cop." Now we had something to talk about—something written by McKinney, who became the author of his own fate.

Our problems were just beginning, as a contract was put out to kill Hall. Hall's only chance for survival was to cooperate with cops, whom he despised.

I first met Hall when he was brought out to the old Santa Monica Courthouse, an archaic building offering only the pretext of security for high-profile cases. Hall was brought to a witness interview room called "the closet," so named because of its four-foot-by-four-foot configuration. I had not made up my mind as yet whether I would call him as a witness. The sheriff closed the door and locked it. Hall was not at all what I had expected to see. This was a kid! A baby-faced youth who looked like he didn't shave and wouldn't for a long time. He possessed clear blue eyes, and, but for circumstances, might have been cast as a neighbor kid in *The Brady Bunch*.

Wendell sat across from me, a tiny table separating us. He studied me with a bemused "So this is the big, bad ol' DA dude?" look. In turn, I tried to see what it was about him that would make George McKinney, a deadly killer, enlist his support. It did not seem credible that such a pro would enlist this innocent's assistance, nor did I think a jury would buy it.

It took a much shorter time to sort out the truth than I had anticipated.

Wendell played with a pencil on the table. He looked at it, twirling it in his fingers, and looked at me with a weird smile. But his eyes were hard. *Unkind* is a better word. I asked him why I should believe that McKinney, an experienced pro, would come to him. I wondered whether this was a reverse setup by McKinney to show how desperate we were—and whether Hall was part of McKinney's own sting.

"You don't look that tough. No offense intended. But why should I believe you can handle guys meaner than you, and twice your size?" I asked in my best-mannered skeptical voice.

Wendell paused, then spun the pencil. He kept his gaze down. "Mr. Katz, there's nothing stopping me from killing you right now," he said softly, still staring at the pencil. "Is there?"

The evenness of his voice signaled a warning. Was I just being paranoid, or was I getting claustrophobic, or was it just hot in this confined space? It's just my imagination, I thought. "So what is it you think you can do to me, Wendell?"

He looked up and smiled, then studied the spiraling pencil in his hands and said, "I just might decide to drive this pencil through your brain." Then he stopped smiling. His eyes narrowed to squiggly lasers.

"And just how might you do that?" I said in the most confident tone I could muster, unsure whether my inner vibrato betrayed my fears.

"Push it through your eye to the back of your brain, Mr. Katz, that's all." Well, if nothing else, he certainly was polite. He held the pencil loosely in his hands. I carefully reached for it. He held on to it for just a moment too long, then rolled it into my sweaty palm. I had no doubt Wendell Hall would be an effective witness!

Wendell's testimony, supported by the undercover videotape, was accepted by the jury, despite the evidence of a deal struck by the people, and despite attacks on his credibility by other gang members called by the defense to impeach him.

The key to a successful presentation of a gang witness's testimony is in the establishment of an underlying rapport and mutual respect. This requires the DA to understand the witness's value system, and to identify with the problems and impediments to the testimony. Gang members need substantial reinforcement that what they are doing is morally right, that it ultimately serves them and their family's own interests and presents their only chance to break the shackles of an association that, with certitude, will lead to their death or lengthy confinement.

On the other side, the defense attorney representing an active gang member will reinforce the witness's identity with the gang and what it means to violate its tenets. Sometimes the defense will arrange an interview between the witness, the defense attorney, and the defendant under the guise of preparation for trial. Enormous pressures are brought to bear, and even if the interview is conducted in a totally scrupulous manner, the witness is torn between his gang loyalties and the need to help himself. Without threatening the witness or telling the witness not to testify, a defense attorney can point out the possible adverse consequences of cooperation with the People. That is why, even under the best of circumstances, a prosecutor cannot count on a gang member's testimony until it actually unfolds!

What happened in the McKinney case was not unexpected. The prisons do their best to separate gang members by spreading them out through the system. It is common practice for a defendant to subpoena scattered gang members for a reunion at the local trial venue, in the guise of testimonial relevancy. In capital cases, character evidence might be presented, for example. Sometimes prison breaks are planned, summit gang meetings consummated, or a contract killing set up or performed. To lifers, with no real fear of the death penalty being implemented, it's no big deal. But it is a big deal for the well-being and security of everyone else, and consequently expensive protective measures are mandated.

Undercover armed guards were everywhere as Doc Holiday, leader of the prison gang the Black Guerrilla Family, and Joe Morgan, founder of the infamous and deadly Mexican Mafia, as well as members of the notorious Aryan Brotherhood, were called by the defense, ostensibly to refute Wendell Hall's gang stature and claim of being solicited for murder.

The trial at times seemed on the verge of becoming a circus sideshow starring some of the most unsavory rogues this side of Universal Pictures's casting department. And the system allowed it to happen. Many courts, indulging in every aspect of a defendant's perceived due-process rights, automatically permit these gang members to be called as witnesses without the requirement of an *in camera* showing of relevance and materiality. This should be required in every case. The judge should look at it outside of the presence of the prosecution, and determine whether the witness should be brought to the trial. Only then should an order be issued.

Witnesses like Jerry Sartain and Mary Brunner are simply the two sides of a double-edged razor. Sometimes it is hard to know which side will cut, or how deeply.

Our justice system is far from perfect, constantly requiring compromises and value judgments. Immunity for Linda Kasabian, but not for homecoming queen Leslie Van Houghton. Immunity for Mary Brunner. Life imprisonment for Jerry Sartain, death for George Patrick McKinney. Favors for Wendell Hall. And so it goes. The old saw still applies: "When a crime is committed in hell, you don't have angels for witnesses." Pay the devil, even if you feel dirty—all in the name of our justice system.

SIXTEEN

The Devil Made Me Do It. Really.

THE ABUSE EXCUSE

> One of the men whom Baldwin murdered, Baldwin had
> notoriously been threatening to kill for twelve years.
> The poor creature happened, by the merest piece of ill
> fortune, to come along a dark alley at the very moment that
> Baldwin's insanity came upon him and so he was shot
> in the back.
> —*Mark Twain, 1875 (paraphrased)*

Dan White, Lorena Bobbitt, and Lyle and Eric Menendez. Their trials and the outrageous results are symptoms of a serious illness in our society and our criminal justice system. Sometimes it seems the more brutal, chilling, and gruesome the assault and mutilation, the greater the likelihood of a successful mitigation of the crime. These cases all share one thing in common, a defense that a criminal is somehow not really responsible for his or her own actions. "Abuse-excuse" defenses should play no role in determining a person's innocence or guilt. They demean our judicial system, they let the guilty escape just punishment, and they undermine the principle that we are responsible for controlling our actions.

If a man commits a crime, I believe that he is responsible for his crime—not his mommy and daddy, not racism, not an abusive spouse, not recovered memories of childhood abuse, not his potty training. He alone is responsible. He made the decision to murder. Then he murdered. He decided to rape. Then he raped. Unless we firmly reestablish that principle in our courts, our justice system will cease to have much real meaning.

All of the modern abuse excuses grew out of the traditional (and very sensible) insanity defense and the doctrine of self-defense. Both self-defense and the insanity defense relate to the *intent* and the *state of mind* of a criminal defendant. Although these doctrines have been with us for a long time, the application of the doctrines to specific facts is the battlefield upon which each society in its time expresses its values and its concept of what it is to be an adult—that is, to be a responsible human.

Our courts have become one of the principal arenas where traditional notions of personal responsibility grapple with new, supposedly more enlightened notions of who is really to blame for a criminal's heinous acts. Isn't society really to blame, or dysfunctional families? We are witnessing an assault by our high courts on all of our traditional notions of personal responsibility. The high courts must stop allowing juries to apply relaxed standards of personal responsibility in response to increasingly creative theories by defense psychiatric experts. The abuse excuses—recovered memory, emotional (not physical) duress, the "Twinkie defense," abused-child syndrome, and imperfect self-defense—are all reflections of the notion that somehow we are not really all that responsible for our acts. The devil made us do it. Such notions should remain between the defendant and his Maker. They belong in the confessional. They do not belong in a court of law.

Intent Is an Essential Element of Most Serious Crimes

Common-law judges in England invented most of our current system of criminal law. Under the common law, and today in the United States, the state has to prove two things in order to convict someone of a serious crime: the wrongful act (the *actus reus*), and a wrongful intent (*mens rea*). So an act without the wrongful intent is not a crime. For example, if you were to accidentally bump into a tourist at the edge of a scenic cliff and the tourist fell to his death, that would *not* be a crime. No intent to kill existed. The same act, however, with the intent to kill the tourist, would be murder. On the flip side, an evil intention without a correspondingly evil act is not a crime. Lorena Bobbitt is probably not the first woman to consider cutting off a man's penis. But thinking about it is not a crime. Lorena Bobbitt actually did it. That made her act a crime. So a wrongful *intent* must coexist with a wrongful *act*; otherwise there is no crime.

Can You Intend to Commit a Crime When You Are Crazy?

The M'Naughten case established the traditional defense of not guilty by reason of insanity. As such, it is the great-grand-daddy of all abuse-excuse cases. The M'Naughten case was as famous and as controversial in 1843 as the Hinckley, Menendez, Bobbitt, and White cases are today. It had famous victims: Edward Drummond was the private secretary to the very prominent Sir Robert Peel, the real target of the assassination. The killer was a severely disturbed man. The House of Lords debated the question and ruled as follows:

> If a man's mind is so ravaged by a mental disease or defect, such that he cannot know the nature and quality of his act, or if he does know the nature of the act, he does not know that the act is wrong, then he *is not guilty* by reason of insanity.

Of course, the M'Naughten rule follows logically from the idea, firmly part of English criminal law, that a killer must have the *intent* to kill. Thus, if a schizophrenic stabs his wife, thinking she is a tree, the killer is not guilty—he had no wrongful intent. Or if he intends to kill her but believes that she is a demon from hell, he would not be guilty because he did not know that the act was wrong.

Of course, it is a long path from the M'Naughten case to Dan White's "Twinkie defense" and the other various abuse-excuse defenses. But M'Naughten was where they all started. I do not intend to spend much more time on the traditional insanity defense embodied in M'Naughten. It is rarely used (in fewer than one percent of cases), and is rarely argued successfully (only about 26 percent of insanity pleas are successful). In over 80 percent of the successful cases, the prosecution and the defense agree that the defendant is insane. I do not believe that our system needs changes in the way that we handle our traditional insanity-defense cases. It is in the abuse-excuse defenses that the system starts to fall apart.

The Modern Diminished-Capacity Defenses

M'Naughten's unruly grandchildren, the diminished-capacity and diminished-responsibility defenses, threaten to tear our legal system apart. Instead of being complete defenses to a crime (like the insanity defense), the modern "Twinkie defenses" and abuse excuses result in people like Dan White and others being found guilty of a crime, but a much lesser crime—or in a jury being hopelessly deadlocked and confused, as in the first Menendez trial.

How did we get to this point? The diminished-capacity defenses are children of the sixties, a decade when a hurricane of anti-death-penalty rhetoric, pseudoscience, behavioral science, psychobabble, and legitimate scientific research into the human mind all came together. Collectively they changed the way many people in our society viewed personal responsibility. Their "enlightened" worldview holds that events from childhood determine who we are and what we do. Indeed, some even say prenatal conditions influence postnatal behavior.

It is easy to ascribe such views only to others. But many of us unconsciously accept some if not most of these tenets in our own lives when it is convenient to do so. For example, we sometimes deny responsibility for our behavior when we could have done better. We end a marriage with statements like "I have intimacy problems," or "I need some space," or "My mother never held me when I was a child. I cannot get close enough to you. That is not fair to you." What we are really saying is that we want to break up a marriage. Somehow our supposed intimacy or "space" problems relieve our guilt for hurting someone else. All of this is fairly mundane—just a little equivocating in our personal relationships. But this way of thinking was forced into our courtrooms in the 1960s by an activist Supreme Court. Because lots of us have started to think that way in our personal lives, it means that a lot of jurors have been open to creative excuses for criminal behavior. The result? A judicial train wreck that is still not over. As the theories of Freud, Jung, and Adler began to attract adherents, a firmament of research, study, and developing theories evolved. New insights into behavior and responsibility invaded the law like killer bees, first a hemisphere away, marching slowly toward our borders, then with increasing speed, penetrating the protective margins of safety.

In criminal law, this enlightened worldview sees our acts as the inevitable result of parents, siblings, and teachers who abused us, friends who tormented us, poor self-images and poorly developed egos and, I suppose, ids and superegos. In this worldview, we are not really responsible for what we do; it was all predetermined long ago. So less "enlightened" people have to understand that the pain and death of innocent victims and their surviving loved ones in the wake of some loser's slaughter-house tantrum is not really the killer's fault; it was all set in motion by forces beyond the killer's control. How often have we heard psychiatrists or psychologists say something that sounds like "The defendant suffered from low self-esteem, like Robert Bardo, who stalked and murdered actress Rebecca Schaeffer, or in a case in which the defendant massacred his entire family. He felt rejected, isolated, alone, detached. So one day he exploded into an uncontrollable rage, butchering his sister, brother, and mother. He needs psychiatric help—not prison." Sure.

Judicial Arrogance: The Conley and Goedecke Cases

It was 1967. I was just two years in the DA's office when a friend stopped by with a copy of the brand-new California Supreme Court decision in *People v. Goedecke*. I read the opinion with amazement. It was a brutal murder case. Here is how the court described the facts:

> Raymond Goedecke, eighteen years old, a religious young man, planned and executed the murder of his father. At a church camp he deliberately announced two or three times that he was sleeping in his car, in order to be able to leave and return undetected. He rolled his car down

the hill, then let the clutch out so he could not be heard. Upon reaching home he parked across the street, and took his shoes off when entering the house. He walked through the garage and picked up an iron bar, wrapping a towel around it. He went to his parents' bedroom and struck his father several times with the bar and then hit his mother a number of times. . . .

Afterwards he went into the bedroom of his fifteen-year-old sister and eight-year-old brother and struck them many times [killing them]. He washed up in the bathroom and then returned to his parents' bedroom and saw his father attempting to crawl towards the door. Defendant smoked a cigarette as he watched his father struggle for a while. On seeing his father's hunting knife on a chest, he thought, "Maybe this will finish him off." He then stabbed his father a number of times. As he left the house, his thought was, "Raymond, get out of here." He did not know what was in his mind during the episode except the two quoted thoughts.

He faked ransacking his parents' house, carefully disposed of the murder weapon, got gas for his car and washed up again at the gas station, and pretended horror and surprise the next day when he discovered the bodies.

The defense claimed that Goedecke was in a "dissociative" state from the time he went to sleep in the car until he awakened the next morning, and *that he was incapable of forming any intent to kill during the night in question.* The prosecution experts testified that he was not in an abnormal dissociative state, but simply experiencing what any "normal" person committing a horrible crime would be feeling. Dr. Alfred Larson summed it up this way:

I have come to the conclusion that dissociative reaction in situations like this very often is the *product of the crime*, rather than the cause of it. It's a way of the mind to protect itself from the consequences of such a brutal thing that is going on in front of the individual, in which they themselves are committing the act.

What Goedecke did sounds like a classic premeditated murder to me. It did to the jury, too; they returned a death sentence. But it did not sound at all like first-degree murder to a liberal California Supreme Court. The Supreme Court bought the defendant's psychiatric excuse argument hook, line, and sinker, and held that Goedecke could not be convicted of the first-degree murder of his father—you see, Goedecke's father may have struck him, he was rejected by his friends at the church camp, and communication between his father and him had broken down. So of course Raymond had to kill his father. As a result, the California Supreme Court reduced the conviction to second-degree murder. This being accomplished, the defendant could not be sentenced to death.

The court's reasoning in the Goedecke case was worse than its holding:

> [A]lthough defendant *knew* the difference between right and wrong and that the intended act *was* wrong, the extent of his understanding, his reflection upon it, and its consequences, with realization of the enormity of the evil, was *materially vague and detached* and fell short of the minimum essential elements of first degree murder. . . ." (Emphasis added.)

Huh? Poor little Raymond knew he was being bad, but was "vague and detached" about just how bad he was being? So what?

Needless to say, the Goedecke defense became a defense of preference in murder cases because it completely changed the elements of premeditation and deliberation. It was also popular because it often let the defense blame the victim: "Dad hit me. What else could I do?"

The Goedecke case changed the law of premeditation so that first-degree murder became second-degree murder. In *People v. Conley*, decided a year before *Goedecke*, the California Supreme Court took a different and more insidious path, undermining traditional notions of murder, by challenging the very underpinnings of the law of murder. In *Conley*, the court launched a frontal assault on the traditional definition of *malice*. This was an astonishing case, because malice is an element required for all murders—first or second degree. If defendants could mount a successful *Conley* defense, their murder charge would be reduced to manslaughter! Here are the facts in *Conley*:

Elaine McCool had promised to leave her husband and marry Conley—but she didn't. Conley responded by threatening to kill Elaine and her husband several times, but never carried through on his threats. Then Conley went on a three-day drinking binge while on medication for an ulcer and a back injury. At the end of the three-day bender, he shot and killed Elaine and her husband. Before leaving to kill the couple, Conley told friends that "I have been hurt by three different women before. I can't take it anymore. She promised to marry me." He was drunk.

The *Conley* court held that Conley could not harbor legal malice unless he had "an awareness of the obligation to act within the body of the laws regulating society." In other words, according to *Conley*, malice requires that we *understand and have the ability to conform our behavior to the law.* Without malice, murder becomes manslaughter.

Conley turned the law of homicide completely on its head. It was a shocking decision. A shockingly bad decision. Before *Conley*, the prosecution had to establish malice to convict for either first- or second-degree murder. Once the prosecution established malice, then the prosecution had to go further and establish the higher mental state of premeditation and deliberation. Premeditation and deliberation changed murder two to murder one. But under *Conley*, a killer could premeditate a killing (traditionally murder one), but still lack the element of malice! So a premeditated murder, a well-thought-out and well-planned killing, was no more than manslaughter under *Conley*.

Needless to say, the Conley case opened the floodgates. This was a dream come true for killers and their counsel. First-degree murder, which carried the death sentence, magically became voluntary or involuntary manslaughter. For an involuntary manslaughter conviction, the murderer serves a couple of years and then gets out. And not much more time is served for a voluntary killing. One after another, cases came down where first-degree murder was reduced to manslaughter by the courts, or by juries given confusing instructions. These cases culminated in the famous and successful "Twinkie defense," mounted by Dan White and his attorneys.

The Twinkie Defense

I have mentioned the Dan White "Twinkie defense" several times in passing. But you really have to understand the facts in that case to understand just how radically the California Supreme Court had reshaped the law of homicide in its ill-advised *Conley* decision.

White was a disgruntled former member of the San Francisco Board of Supervisors. He shot and killed Mayor George Moscone and San Francisco city supervisor and gay rights activist Harvey Milk. White was charged with two counts of first-degree murder, for which the prosecution sought the death penalty. The facts were simple. White was mad at Moscone and Milk. White had impetuously resigned from the Board of Supervisors. Shortly thereafter he wanted to be reinstated, and asked Moscone to do so. Moscone refused. They had an argument. White got a gun and then calmly and purposefully walked into the San Francisco City Hall, entering the building through a side ground-level window, thus enabling him to avoid the metal detectors located at the main entrance. White then walked directly to the mayor's office and killed Moscone. He reloaded his gun and then went to supervisor Harvey Milk's office and killed him.

At trial, White's lawyers contended that White had eaten so many Twinkies (a packaged cake confection with a creamy sugar filling) shortly before the murder that his blood sugar was elevated to the point that he was incapable of harboring malice, as it had been reshaped by *Conley*. Honest, I am not making this up. The jury found White guilty only of voluntary manslaughter. He was sentenced to the maximum for the crime, seven years and eight months for a double slaying. Dan White served only a few years in prison, and committed suicide a short time after his release. Perhaps he realized himself, better than did the high court, and better than did the jury, that he alone was responsible for his hideous acts, acts that deprived the city of San Francisco of its popular mayor and a much-loved member of their Board of Supervisors.

Although California led the way, concepts like the Twinkie defense are not unique to that state. By 1975, twenty-five states and several federal courts of appeal had adopted diminished-capacity (*Conley*-style) defenses. Other states adopted the pathological gambling syndrome, the battered-woman syndrome, post-traumatic stress disorder, temporary insanity, and other similar syndromes as defenses that would excuse defendants of crimes like murder, armed robbery ("I was a pathological gambler, I needed the money"), and so forth.

The People Strike Back

After the Dan White Twinkie-defense debacle, the people of California responded firmly to the Supreme Court's assault on the concept of personal responsibility. The judicially crafted law of diminished capacity (or diminished responsibility) was *expressly eliminated* in a series of carefully drawn and crafted laws. The statutes were unambiguous and absolutely clear that the diminished-capacity defenses, the Twinkie defenses, and the *Conley* and *Goedecke* doctrines were gone. History.

The Court Ignores the Will of the People

So how did the high court of California react to the new law? Easy. It just ignored the law through judicial sleight-of-hand. The court set twenty thousand angels dancing on the head of a pin and discovered that the legislature did not mean that *People v. Conley* was dead per se. Thus was born the doctrine of "imperfect self-defense." Imperfect self-defense allows defendants to claim that they were afraid another person was about to kill or seriously injure them. Normally the law requires that the defendant's belief that he is about to be killed be an objectively reasonable belief. But imperfect self-defense kicks in when the defendant's belief that he is about to be killed is *unreasonable*. In that case, imperfect self-defense reduces murder to manslaughter, because malice, an essential element of murder, does not exist. Simply put, he honestly but unreasonably believes he has a right under the law to use deadly force and therefore believes he is acting within the law. Now this is how it works in the real world. Suppose you are repeatedly harassed by a school bully. One day the bully says he's going to "get you real good." The next day you see him coming in your direction. His hands are in his pockets. You think he may have a concealed weapon. He yells for you to come over to him. Fearing that he is going to hurt you badly, you shoot him with a gun that you took from the house that morning. Your fear of imminent danger is real—but un- supported by objective facts.

This doctrine is truly a dream come true for any criminal de- fendant accused of murder or of maiming another person. For one thing, it radically reduces the sentence. Also, the defense is not really based on any facts; it is based on what the defendant says he was feeling. It is further based on paid psychiatrists, who make their living by testifying that defendants were actually, but unreasonably, afraid. To support their conclusions, these experts invent whatever syndromes are necessary for them to be able to reach that conclusion. To the extent that the defense is sup- ported by facts, the only person who can deny the facts is usually dead.

Imperfect self-defense also lets the criminal muddy the wa- ters by putting the victim on trial. The issue is no longer whether the defendant murdered someone. It is how the defendant felt and what he was thinking when he was committing the murder. Was the victim mean to the defendant? For how long did the vic- tim's meanness last? How did it make the defendant feel when the victim was so mean? Was the victim mean just before the murder? And we instruct our juries to come back with manslaughter verdicts if they empathize sufficiently with the de- fendant's feelings and thoughts.

The Menendez Monsters

And then came the Menendez case. Lyle and Eric Menendez were two rich Beverly Hills kids with a domineering father and an alcoholic mother. They murdered their parents. The mur- ders were carefully planned. Two days before the killing, Lyle and Eric bought shotguns under false identities in San Diego. San Diego is 120 miles from their home, making it unlikely that anyone local would remember them buying the shotguns. They loaded the shotguns and waited until their parents were watch- ing a movie on a big-screen TV, eating ice cream.

They shot their parents at close range in the back, the head, and the side. They kept shooting when their parents were sitting on the sofa, slumped on the floor or crawling for God knows what. They smashed their parents' heads with some hard object—probably the shotguns. They shredded their kneecaps with buckshot to make it look like a Mafia hit. Eric and Lyle then went outside, reloaded their weapons, and came back in and finished off the mother, who was, as the boys so delicately put it, "sneaking away," dragging her body across a lake of her own blood pooling on the floor.

The boys set up an alibi, buying tickets to a movie and making plans to see Eric's tennis coach on the night of the killing. Within twenty-four hours of the killings, Lyle and Eric took their father's safe to the home of a probate attorney, afraid their father had changed his will as he had recently threatened to do. In quick order, Lyle and Eric moved to the trendy Marina district while Lyle negotiated to buy a $1.1-million condo and a $90,000 Porsche. In a moment of generosity, Lyle even sent Eric to Israel for a tennis tournament.

Then Lyle and Eric made the mistake of telling their therapist that they had killed their parents because their father was cheating on their mother and making her miserable and suicidal. Once they'd killed their father, they said, they'd done their mother a favor by killing her, because she couldn't do anything without her dead husband. Those were the objective facts.

The murdered victims were victimized again—their every act and deed presented to the whole world for its judgment. The defense contended that Lyle and Eric, acting out of fear, conditioned by years of physical, emotional, sexual, and verbal abuse, had an actual but unreasonable belief that they were going to be killed by their parents. So they struck first, and killed their parents before their parents killed them. In support of this contention the defense offered the following: Both Eric and Lyle had been sexually abused by their father. Until the last week before the killings, Lyle was unaware of Eric having been abused, and vice versa. Their father had threatened to kill Eric unless he kept the molestation a secret. When Eric told Lyle of the molestation, Lyle confronted his father, demanding that he stop. The father laughed, then angrily said that "they were through," which Lyle took to mean that they were going to be killed, because the father said "the things Lyle was planning don't matter anymore."

Note how all of the facts pertaining to imperfect self-defense are things that only Lyle and Eric's parents could verify or deny. And they are, of course, conveniently unable to testify. There was never any objective evidence of sexual abuse. Never. The lack of objective evidence is typical of imperfect-self-defense cases. By way of contrast, a traditional self-defense case is usually accompanied by physical evidence that confirms or rebuts the claim of self-defense. For example, ballistics can usually tell whether the victim was coming toward the defendant when a gun went off, how close the two of them were, and whether the victim was facing the defendant or was turned away when the gun was fired.

An abuse-excuse defense profoundly affects the course of a trial. In the first Menendez trial, that defense allowed the highly skilled attorney Charlie Gessler and the brilliant Leslie Abramson to put Eric and Lyle's parents on trial. The jury in the first trial was confused. It hung hopelessly between a murder verdict and a manslaughter verdict. After the hung verdict, the Menendez brothers were retried. In the second trial, the court did not permit the boys to raise the abuse-excuse defense. Although Gessler and Abramson were still on the defense team, the jury had no difficulty returning a verdict of murder in the first degree.

The Lorena Bobbitt case was similar to *Menendez*. However in Bobbitt, there were facts supporting her claim that she was a battered wife. She had apparently suffered years of abuse at the hands of her husband. Several options were open to Bobbitt— she could have stayed with her neighbor (who had offered to let Lorena stay with her), called the police or a spousal abuse hot line, or just packed and left. She had a number of options short of mayhem and mutilation. But she waited until her husband was asleep, then cut off his penis.

Lorena Bobbitt's defense was geared toward getting the jury to concentrate on what a terrible person her husband was, rather than on what she herself had done. The imperfect-self-defense doctrine, coupled with the doctrine of temporary insanity, also let her play the sex card, just as Johnnie Cochran played the race card in the Simpson case. Women who had fantasized about cutting off some guy's penis finally had a hero who actually did it. Opinions just about that silly were expressed by many women during the thrill of the Bobbitt trial. As Rush Limbaugh pointed out in an article published in *Newsweek*, "Just imagine what their [the feminists'] reaction would be if someone had tried to cut off a woman's breast." Just suppose. Would the poor fellow's feelings excuse his act of mutilating a woman? Suppose the poor fellow's mother had withheld affection and hit him when he was a child. So now he claims that he fears all women. He claims that the victim reminded him of his mother. Of course he had to cut off the victim's breast before she hit him, just like his mother used to hit him. It is insane that this argument does not reduce us to giggles. It is insane that serious defense attorneys could and, in fact, will make this argument someday if the law is not changed.

The main effect of the abuse excuses in *Menendez, Bobbitt*, and similar cases is to allow the defendant to blame the victim for the defendant's own evil acts. The subliminal message to the jury in the Menendez case was that *Jose Menendez was a bastard and had it coming.* In the Bobbitt case, Bobbitt's husband was abusive. He probably *was* a real bastard. But she cut off his penis when he was asleep. The fact that someone is a bastard is not grounds for murder. It does not justify cutting off a sleeping man's penis. It does not justify cutting off a woman's breast.

This is about much bigger issues than child or spousal abuse. We are a society of laws. The law does not provide for a "self-help" death penalty. Even if everything the Menendez brothers claimed was true, the law still does not provide the death penalty for what Jose Menendez did. Nor does the law provide for Bobbitt's maiming her husband as a punishment for his sins. If we want to change the law, we can. After all, in common-law England, virtually every felony resulted in the death penalty. So we could pass laws making child abuse a capital crime. We could punish spousal abuse by removing the genitals of the husband. There is a precedent. In some Arab countries, theft is punished by cutting off the thief's hand. But until we are ready to do that directly and as a matter of law, why should we allow self-help to accomplish the same end?

Do we really want a society in which each person is left to judge when enough is enough? And, having decided that, should each person be empowered to take a human life? The days of the Old West are over. Self-help belongs in Charles Bronson movies, not in our everyday life. That is still why criminal charges are brought in the name of "the People," not in the name of the victim. The government brings the charges, not the victim or the victim's family. Hence, "The *government* charges Paul James and Kenneth Green with murder in the first degree."

And so we are back to where we started. These special defenses are a reflection of a sickness in our society. For some reason, we of the collective-guilt age have a hard time dealing with the fact that people are responsible for their own actions. The real culprit is racism or child abuse or spousal abuse or government funding cutbacks. . . . The list is endless. The message our judicial system sends when it buys into this nonsense is that everyone is a victim; that the killer and the dead person are morally equal; that both are victims; that, in fact, the killer is in some ways morally superior to the dead person because the dead person was a bastard. I do not accept that reasoning. Nor should our judicial system.

If you think that absurd excuses and blaming everyone else is unique to big criminal trials like *Menendez* and *Bobbitt*, think again. Kids have figured out that if they claim abuse, the shrinks treat them differently and so does the court system. I frequently sat in amazement in juvenile court as one teen after another explained to me why they did what they did. "My mother wouldn't let me stay up and watch TV." "She wouldn't let me play with my friends." "She was always making me read things I didn't want to read." "I had to take care of my sister." "I never could do anything I wanted." "My mother called the cops on me . . . we were just smoking a few joints." "She made me go to school." "She wouldn't let me drive the car." "She hit me." "I was abused." It wasn't my fault. Mom did it. In other words, I and the person I just killed, the woman I just raped, are really both victims. They are learning young these days. At fourteen years old, they already know how to play the professional victim.

Get Rid of Imperfect Self-Defense

I would immediately cast the doctrine of imperfect self-defense and all other diminished-capacity defenses, including the temporary-insanity defense, on the junk pile of noble but failed experiments—perhaps right next to the discarded statues of Stalin in the former Soviet Union. It is not unreasonable for society to expect people to act reasonably and in accordance with traditional notions of behavior. Nor is it unreasonable to hold them to account for their acts that do not fit our laws. Nor is it unreasonable to require people to have due regard for the sanctity of human life.

If there are mitigating circumstances that the killer thinks are relevant, then they should only be admissible at the probation and sentencing hearing before a judge, not in front of the jury. At the sentencing hearing, a judge can assign the degree of culpability and moral turpitude of the offender and mete out the appropriate sentence reflective of all the circumstances of the crime. In this way we still discourage personal retribution and self-help, while recognizing the infirmities and weaknesses in people that cause us to act beyond the pale of acceptable behavior.

SEVENTEEN

Hang 'Em High.
Well . . . Sorta.

POLITICAL SMOKE AND MIRRORS

A lie which is half a truth is ever the blackest of lies.
—*Alfred, Lord Tennyson, 1864*

We all want to be tough on crime. The truth is, we've had enough. We can't go to the store late at night because we might be robbed. Can't walk the streets because we might be assaulted. Won't let our children go to a party because there might be drugs, or worse. Can't take the kids to the stadium because it's in a drug-infested, crime-ridden neighborhood, where routine shootings take place. Won't drive on the freeways late at night after the dance, because there might be a drive-by. We can't drive a nice car because we might be carjacked, our bodies dumped unceremoniously on the pavement. We don't feel in control of our own lives. We choose carefully where and when we go, where and when we park our cars, surrendering territory to the criminal predators and the gangs, block by precious block.

If any of this resonates with you, then you're mad, plenty mad. You want to do something about it. "Let's get the bastards, let's hang 'em high." But first let's talk about politicians. Politicians identify key issues, reduce the key issues to buzzwords, and then persuade you to vote for them. It may not surprise you that the politicians often do not give a damn about solving the problem that makes the buzzwords resonate. They care about getting your vote. "Let's get tough on crime" is exactly that kind of buzz. Democrats and Republicans are falling all over themselves to prove that they are the toughest of the tough guys on crime.

So politicians offer us a quick fix and we jump at it. We say okay. It sounds good to us. We can get back at the predators. Keep 'em off the streets. Lock 'em up. Yep, that's what we're going to do. The honor roll of important-sounding anti-crime legislation or initiatives over the past thirty years is impressive. The "three strikes" law; the Racketeer Influenced Corrupt Organization Act (RICO); the "war on drugs"; the Omnibus Crime Control Act; heck, we even had a "drug czar." And on it goes. So what I want to know is, Why do we feel less secure than we did a year ago, five years ago, ten years ago, thirty years ago? Why didn't all these impressive-sounding laws seem to have any effect at all? Why are things getting worse?

What is really going on is that our politicians are playing "let's pretend." Our political leaders are lying to us about crime. They will pass all the tough-sounding measures that we want—as long as they can make us think that they are actually doing something. What they won't tell you is that they aren't going to spend enough money, your tax dollars, to do what it takes to *keep* the dangerous felons off the streets. Not unless we make them do it. Period.

It should not be too tough for the politicians to figure this one out. To put a bad guy in jail, what we have to do is (1) arrest him; (2) try and convict him; (3) put him in jail; and (4) keep him in jail. A straightforward formula. It means that we have to have enough police, enough courts, and enough jails to handle all of the bad guys. So why is it that the politicians have systematically withheld money from the police, the judicial system, the jails, and the prison system for thirty years at the same time that crime, ugly violent crime, has been skyrocketing? The reason is simple—the politicians do not want to spend the money. *But unless we have enough police, courts, jails, and prisons, all of the tough-sounding laws in the world don't mean a thing, except votes.* Hang 'em high. Sure.

The situation in L.A. is analogous to that in other cities. The voters, tired of habitual criminals, approved a bond issue a few years ago to build a new $373 million adjunct jail facility in Los Angeles. "State of the art," the politicians squealed. "We'll show 'em who's tough on crime." When it came time to open the new jail, when it came time actually to put bad guys in it, the politicians couldn't find the money to run it. As of this writing, this $373 million monument to getting tough on crime has been vacant and unused for nearly two years. It's not that there is no money; it's that there are other priorities for the money. And as long as the politicians can buy your vote with buzzwords and political chatter and without changing their spending priorities, that is exactly what they will do.

Meanwhile, the L.A. County Sheriff, lacking the space in his other jails, uses existing dormitory-style facilities to house rival gang members together. Crips, Bloods, Mexican Mafia, white supremacist gangs, Asian gangs, all cleaving to one another like killer wasps and poisonous spiders. If these guys were on the street in a natural setting, they would kill one another in the blink of an eye. Some jail facilities have been closed because they are regarded as too antiquated to house the inmate population humanely. Others were closed because the sheriff had to shift members of his force from jail operations to street patrols.

These are jails I'm talking about, not prisons. Jails are supposed to be the place for the lightweight criminals. The only really bad guys who are supposed to be in jail are the ones waiting for trial or for a place in a real prison like San Quentin or Folsom. But the prisons are so grossly overcrowded that the Wayside Honor Rancho, formerly a minimum-security jail, is now a maximum-security facility, holding very bad guys together in dormitories who can't be housed in adequate prisons because there is no space. Jails and prisons happen to be the fastest-growing sector in the U.S. economy. And still no space!

Politicians are looking to the private sector to provide more cost-effective management of our jails and prisons. The private sector, however, is not a panacea; profit being their primary motivation, costly training of personnel is often compromised, not to mention the quality of guards hired. You get what you pay for. Cut-rate guards mean diminished professionalism and dangerous incompetency.

This problem is not unique to Los Angeles or California. It's happening everywhere. The L.A. County Sheriff is now releasing jail inmates after they have served only 25 percent of the court-ordered sentence. Read that again. *Only 25 percent of the court-*

ordered sentence. Look at the consequences. This means a defendant who drew a weapon will serve six nights on a thirty-day sentence, a wife-beater six weeks on a six-month sentence. So here's a real for-instance—a recent one. A husband beat his wife. He vowed he would kill her. They put him in jail. But the sheriff released him in just a few days—no room. He promptly killed his wife. A running joke among those in the know about criminal law is that knowledgeable defense attorneys refuse probation for their clients on misdemeanor charges, demanding that the judge impose the maximum misdemeanor jail time of one year. They know that the sheriff will release the defendant after he serves only three months. That beats two years' probation for most of their recidivist clients.

Our jail and prison populations will triple by 2006. Where are we going to put the people? Who's going to pay for it? If we are really serious about violent crime, serious about keeping violent offenders off the streets, then we have to make our politicians pay for it. That means paying to put an entire infrastructure in place: more cops, more courts, more prosecutors, more defense attorneys, more jails, more jailers, more prisons, more prison guards. California alone will need twenty new prisons by 2005. Its current prison population of 135,000 (exclusive of jails) will explode to over 306,000 by 2005. When we extend this to the rest of the country, we are talking abut a lot of money—maybe several hundred billion dollars over the next twenty years. It will be a big job, and it will require that the politicians spend money according to our priorities rather than theirs. Keeping civil order is the first job of government. This cost would indeed be worth it, if we finally got what we wanted—civil order, peace of mind. *If* is a mighty big word in this equation.

I want to take you on a guided tour of some political smoke and mirrors. The latest, greatest get-tough anti-crime programs are the three-strikes-style laws. There is nothing special about them; I could analyze just about every get-tough anti-crime measure that the politicians have sold us in the past thirty years in about the same way. They all look tough. But all are seriously flawed because they fail to supply the infrastructure necessary to make them work. So let's look at the three-strikes law. Is it an effective and efficient means of reducing violent crime, or is it counterproductive?

Here is a quick demographic lesson. Most active, violent criminals are between thirteen and twenty-nine years old. This age group commits the vast bulk of all violent and serious felonies. As criminals move into their thirties, the incidence of violence tapers off. In the past couple of years there has been a small decrease in the amount of violent crime. The politicians, of course, are taking credit for the change. They got tough! Not really. The actual reason violent crime has dropped in the past few years is that the baby boomers are getting old, most now in their forties. People in their forties do not commit very many violent crimes. Because a smaller percentage of the population is in its "prime crime" years, there are fewer crimes. Here's another piece of news the politicians won't tell you: The baby boomers had children. The children of the baby boomers will soon be into their "prime crime" years. If this fact does not scare you, it should. I sat as a juvenile court judge. I know what's going on out there. Today's kids are already showing signs of being the highest crime generation ever in America—both qualitatively and quantitatively. The crimes committed by young people today are unimaginable compared to a few decades ago. Fourteen-year-olds executing their parents and siblings. Children putting rat poison in a teacher's drink. Shooting teachers. Shooting schoolmates. AK-47s. Drive-bys. A six-year-old boy beating a four-week-old baby with hands, fists, and a stick. We will have to deal with them right off the bat. Early. Effectively. It will be too late if we wait for their third strike. We're going to have to start acting on the first strikes.

There are different kinds of proposed three-strikes laws. Some require a defendant's prior crimes to have been violent felonies; others require *serious or violent* prior felonies (a "serious" felony is actually considered to be less serious than a violent felony). Some three-strikes laws require the third strike to be a serious or violent felony. Others, as in California, specify that the third strike may be *any* felony, including theft. So, for example, in California, the third-strike felony could be a petty theft, possession of a tiny amount of cocaine, or walking into a department store and stealing a pair of underwear. Or it could mean taking a piece of pizza from some kids on the beach boardwalk.

Regardless of the nature of the third-strike felony, California DAs are required to file the felony as a third strike. While the DA can then have it removed as a third strike (with court approval), DAs are political animals, loath to remove a third-strike count because they are fearful that they will be labeled as "soft on crime." (There are DAs who refuse to file "three-strikes cases" in nonviolent felony cases—San Francisco DA Terrance Hallinan, for one. Of course, that's San Francisco. So if you have two priors and you're a thief in San Francisco, a little jail time will do you. But if you're in L.A. County, you're looking at twenty-five years to life. That's not exactly evenhanded justice.)

Many states' three-strikes laws are like California's; they do not distinguish among different types of felonies on the third strike. So the auto thief, the addict with a small amount of cocaine, and someone boosting food from the local 7-Eleven can end up doing as much time as, and more time than, a person convicted of second-degree murder, rape, or child molestation. What does it say about a society, when it would send a person to prison for twenty-five years to life for the theft of a can of oil, a piece of clothing, a slice of bread? The teachings of the Old Testament were far more humane: "An eye for an eye, a tooth for a tooth, hand for hand, foot for foot." At least this connotes some proportionality between the crime and the punishment.

Let's look at a couple of additional problems with the third-strike laws. Let's say you are a street mugger. You already have two strikes. You are robbing someone. You have to choose now. Do you kill the victim or not? Before three strikes, killing the victim was not a high-percentage move. Murder carried a much higher sentence than a mugging. But if you have two strikes, you are going to do twenty-five years to life for the mugging anyway. Second-degree murder carries only fifteen years to life, and first-degree murder (noncapital) carries twenty-five years to life in California. You might as well kill the victim—it's cleaner, and there are no witnesses. And if you think criminals are too stupid to figure this one out, think again. They are evil, not stupid. Cops are also in greater danger when they arrest a suspect who knows he will be subject to the three-strikes laws.

Now it's time for some more demographics. It is axiomatic that criminals up on their third strike will have committed their prior felonies over a period of years. By the time the third strike is committed, the felon may present no serious threat of violence to anyone. Remember, the third strike does not have to be violent. So our typical third-strike felon is likely in his late thirties or forties, and he is charged with "*any* felony." Third-strikers tend to be older. On the other hand, the first- and second-strikers in jail right now are younger and are more likely to commit violent felonies on release. So whom should we keep in prison—the older, less violent third-strikers or the younger, more violent first- and second-strikers? You say, "Let's keep all of them in jail." That's a great idea, but today it is impossible. Remember, the politicians have starved the prison system of funds for thirty years. There is no space to hold both the first-strikers and the third-strikers. That's reality. The politicians don't want to tell you, but that's a fact.

So look at the effect of the three-strikes law. Every time we send a non-violent third-striker to jail or prison for twenty-five years to life, other criminals, probably younger than the third-striker, and probably more prone to violence, must be released to make room for him. So here's another dirty little secret that the politicians won't tell you: Young, violent, and dangerous felons are being paroled at this very moment to prey on society because their early release frees the space required to incarcerate the pizza thief and the department-store thief and the drug addict on the corner for twenty-five years to life. These young felons are the most dangerous people in our society. And we are releasing them upon ourselves during the years when they still have the drive and the adrenaline to hurt us badly. I know we did not intend this when we voted for politicians to pass the third-strike laws, but what I described is happening right now, today. This is crazy. To be sure, many three-strikes defendants are charged with violent felonies. Putting them in jail for a very long time is the satisfying part of the three-strikes laws. We will always be able to find examples of really bad guys sitting in prison right now for a long time because of the three-strikes laws. But as a group, the three-strikes population is less dangerous than the young men who have committed violent first felonies.

I am not going to pretend, like a politician, that there are any quick fixes. No "get tough" measure is going to make a big difference without more police, more courts, more prosecutors and public defenders, and more jails and prisons. Until we have enough jails and prisons, we will just be shuffling bad guys in and out, when *all* of them should be incarcerated.

I believe, however, that we would be better served, as argued by Victor Sze in a fine *Loyola University Law Review* article, by a *guaranteed full-term* policy, instead of a three-strikes policy. That means people who commit violent and serious felonies the *first* time must do *all* of the time. No early parole, no good-time/work-time credits of one day for every day a criminal predator serves in prison. Do the crime, serve the time. If they commit a second violent or serious felony, they do the "guaranteed full term," which under the law is enhanced by the prior felony. By the time they get out, they are older and less likely to commit the crimes of a twenty-year-old—the crimes that maim and kill us in just milliseconds of explosive aggression.

In addition to its impact on the jail and prison system, the California three-strikes law has brought a teetering court system to its knees. Remember, for thirty years, the legislature has starved the courts, as well as the penal system, of funds. The courts have had to compensate by *not* going to trial in criminal cases. Trials are too time-consuming, too costly. The DAs and the courts avoid going to trial with plea bargains. A plea bargain is a deal by which the defendant agrees not to try the case, or pleads guilty to a lesser charge, in exchange for less time in jail or prison. Not an elegant solution, but at least it keeps things running. Without plea bargaining, and lots of it, the system would collapse. When I was a DA, over 90 percent of all felonies were disposed of by plea bargains. Just before we passed the three-strikes law in California, the percentage was up to about 94 percent. The reason for the increase? More criminals, no additional courtrooms, no additional judges. Sze points out that since the three-strikes law was passed, only 6 percent of three-strikes cases and 14 percent of second-strike cases have been settled by plea bargain. If but an additional 5 percent of the total number of felony cases go to trial, in Los Angeles County alone we will have to conduct nearly five thousand trials per year. We don't have enough judges and courtrooms to come even close to being able to conduct that many trials. This will affect you directly. Criminal cases have priority over civil cases. This means that the three-strikes law will likely bring the civil courts to a halt. So, if you are in a car accident, forget about collecting money from the insurance company; you will not be able to get to trial to sue them. All of the courtrooms will be busy trying third strikes.

Amazingly, when members of the "get tough" public sit as jurors, they do not want to sit on three-strikes cases. They do not want to send someone to prison for twenty-five years for stealing. So they do what jurors do. They nullify and play with the facts, or they refuse to sit on the case if they are informed that it is a three-strikes case. Mind you, these are the very members of the public who thought they wanted three-strikes laws. Intuitively, we who have to pay for the three-strikes law have drawn a line in the sand. We don't think it makes good sense to send people back to prison for life because they stole something when there isn't enough prison space to house violent, predatory criminals. How much are you willing to pay for "getting tough on crime"? How much pressure are you willing to bring on your politicians to stop lying, to stop pretending that they are solving crime with buzzwords? I have some suggestions about which items on our get-tough wish list need the highest priority and where to spend the limited funds available.

1. *Infrastructure.* First and foremost, more police, more courts, more jails and prisons. Of those, more jails and prisons are the most important. There is not even a close second in priorities.

2. *Guaranteed Full-Term Sentences.* Since three-strikes cases do not embrace first-time offenders, we must ensure that first-time offenders who have committed violent or serious felonies serve the full term ostensibly promised by the legislature. No early release. No time credits. (While the initial cost is higher, in the long run it will stop criminal recidivism at an early phase, act as a deterrent, and reduce the number of third-strikers.) Remember, when felons move into their thirties and forties as a group, they statistically commit less violent felonies than those between the ages of thirteen and twenty-nine.

3. *Three-Strikes Laws for Violent or Serious Felonies Only.* Three-strikes laws should be tailored to the demographics of the prison population. The only three-strikers that we want in jail for the long term are the ones who are still violent or dangerous. Therefore we must require that the prior felonies be serious and violent, and that the third strike be a violent and serious felony. No two-bit felonies. No misdemeanors masquerading as felonies. Burglaries in the night, robberies, kidnappings, deadly assaults, murders, rapes, forcible child molestation, yes. Stealing clothes or food, possessing small quantities of drugs, stealing a wallet without violence, no.

4. *No Early Parole.* No good-time or work-time credits for violent or serious felons. You do the crime, you do the time. (But this means we have to make the politicians build more prisons and prison infrastructure.)

5. *Alternative Sentencing.* All non-violent and non-serious felonies should be subject to alternative sentencing such as work programs, community service, house arrest with electronic monitoring anklets, and the like. This will free up much-needed space and resources required for violent offenders. (We save money here.)

6. *Juvenile Justice.* The most dangerous felons are the young ones. I wish I knew how to save them. But by the time they are sixteen, seventeen, or eighteen and have committed several violent or serious felonies, my experience is that there is little hope for them. If they are let out of juvenile detention facilities, the overwhelming odds are that they will rape or kill or commit other crimes again and again. They need to be incarcerated just like adults for the guaranteed full term in the prisons for youthful offenders while they are being educated and given job skills. (That means more money.) Regarding three-strikes laws, serious or violent prior felonies, even if the perpetrator is a juvenile, should count as priors. (This reaches those in the most dangerous demographic group, who must be stopped at the earliest possible phase of their violent criminal careers.)

7. *Prosecutorial Discretion.* Finally, the prosecutor and the judge should have the discretion to remove a prior in the interest of justice. But it must be done on the record so that the public may track those dispositions. No hidden deals, just a little occasional humanity when the circumstances dictate and the DA and judge can justify it to a public fed up with crime.

Now we know what we should do. But here's the hard part: we have to make our politicians do it. That means no lies. No deceit. They must do what they say, and say what they do. No empty jails and unused prisons rotting away. We're willing to pay a fair amount to free ourselves from the imprisonment of our violent criminal captors. That's more important than a nominal 15 percent tax cut across the board. We can't afford that right now. So just tell us what it will really cost, and we'll tell you where from our tax dollars you can take our money. These solutions, while not perfect, impart some sanity to the hot rhetoric of toughness.

E I G H T E E N

Open the Windows

TV in the Courtroom

The Government's power to censor the press was abolished
so that the press would remain forever free to censor the
government. The press was protected so that it could bare
the secrets of Government and inform the people.
—*Justice Hugo Black, 1971*

As I view it, TV and radio, as well as the more conventional
methods of disseminating news, are all included in the
concept of "press" as used in the First Amendment and
therefore are entitled to live under the laissez faire regime
which the First Amendment sanctions.
—*Justice William O. Douglas, 1973*

All government functionaries, including the judiciary,
need a watchdog. Thomas Jefferson said, "There is no
safe deposit [for the liberty and property of the people]
but with the people themselves; nor can it be safe with
them without information. Where the press is free, and every
man able to read, all is safe." TV is our principal means of communication, our principal watchdog, as we edge toward the
twenty-first century. It has become our eyes and ears, our window to the world, the tube that allows us to see where we could
not otherwise see. It ended the Vietnam War. It stoked racial
fires in major cities. It gave us back American pride during the
Persian Gulf War. It brought down a presidency by showing us a
corrupt president.

The TV camera in the courtroom is one of the best things that has happened to our criminal justice system in many years. We must insist that our state court judges use courtroom cameras more often. We must demand, through legislation if necessary, that the insular federal courts reverse their complete ban on cameras in federal court. We should bring pressure to bear on federal judges to open their courtrooms to public scrutiny. As life appointees, they enjoy great entitlements and wield enormous power. They bear close watching by an informed public. I guarantee that the public would be amazed at what goes on in some federal courtrooms.

Public trials are an American tradition, and cameras in court are very much a part of that tradition. As soon as cameras and live radio transmitters could be placed in courtrooms, they were. Live coverage was as controversial then as it is today. So you might not be surprised to learn that the first attempt to ban cameras and live radio coverage of criminal trials took place in the 1930s. Those who would ban the cameras are still busy today. So let's take a step back in time for a moment and look at just how much public trials and cameras in court are part of the fabric of American life.

Colonists in rural America regularly attended criminal trials in person. Courthouses were the centers of community life from which counties and townships emerged. Trials were scheduled on designated days. Those designated days were a community event—a family holiday of sorts. The trials were frequently followed by festivities. Everyone participated in the process. We citizens were knowledgeable about our courts. We knew if the judge was stupid. We saw when justice was being perverted. We were there, and the courts belonged to us.

Courthouses continued to be the center of much of our communal life until long after the Civil War. The history of the Civil War is replete with famous battles named after various courthouses. One of the bloodiest encounters of the war took place at Spotsylvania Court House in the Wilderness. Lee surrendered to Grant at Appomattox Courthouse. It was not so much that opposing generals liked to fight or surrender at or near courthouses. It was that courthouses were usually centrally located and often at the intersection of the important roads.

Why? Because they were still the most prominent and important buildings around, even as late as 1864.

It is not like that anymore in America. Many of us could not even locate the courthouse in our community. Even fewer have ever attended a criminal trial just to see what is going on. We work too hard. We live in an urban, postindustrial society. Our sense of community no longer exists. We view our justice system, if at all, from a distance. As our personal involvement in the criminal justice system waned, the media rushed to fill the void. The media have an absolute right to report on a trial—before, during, and after. That means the media have the right to be in the courthouse (although not necessarily with a camera). This right is guaranteed by the First Amendment and is an essential part of the fabric of our free society.

Information is, however, a two-edged sword. Press coverage of trials has not always been a constructive influence, to say the least. By the 1920s, tabloid-style reporting of criminal trials was commonplace. In the trials of Sacco and Vanzetti in 1921 and of Leopold and Loeb in 1924, unruly and aggressive media fanned the flames of passion, convicting the defendants in the press before a word was uttered in court.

In 1925, Clarence Darrow and William Jennings Bryan held the world spellbound in the notorious Scopes "Monkey Trial." An outraged public, throughout the entire world, followed the proceedings blow-by-blow on newsreels and, for the first time ever, live radio. "Turn your face a little more this way, Your Honor," the photographers yelled, as if directing a commercial. "Step a little farther forward," they stridently demanded of Clarence Darrow. The trial judge in the Scopes case, John T. Raulston, boasted that his gavel would be "heard around the world." And it was.

Everything changed in 1935, when Bruno Hauptmann was accused of kidnapping and murdering the son of an American icon, Colonel Charles Lindbergh. The world was sated with gavel-to-gavel coverage by radio and movie cameras in the courtroom. More than six hundred reporters and one hundred camera operators fought for their place in the sun. Ungovernable photographers scampered like frenzied mice atop counsel table, blinding witnesses and attorneys with flashbulbs for the evening edition. Media coverage of the Lindbergh case was a travesty. As a result, the American Bar Association added Canon 35 to its Judicial Canons of Ethics in 1937, prohibiting the broadcasting or photographing of court proceedings. The ABA extended its prohibition to TV cameras in the courtroom in 1952. But the courts intervened and allowed cameras back in. So, in 1954, Dr. Sam Shepard was lynched and convicted by the print media and TV cameras in the courtroom. F. Lee Bailey secured a reversal of the conviction because of the pervasive inflammatory and prejudicial media coverage. On retrial, Shepard was acquitted. (The Shepard case continued its telegenic run after the retrial. *The Fugitive*, one of the most popular series in TV history, was based on the Shepard case.)

Today some thirty-five states allow cameras in criminal courtrooms under designated circumstances, almost always requiring the consent of the presiding judge and giving control over the cameras to the judge. Federal judges, however, have voted overwhelmingly not to permit any television cameras in their courtrooms.

The Benefits of Cameras in the Courtroom

In the Prologue to this book, I noted how profoundly the media coverage of recent trials has changed the nature of the public dialogue about our judicial system. The callers I talk to on my TV and radio shows have seen what is going on, they understand what is going on, and they do not like what they have seen. In fact, one of the reasons you are reading this book is probably the disquieting sense you got when the cameras rolled and you saw real criminal justice—not *L.A. Law*—served up on prime-time TV.

Many of the players in the system—the attorneys, the judges, and the professional experts—are not pleased that the public is looking so hard at the judicial system. Something might change. The system has been developed by and for judges and lawyers. Many really don't want the system to change. They like the status quo. So you will hear a lot of people arguing that we should bar cameras from the courtroom. They will talk about the dignity of the proceedings and the majesty of the law. They will argue that cameras demean the nobility of the law. Hogwash.

There is nothing noble about disrespectful, shameful, and abusive behavior in our courts, or about runaway jury verdicts. Cameras merely record and play back what happens, warts and all. This is just like the Rodney King beating tape. The camera was not the problem; it was only the messenger. *What* the camera recorded was the problem. If we don't like seeing police batter people senseless, let's stop police beatings. If cameras show us scenes that are demeaning to the criminal justice system, then it is time to change the system. If the players misbehave, we can stop it because we see it. Putting the cameras away and expecting things to get better is as futile as killing the messenger, burning the message, and hoping it will all go away. Interestingly, in light of Judge Fugisaki's ban on TV cameras in the Simpson civil trial, the "E" entertainment channel presented reenactments of courtroom testimony performed by actors using the trial transcripts as a script. While they tried to reflect the courtroom proceedings accurately, of necessity they had to decide what was important and what was not. Having attended the trial, I can tell you that the actors could not and did not accurately portray the ambiance, body language, and essence of the attorneys and the witnesses' testimony. I say that we keep the cameras in sharp focus—so they can do their job, one that they do better than anyone—revealing intimate details about how our system works or fails to work *and* informing us of the good to be savored and preserved.

Normally, when we think about cameras in the courtroom, what comes to mind are regular criminal trials of adults. But a huge part of our justice system deals with juveniles. Juvenile justice, in the long run, has a greater impact on crime than any other component of the justice system. It is the feeder to the adult system. We know little about our juvenile system. The theory is that juvenile courts are designed to change criminal behavior, not to convict children. Therefore, the theory goes, anonymity facilitates rehabilitation. It also allows the juvenile justice system to remain hidden from view, even though some of our most vicious criminals are juveniles.

The public needs to be informed about this very insular and protective enclave of the justice system. What kinds of deals are being made? How do we treat juveniles? What programs are being implemented to change vicious behavior? What additional resources do we need? Is juvenile probation effective? Do juvenile camps work, and what goes on there? Does the youth authority do its job? Accordingly, TV cameras should be allowed in all juvenile cases involving rape, attempted rape, murder, attempted murder, or any case in which a gun or other deadly weapon is used, *and* where the DA's petition to have the juvenile tried by the adult court was denied.

Look what this would accomplish. For juvenile recidivists, anonymity only promotes the continuation of repeat criminal behavior because they are not held up to public accountability and judgment. Public knowledge and commentary would impose pressure in the form of public opprobrium to change delinquent behavior lest the delinquent's family suffer the associated stigma and shame. Keeping things secret is of no benefit to the court system. The public ought to know how we are dealing with youngsters who, at sixteen, already appear to be turning into monsters.

Of course, stringent guidelines for such coverage must be developed by the appellate courts to promote fairness and uniformity and to ensure that the legitimate purposes of the juvenile law will be carried out. The juvenile judge must, of course, make the final determination whether or not it is in the interest of the minor *and* society to allow cameras in a particular juvenile court hearing.

One final reason for allowing TV cameras in the courtroom is that minorities, not without justification, feel disenfranchised. They are anxious and angry. They believe that the system is skewed against them, favoring whites. They point to harsher sentences against blacks. It is important that they and we see that the justice system is evenhanded and fair. No backroom deals. No harsher sentences for minorities. No racial animus dictating verdicts. No disparate treatment of people based on their class.

Notwithstanding all the tasteless, inaccurate, and hysterical coverage of the Simpson case, the Menendez case, and the Rodney King beating case, cameras in the courtroom have been an enormous asset to the entire criminal justice system. We need to keep them there and use them more often.

Courthouse Cameras Should Observe, Not Participate

No one except paparazzi-style reporters wants to return to the Lindbergh-Shepard style of live trial coverage. But there is absolutely no reason why cameras in the courthouse must be an obnoxious or intrusive element. I advocate a passive camera, one that merely observes and does not editorialize. A few simple rules will suffice:

• The camera should be at a fixed, unobtrusive location. Close-up shots should be prohibited. The camera just observes what is there without doing dramatic cuts, fades, and close-ups, except where evidence is concerned. This is not entertainment; its purpose is to provide information and knowledge.

• Jurors should at no time be identifiable, and therefore should never appear on camera.

• Except under extreme circumstances, such as bona fide concerns about physical safety, witnesses (including the defendant) should be *on* camera.

• The camera should never be permitted to invade the privacy of the defendant or the lawyers at the counsel table. To preserve privacy and to prevent grandstanding, it should not show the lawyers or the defendant there. It should only display the witnesses, any demonstrative evidence, and the judge. Attorneys should be on camera only when they address a witness or the court.

• Microphones should be controlled by the judge or a designated person, making sure that private conversations of the defendant, attorneys, and witnesses not be overheard.

• The judge or a court designee, under the judge's direct supervision, should control the TV pictures, using a kill/delay device to prohibit offensive and prejudicial material from being transmitted.

• Child-abuse cases, cases arising from sex crimes, and cases involving "flashpoint" issues such as allegations of racism must be handled with extreme sensitivity, in accordance with strict guidelines established by our appellate courts and with absolute control by the trial court judge.

The key to making cameras in the courtroom work is the judge, who must maintain strict control over the proceedings. Passive cameras in our courts will soften the hype and the irresponsible and misleading media coverage all of us have witnessed.

Placing the Blame

I want to end this chapter with a very personal example of how cameras in court can be used constructively. You already know I feel strongly that the people mostly to blame for the mess we are in usually manage to blame someone else. Frequently the people who get blamed in the media are the trial judges, who are only applying the laws and rulings of the legislatures and the high courts.

This happened to me. I have written earlier about the John Sweeney case. Because of poorly decided appellate decisions, I had to exclude some very important evidence about Sweeney's multiple beatings and hospitalizations of his girlfriend before he killed actress Dominique Dunne. The jury returned terrible verdicts, not nearly severe enough for the crime committed. I was excoriated in the print media and by some TV commentators for my ruling, owing in part to the efforts of Dominique's prominent father, Dominick Dunne, who was infuriated over the verdict.

Dunne had every right to be angry, but his anger was misplaced. By blaming me, he unwittingly helped the real culprits avoid responsibility. The parties actually responsible for what happened in that case were a liberal California Supreme Court supportive of expanding criminal procedural rights, and a hypocritical California legislature, which has knowingly underfunded the California prisons for years, leaving us with inadequate prison space to accommodate the ever-increasing prison population. Thus, Sweeney, a brutal murderer, was out on the street barely three years after I sentenced him.

As a judge I had no platform or ability to respond to these charges during the trial. I had no effective way of informing the public about why I was compelled to keep this evidence out, or why I felt that the verdict and the sentence represented a miscarriage of justice. I had no platform to inform the public that trial judges are not soft on crime. The probation and sentencing hearing was the first time that I could ethically comment on the case.

I allowed an unobtrusive CNN camera into the courtroom for the emotionally charged sentencing hearing. Even the people who had been picketing outside the courthouse during the trial came inside and attended this hearing. I allowed the camera because it was the first time I could speak to the public. I could finally talk about what was really going on in this case. I could finally tell of the rage I felt over the jury's unjust manslaughter verdict, and the decisions of the California Supreme Court. It was my turn to speak.

> No one has heard from this court regarding the views with respect to the evidence or, indeed, the verdict. This was a killing with malice. This man held on to this young, vulnerable, beautiful, warm human being who had everything to live for, with his hands. He had to have known that as she was failing to get oxygen, that the process of death was displacing the process of life.
>
> He had to have known that he was squeezing the hope from Dominique Dunne, and he did it not for thirty seconds, not for forty-five seconds. "Hey, Sweeney, stop here, because that is it." He squeezed it for a minute. Then he squeezed it for a minute and ten seconds and he squeezed it for a minute and twenty seconds. And he went on for two minutes. He didn't say, "Hey, Sweeney, get hold of yourself. Stop. I can see what is happening. She is flailing around." None of that happened. He continued to squeeze. He continued to squeeze the life out of her. That is malice. If that isn't malice, I don't know what malice is. . . . [W]ere I the trier of fact in this case, given all of the evidence before this jury, I would have unhesitatingly returned a verdict of murder in the second degree.

I then imposed the maximum lawful sentence on Sweeney. It was outrageously low, given the crime committed—six years and six months. I then had to use the special math mandated by the legislature to reduce the sentence by almost one and a half years.

Even worse than the legislature's special math was the shortened term Sweeney would actually serve because of overcrowded prisons. So I continued,

> In order to relieve the congestion of the prison system, you will get one day off for each that you have served. This is the mandate of the legislature. Thus you will be required to serve probably less than the full term and less than one-half of the full term! So, you will be doing one-half of your sentence. . . . Indeed, Mr. Sweeney, life is really cheap!
>
> If the public is shocked over the disproportionate term—you and others . . . convicted of voluntary manslaughter actually serve for the intentional taking of a human life—you should channel your energy and make the legislature and the representatives hear your voice and change the law. The court's hands are tied.

TV opens the windows and lets in some fresh air, some light. In the light, we see what is. In the dark, we wonder what might be. You saw Simpson try on the gloves. You didn't rely on a commentator to tell you whether they fit or not. That is the power of seeing for yourself. If we think the government is hiding something, that perception undermines our confidence in justice. Perceptions become reality, and can bring down an insensible nation that becomes, by definition, inaccessible to its people. To paraphrase Thomas Jefferson, where TV is free to record our affairs of state in the courtroom, and every person is able to *see*, all is safe.

E P I L O G U E

The Noble American Experiment

PAY NOW OR PAY LATER

Justice is not blind, nor is she evenhanded. The scales do not balance. Not, that is, until we are freed of our humanity and turned to demigods. And then justice will no longer be needed.
—*H. L. Mencken, 1925*

Remember the rape-murder case I told you about in chapter 9? I was the DA. The killer had raped a beautiful young woman and then stabbed her twenty-seven times. It wasn't his first time. He had a previous juvenile conviction for rape. The appellate court reversed his conviction because the veteran trial judge had given an instruction to the jury that had been previously approved by the same high court. The jury was initially deadlocked eleven to one. Here is the "erroneous" instruction. The judge told the jury to "deliberate some more. . . . [Y]ou are just as capable of arriving at a verdict as any other jury." I also showed the jury a picture of the victim in life, beautiful and seated next to her proud mother. The high court said the picture was prejudicial to the killer. I hated those judges. I hated the system, a system in which I was a player, a system in which justice seemed to have little to do with the truth. Later I became a judge—an inside player. More recently I have been an observer, a member of the public, like you. And, like you, I have a feeling we are losing our sense of values and morality.

A system that exalts a criminal's rights over the victim's, procedure over substance, and adversarial supremacy over the quest for truth and justice is on the verge of moral bankruptcy. It will not survive, because the people will not support it. That system, with all its imperfections, is all that stands between us and tyrannical government or—worse—anarchy. If we haven't the faith and courage to fix the justice system while that is still possible, we will all eventually lose our freedom. And all it would have taken is some faith and courage.

I know you know this is true. You have told me so—maybe not you yourself, but Americans from all over. I have talked with a lot of citizens on my TV and radio shows. My callers tell me something is wrong. A feeling deep within them triggered the alarm, a feeling that things are out of control, that we are crumbling as a society, unable or unwilling to accept responsibility and impotent to do anything about it. My callers tell of their anger toward a justice system that mocks the truth, that never seems to fulfill its promises. They are tired of a system that is more sympathetic to murderers than to the slain victim. I listen. I agree. The system is broken and needs fixing. The bad news to date is we've done little to fix it. The good news is we can.

We will never have a perfect justice system—that I can promise. We're human and flawed. But thank God we have our humanity—which is better than "perfect" justice "by the numbers." Our task is at hand. It can be accomplished. In fact, there are some encouraging signs. To begin with, we would not be having this dialogue were it not for the positive effect of cameras in the courtroom. In the twenty-first century, our main means of communication will be the transmission of information by media not yet discovered or refined. The ubiquitous TV camera has led the way. Say what you will, the O.J. Simpson case has drawn all of us together, forcing us to focus on a criminal justice system we thought we knew. The camera makes us intruders on a process, uninvited by its players, who have always kept us at a distance that allowed them to perpetuate an insular, arcane system serving a privileged few who had been escorted through the thicket of rules and regulations by the players themselves. A system where one needs, pays for, and travels with a guide through its byzantine twists and turns—a tortuous path invented by the guides themselves. Today we are watching and talking. That was not true five years ago, and it is a very good sign.

We must begin with the police. They're out there all the time, protecting our hides every day. Hire more; they need the help. Support them better. Give them a sane set of rules within which to work—a set of rules we and the police can live with and respect, rules that hold truth as their principal objective, but that are not out of step with a nation committed to the preservation of its citizens' individual rights. Such rules respect crime victims as much as criminals. To do this, we must insist on effective civilian oversight over the cops and their departments who serve us.

Then we must build the rest of the infrastructure. Courts, judges, prisons, jails.

Finally, we must look hard at our adversary system. What is it? What does it do for us? Who are the key players, and how are they doing? Judges, lawyers, and juries. Each has a more refined role to play. Each can do much better.

Justice is only a mirror of our society. So there is more to do, such as declaring a war on poverty and illiteracy with the same commitment and resources we bring to the war on drugs. A war in which money is not doled out to perpetuate a growing subclass of citizens, but one in which opportunities are created and citizens are enfranchised and made productive. Training, education, and job opportunities must be real and not illusory. They must reach the *same* people we now imprison. We need safer schools, with more and better-paid teachers working in better facilities and with more teaching resources. We must acknowledge that our children are the future, and we must give them the tools of survival.

The government can do only so much. It's up to us to teach our children the values that keep them out of the "system." It's up to us to spend quality time with our children, reinforcing their sense of worth, acting as positive role models. It's up to us to say no to violence, to keep our kids from watching violent TV shows that desensitize us to human suffering, pain, and death. It's up to us to teach our children it is unacceptable to resolve disputes with violence. It's up to us to keep our families together—stable families, loving families, productive families.

American values, human values, are not the property of Republicans or Democrats, Conservatives or Liberals. They are just sensible things we all know deep down must be done if we are to survive as a society much past the turn of the century. In the long run, these are more important than any government initiative or any tough anti-crime laws.

Learned Hand said in 1916 that the law "must feel the circulation of the communal blood or it will wither and drop off, a useless member . . . the form of justice will be without content till we fill it with the ardor of life." It is we who must fill the justice system with the ardor of life, with our communal blood, our values, our ethics, and our humanity. The human and monetary costs of the tasks ahead seem enormous. But they are just pebbles in a sea of a thousand tides. If we don't pay for real reform now, our children and grandchildren will bear witness to the unraveling of a once proud nation.

Rabbi Hillel asked, "If not now, when?" He is right. This is *your* justice system. Not mine, not Chief Justice Rehnquist's, not Johnnie Cochran's. Yours. It is in your hands. So lay down this book, dial your state representative, write your member of congress. Let them know it's way past time, and some overdue bills must be paid.